The Jewish World in Stamps

The Jewish World in Stamps

Ronald Eisenberg

Schreiber Publishing
Rockville, Maryland

Ronald L. Eisenberg

The Jewish World in Stamps

Publishing by:
Schreiber Publishing, Inc.
P.O. Box 4193, Rockville, Maryland 20849   www.schreiberpublishing.com

Library of Congress Cataloging-in-Publication Data

Eisenberg, Ronald L.
  The Jewish world in stamps : 4000 years of Jewish civilization in
postal stamps / Ronald Eisenberg.
      p. cm.
Includes index.
  ISBN 1-887563-76-8
1. Jews on postage stamps. 2. Jews--History. I. Title.
  HE6183.J4 E37 2000
  769.56'4990904924--dc21
                      2002008824

Printed in the United States of America

For Avlana Kinneret and Cherina Carmel,
May the rich treasure of your Jewish heritage be forever stamped in your hearts,
and may you continue the unbroken 4000-year chain of Jewish tradition

Introduction

Ever since my first visit to Israel 30 years ago, I have been a collector of Israeli stamps. However, I never considered them for literary inspiration until I had the opportunity to use a variety of medical-related stamps on the chapter title pages of my book *Radiology: An Illustrated History*, written to commemorate the 100th anniversary of Roentgen's discovery of x-rays. While diligently poring through the Scott Catalogue in search of appropriate stamps, I noted the large number from countries throughout the world that depicted synagogues, Holocaust memorials, and famous Jews. This experience provided the seed for *The Jewish World in Stamps*—a journey through 4000 years of Jewish civilization on postage stamps.

The book opens with the formative years of the Jewish people, from the patriarchs and matriarchs at the dawn of monotheism to the Exodus from bondage in Egypt and the Revelation at Mount Sinai. Stamps depicting masterpieces by renowned artists illustrate this early biblical period, as well as the subsequent days of the Judges, Prophets, and Kings of Israel. Next is a whirlwind tour of Jewish history from the Babylonian Exile in 586 B.C.E. through the first half of the 20th century and the incomparable tragedy of the Holocaust.

In the Diaspora, Jews have distinguished themselves across the spectrum of human activities. The book details the accomplishments of Jews in art, literature, music, theater and movies, science and industry, and politics. This section closes with Jews who constitute a remarkably high percentage of those who have been awarded Nobel Prizes.

The scene then shifts to the State of Israel. After a brief history of the Zionist movement, the waves of aliyah and early settlements, and the wars that were required to establish and preserve the Jewish State, there are richly illustrated descriptions of the flourishing cultural life and institutions in Israel, the city of Jerusalem and other sites in the Holy Land, and the flora and fauna of the region. Finally, there is a section on Jewish traditions and values, featuring stamps related to the Sabbath and festivals and the synagogue.

Each stamp throughout the book has a legend that describes the person or scene depicted, followed by a citation consisting of three parts - the country, the Scott number (based on the major stamp catalogue, which is available in most libraries), and the year of issue.

Unfortunately, some illustrious Jews have never been featured on postage stamps. For example, it is inexplicable that there are no stamps honoring two towering virtuosos of the 20th century, violinist Jascha Heifetz and pianist Vladimir Horowitz. For religious reasons (not wanting to discard a stamp bearing his image), Chabad has refused to permit a stamp of the late Lubavitch Rebbe, Menachem Mendel Shneerson. Many current celebrities are not featured on stamps because of the general policy of some countries, such as the United States and Israel, to not issue stamps of individuals while they are still alive. Finally, a few Jews with stamps listed in the catalogues have been omitted because their stamps were simply not available, while others may not have been included because I did not realize that they were Jewish. I would greatly appreciate hearing from readers about other Jews featured on postage stamps, so that I can include them in a second edition of *The Jewish World in Stamps*.

Some may argue that certain of those listed in the book are not truly Jewish, either

because they had only a Jewish father (and thus are not Jewish according to *halacha*) or converted to Christianity. Inclusion of the former merely acknowledges their unmistakable Jewish descent. The prominent figures who converted to Christianity, or were baptized by their parents as children, as a way to be spared from discrimination in order to achieve academic, financial, and social success, are included because, as the Talmud observes, according to *halacha* a Jew remains a Jew, "even if he has sinned."

I want to thank Zina Schiff, my wife and editor extraordinaire, whose passion for Judaism nourishes me. Thanks also are due to publisher Morry Schreiber, whose initial support, superb suggestions, and ceaseless encouragement were instrumental in making *The Jewish World in Stamps* a reality.

Ronald Eisenberg

A Word From the Publisher

For over half a century I have been involved in either reading, writing, reviewing, editing or publishing books on Jewish subjects. For nearly twenty years I have entertained the dream of some day publishing a book on the Jewish world in stamps. As a stamp collector back in elementary school, I knew there was a wealth of stamps on Jewish subjects around the world, waiting to be put into a book form.

Last year I was approached by Dr. Ronald Eisenberg, an avid stamp collector with a special interest in stamps on Jewish subjects, and the author of books in both medicine and Judaica. Dr. Eisenberg did not have to twist my arm. I was ready before he even finished the sentence. We both understook the task with unabashed enthusiasm, and we kept going until we finished covering all the areas we wanted to see included in this kind of a project.

What strikes me as remarkable is the fact that after so many years of living intimately with Jewish history, culture and in many different Jewish communities, including Israel, the United States, and both South and Central America, I never fully experienced the incredible scope and depth of Jewish involvement in all aspects of civilization in practically every corner of this planet until I saw all those hundreds of stamps come together as they do in the following pages. Is it because pictures are so much more immediate and powerful than words? I will let the reader decide. All I can say is - you are in for a treat!

Mordecai Schreiber

Table of Contents

The Bible

Introduction

The Bible is the most widely translated and influential book of all time. The English word is derived from *biblios*, a Greek word meaning "book." The Hebrew term most frequently employed for the Bible is the acronym *Ta-Na-Kh* (*Tanach*), which is derived from the initial letters of the names of its three major divisions: *Torah* (Law), *Nevi'im*, (Prophets); and *Ketuvim* (Writings). The Christian term "Old Testament" is not accepted in Jewish tradition because it expresses the belief that there is a "New Testament" (i.e., "covenant") that has somehow superseded the special divine relationship with the Jewish People.

Gutenberg prints the first Bible.
U.S.A. 1014 (1952)

The first five books of the Bible are known as the *Chumash* in Hebrew and the Pentateuch in English. In Hebrew, the name of each individual book reflects its initial (or first significant) word - *Bereishit* (in the beginning), *Shemot* (names), *Vayikra* (and He [God] called), *Bamidbar* (in the wilderness), and *Devarim* (words). The English names for these five books - Genesis, Exodus, Leviticus, Numbers, Deuteronomy - are descriptive of the contents or major themes of the respective books.

The second division of the Bible, *Nevi'im* (Prophets) includes the narrative historical works (Joshua, Judges, Samuel, Kings) and the largely poetic literary creations of the three "major" prophets (Isaiah, Jeremiah, Ezekiel) and the twelve "minor" prophets (Hosea, Joel, Amos, Obadiah, Jonah, Micah, Nachum, Habakuk, Zephaniah, Haggai, Zechariah, Malachi). The popular epithet "minor" has a solely quantitative connotation and is no indication of relative importance.

The third division of the Bible, *Ketuvim* (Writings), is a varied collection comprising liturgical poetry (Psalms, Lamentations), love poetry (Song of Songs), wisdom literature (Proverbs, Job, Ecclesiastes), historical works (Ruth, Chronicles, Ezra-Nehemiah, Esther), and a blend of history and prophecy (Daniel). The five *Megillot* (scrolls) are often grouped together because of the custom of reading these books on festivals: the Song of Songs on Passover; Ruth on Shavuot; Lamentations on Tisha b'Av; Ecclesiastes on Sukkot; and Esther on Purim.

Sometime during the first century, the final decision was made as to which sacred books were to be considered part of the biblical canon, or Holy Scripture. Some books in Hellenistic Bibles that were not accepted into the official Hebrew canon, known as the Apocrypha ("hidden books"), include such works as the books of Judith and Tobit and the four books of the Maccabees. The Gutenberg Bible, printed in Mainz around 1454-5, was the first major book printed in the west. The first complete printed version of the Hebrew Bible was published by

100th anniversary of the publication of the Bible in Maori. *New Zealand 408 (1968)*

The word Bible in 76 African languages.
South Africa 702 (1987)

Soncino in 1488. Since that time, the Bible has been translated and printed in virtually every language on earth.

Torah

The Story of Creation

500th anniversary of the first printed
Hebrew Bible. *Italy 1733 (1988)*

In the beginning God created the heaven and the earth. The earth was without form and void, and darkness was upon the face of the deep. Then the Spirit of God moved upon the waters, and God said, "Let there be light;" and there was light. God saw that the light was good, and God separated the light (which God called Day) from the darkness (which God called Night). And there was evening and there was morning, one day.

On the second day God made a firmament and called it Heaven, and it separated the waters above from the waters below. On the third day, God gathered together the waters under the heaven into one place called Seas, allowing the appearance of dry land called Earth. Then God made all forms of vegetation that grow upon the earth. On the fourth day, God created the two great luminaries of the sky – the larger sun to shine during the day and the smaller moon to brighten the night (with the stars). On the fifth day, God made the fish and the birds to fill the seas and the sky. On the sixth day, God created the land animals, the cattle and wild beasts and creeping things. Finally, God said, "Let us make a man in our image, after our likeness." So God blessed Man, saying

Creation of the sun and the moon
by Michelangelo. *Vatican City 944-945 (1994)*

The creation of man
by Michelangelo. *Hungary 2362 (1975)*

"Be fruitful, and multiply," and gave man dominion over the earth and all the creatures on land, in the sea, and in the air. God looked at everything God had created during these six days and saw that it was very good. Thus the heavens and the earth were finished, as well as all the creatures that God had made. And on the seventh day God ceased from work and rested, blessing the seventh day and making it holy.

The six days of creation. *Israel 298-303 (1965)*

ECOLÓGICA 92

GENESIS ∞ Creation of the World

In the beginning God created the heaven and the earth.
And the earth was without form, and void.

IN OUR HANDS
EARTH SUMMIT '92

And on the seventh day God ended His
work which He had made; and He rested
...And God blessed the seventh day, and sanctified it.

The story of creation and ecology. *Palau 303 (1992)*

From left: "And there was light." *Vatican City
550 (1974)*; "In the beginning" (*Commemorating the first
mission to the moon*). *U.S.A. 1371 (1969)*

Adam and Eve

"And the serpent was more cunning than all the animals of the field." The jealous serpent seduced Adam's wife into eating fruit from the forbidden tree, and she in turn shared some with her husband. Suddenly, the eyes of both of them were opened, and they knew that they were naked; they sewed fig leaves together and made themselves aprons, and hid when they heard the voice of God. The serpent was condemned to crawl on its belly and eat dust, perpetually hated by human beings. The woman was sentenced to the pain of childbirth, a craving for her man, and subjugation to him. For listening to his wife and violating the prohibition, the man was destined to toil and sweat in order to wrest a bare living from an accursed and hostile soil. Henceforth, human beings would be mortal, eventually dying and returning to the dust from which they came.

After this incident, Adam called his wife's name Eve, because she was "the Mother of all the Living." God expelled Adam and Eve from the Garden of Eden and barred access to the Tree of Life by means of the cherubim and a flaming sword.

Adam and Eve by A. Dürer.
Paraguay 1804 (1978)

From left: *Adam and Eve* (detail) by Rubens. *Grenada Grenadines 1226-27 (1991); Expulsion from Eden* by Michelangelo. *Vatican City 948-949 (1994)*

Cain and Abel

Adam and Eve had two sons. The elder, Cain, became a farmer; the younger, Abel, was a shepherd. Both brought offerings to God, Cain taking some of his produce and Abel selecting the best of his flock. When God showed respect for Abel's offering but ignored his own, Cain was bitter and downcast. Ignoring a divine warning on the seductive nature of sin, Cain killed his brother Abel. For this act Cain was doubly punished. A farmer, Cain was to be denied the fruits of the soil and doomed to be a homeless wanderer. To allay Cain's expressed fear of being killed by anyone who might come across him, God placed a protective mark upon his forehead; and Cain settled in the land of Nod, east of Eden.

Cain slaying Abel (detail) by Rubens. *Grenada Grenadines 230 (1991)*

Cain and Abel by Titian. *Uganda 636 (1988)*

God chastising Adam and Eve *(native painting). Micronesia 292 (1998)*

Top: The story of the flood, beginning with the building of the ark and ending with the covenant of the rainbow. *Israel 394-398 (1969)*.
Bottom, from left: Construction of the ark. *Grenada 1145 (1983)*; the ark and the rainbow; the ark and the animals.
Vatican City 548, 551 (1974)

Noah and the Flood

As punishment for their corruption and injustice, God decided to bring a universal flood to destroy all humanity. Only a single blameless and righteous man named Noah, who "walked with God," together with his family, was to save the human race. God gave Noah detailed instructions for building an ark of gopher wood that would preserve him, his family, and representatives of each species of living creature so that there could be continued life after the flood. Noah was ordered to bring two of every kind of animal, bird, and creeping thing into the ark, one male and one female; of every clean beast, he was to take seven pairs. When all the preparations were completed and sufficient food was placed on board, the deluge began. Torrential rains fell upon the earth for forty days and forty nights, blotting out all earthly existence. Finally the rains ceased, the waters subsided, and the ark came to rest upon the mountains of Ararat. Noah sent out a raven, but it soon returned to the ark because it could not find a place to land. Seven days later he released a dove, which flew back with an olive branch in its beak. After a last delay of seven days, Noah again sent out the dove, but this time it did not return and Noah knew it was safe to disembark.

Noah's rainbow and dove. *United Nations 271 (1976)*

Tower of Babel

The descendants of Noah multiplied greatly, spoke one language, and migrated toward the plain of Shinar (Babylonia). They decided to erect "a city and a tower with its top in the heaven" so that they could "make a name for ourselves" and avoid being scattered over the entire world. God was displeased by this building project and, since it had only been possible because all people spoke one language, God confounded their language so that they no longer could communicate with one another. Then God scattered these people speaking multiple languages over the face of the earth. The unfinished tower was called Babel, for the "babble" of languages that began being spoken there.

From left: Tower of Babel. *Cuba 3205 (1990); Belgium 1119 (1982)*

Noah's ark. *St. Vincent 1152 (1989)*

Abraham and Sarah

Born in Ur of Chaldea in southern Mesopotamia, the 75-year-old Abram was commanded by God to leave his birthplace and his ancestral home and go to "a land that I will show you." So Abram set out with his wife Sarai and his nephew Lot and traveled to Canaan. Lot settled in Sodom, while Abraham remained in Canaan.

Then God came to Abram in a vision, promising that his descendants would be as numerous as the stars in the sky and that they would have all the land of Canaan as an everlasting possession. The sign of this covenant was to be the circumcision of every male child on the eighth day of life. God changed their names to Abraham and Sarah, an indication that they would become a father and mother of many nations. However, Abraham pointed out that, at age 99, he and his 89-year-old wife Sarah had no children; would Eliezer, the steward of his house, be Abram's heir?

God then revealed the decision to destroy the evil cities of Sodom and Gomorrah, but Abraham pleaded for a revocation of the sentence, bargaining with God to spare these cities if even ten righteous men could be found within them. Since there apparently were

God's promise to Abraham by Lilien ("Your descendants will be as numerous as the stars in the sky"). *Israel 626 (1977)*

none, two angels ordered Lot to flee with his family but not look back as fire and brimstone from heaven destroyed the city. However, Lot's wife did look back and she was turned into a pillar of salt.

Just as God had promised, Sarah gave birth to a son whom they called Isaac (from a Hebrew root meaning "to laugh"), since Sarah had laughed at the thought of having a child in her old age. Several years later, Sarah saw that Ishmael, Abraham's son with Hagar the Egyptian servant, was a bad influence on Isaac. She told her husband to send them away. Abraham hesitated, but God told him to obey his wife, as both Isaac and Ishmael would give rise to great nations.

Then God tested Abraham, commanding him to sacrifice Isaac in the land of Moriah. Abraham obeyed unhesitatingly; after a three-day journey to reach the appointed place, Abraham built an altar, carefully covered it with wood, and placed the bound Isaac upon it. As Abraham picked up the knife and prepared to slay his son, a voice from heaven stayed his hand, for Abraham had passed the supreme test of faith by not withholding his son. Seeing a ram caught by its horns in a thicket, Abraham took the animal and offered it as a sacrifice in place of his son. God reiterated the promise that Abraham's descendants would be as numerous as the stars of the heaven and the grains of sand on the seashore. Then Abraham returned to his young men, and together they returned to his home in Beersheba. But Isaac went his own way.

Lot's flight from Sodom by Rubens. *Grenada Grenadines 1231 (1991)*

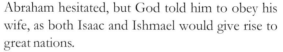

Hagar sees the angel by Tiepolo. *Italy 1184 (1975)*

Sarah and the three visitors. *Israel 638 (1977)*

Abraham and Isaac at Mount Moriah. *Israel 701 (1978)*

Isaac and Rebecca

Cave of Machpelah
in Hebron.
Israel 1344 (1983)

When at age 127 Sarah died in Kiryat Arba (also known as Hebron), Abraham buried his beloved wife in the Cave of Machpelah, which he bought from a local citizen as a family grave. Abraham commissioned his servant Eliezer to travel to Mesopotamia to find a wife for Isaac, for he did not want his heir to marry a Canaanite woman. Eliezer selected Rebecca, a beautiful woman who demonstrated both hospitality to strangers and kindness to animals. After Eliezer explained the purpose of his quest, Rebecca agreed to return with him to marry Isaac. As the caravan neared Canaan, Isaac was walking in the fields. Informed that the handsome young man was her future husband, Rebecca dismounted from the camel after modestly veiling her face.

Sacrifice of Isaac
by Rembrandt.
Russia 5133 (1983)

Isaac views Rebecca.
Israel 702 (1978)

From left: *Rebecca at the well* by Murillo. *Spain 922 (1960); Rwanda 212 (1967)*

Rebecca at the well with Eliezer.
Israel 639 (1977)

Isaac taking Rebecca as his wife (native
painting). *Micronesia 293 (1998)*

Jacob, Leah and Rachel

Twenty years after they were married, when Isaac was 60 years old, Rebecca finally conceived. During her difficult pregnancy, God informed Rebecca about the destinies of her unborn twin sons – how the elder would be the stronger but would serve the younger. The red and hairy firstborn was called Esau; the second held the elder's heel in his hand and was called Jacob. Esau became a skillful hunter and Isaac's favorite, because he brought home fresh meat for his father's dinner. Rebecca, however, loved Jacob, a quiet man who stayed at home. Jacob bought the family's birthright from Esau "for a mess of pottage."

Jacob's vision with ladder and angels.
Israel 703 (1978)

Jacob's dream by Raphael.
Grenada 1146 (1983)

When Isaac in his old age expressed his intention of bestowing his farewell blessing on Esau, Rebecca skillfully induced Jacob to supplant his brother so as to obtain it for himself. Fearing Esau's revenge, Jacob was forced to flee his home. That night, Jacob slept in a field with a stone for his pillow and dreamed of a ladder reaching up to heaven, with angels ascending and descending it. He then heard God repeat the promises of land and numerous progeny that God had made to Abraham and Isaac. Jacob's offspring would be a source of blessing to the whole earth; he would enjoy Divine protection wherever he would be, and would return one day to the land from which he was fleeing.

Leah with her many children.
Israel 641 (1977)

Arriving in Haran, Jacob was welcomed into the home of his uncle Laban, who had two daughters. The elder, Leah, was a plain girl with weak eyes; the younger, Rachel, was beautiful, and Jacob loved Rachel. Jacob arranged to work for Laban for seven years as the bride-price for Rachel, but the years seemed like a few days because of his love for her. When the day of the marriage arrived, however, Jacob discovered that Laban had substituted Leah for Rachel. Only by promising to serve another seven years was Jacob permitted to marry Rachel. Seeing that Jacob had little affection for Leah, God blessed her with many children. The beloved Rachel, however, was barren.

Jacob wrestling with the angel by Delacroix.
France 1054 (1963)

Rachel. *Israel 640 (1977)*

After Jacob had worked for Laban for twenty years and become wealthy, God ordered him to return to the land of his birth. Jacob was attacked on the way by a mysterious stranger, a Divine being with whom he wrestled with all his strength throughout the night. When the stranger, desperate to get away before dawn, realized that he would not prevail, he pulled at Jacob's thigh until the hip dislocated. Still Jacob refused to let go unless the stranger blessed him. "No longer shall you be called Jacob," the stranger announced, "from now on your name shall be Israel, for you have struggled with God and men and prevailed."

Joseph

Jacob was the father of twelve sons, but his favorite was Joseph because he was the first son of his beloved Rachel. To demonstrate this love, Jacob made the 17-year-old Joseph a special long-sleeved coat of many colors, unlike the plain garments worn by his brothers. The brothers hated Joseph, not only because of this obvious favoritism, but also because Joseph tattled to his father about their misdeeds and related a series of dreams intended to lord it over them (of sheaves of wheat and then celestial bodies bowing down before him).

Joseph interprets his brothers' and Pharaoh's dreams. *Grenada 1147-1148 (1983); Grenada Grenadines 1397 (1992)*

Jealous of Joseph, the brothers sold him as a slave to a caravan of Ishmaelites who took him down to Egypt, where he wound up in prison on false charges. Two years later, Pharaoh had two strange dreams that baffled all the magicians and wise men of Egypt. Then the chief cupbearer remembered the Hebrew slave who had correctly interpreted his dream and that of the chief baker. Pharaoh immediately summoned Joseph and related his dreams: seven fat and sleek cows that were eaten by seven thin and gaunt cows; and seven full ears of ripe corn devoured by seven deformed ears that were withered and thin. Joseph told Pharaoh that both dreams had the same meaning – seven years of plenty followed by seven years of famine. Then Joseph offered some unsolicited advice on how to deal with the situation. He proposed the appointment of a man to organize a reserve bank of food during the years of plenty that could be used to feed the people during the years of famine. Pharaoh and his advisors thought that this was an excellent solution and selected Joseph to fill the position. So the 30-year-old Joseph became the second-in-command over all the land of Egypt.

The twelve tribes of Israel. *Israel 105-116 (1955-1956)*

Moses

The Children of Israel became wealthy and increased in power. Fearing that they might join with the enemies of Egypt in case of war, a new Pharaoh "who knew not Joseph" enslaved the Israelites and made their lives bitter, forcing them to rigorously toil in the fields, as well as to make bricks and build great cities for Pharaoh. However, the more the Egyptians afflicted them, the more the Israelites multiplied. To solve this problem, Pharaoh devised the simple solution of killing every newborn Israelite male by throwing him into the Nile.

One Israelite woman named Yocheved hid her baby rather than allow him to be killed. But when he had grown too active and noisy to hide, she carefully laid the child in a large basket made of reeds and placed it in the bulrushes at the edge of the Nile, while her daughter Miriam watched from a distance. Soon the daughter of Pharaoh came to the river to bathe, and she discovered the basket among the reeds. The princess took pity on the crying infant and decided to adopt him. She called his name Moses, a name meaning "I drew him out of the water."

Pharaoh's daughter discovers baby Moses by Tintoretto. *Uganda 1296 (1994)*

The Burning Bush, the Ten Plagues, and the Exodus from Egypt

Although reared and educated as an Egyptian of the highest caste, Moses remained conscious of his origin and sympathetic to his people. One day while protecting a Hebrew slave from his taskmaster, Moses caused the latter's death and had to flee to the desert of Midian. In Midian, Moses saved the daughters of the priest Jethro, who came to water their flocks, from local shepherds who were bullying them. He subsequently married Jethro's daughter Zipporah and became a shepherd. One day while tending his sheep, God appeared to him in a bush that was burning but not consumed. Moses was told to go to Pharaoh and order him to free the Israelites.

As commanded, Moses spoke to Pharaoh, telling him that God commanded the Egyptian monarch to "Let my people go." Haughtily stating that he did not know this "God of the Hebrews," Pharaoh not only refused the request but even ordered the Egyptian taskmasters to make the Israelites work harder. Then God demonstrated His awesome power by inflicting a series of plagues on Egypt, each time hardening Pharaoh's heart so that he would not let the Children of Israel go. After an initial plague of the waters of the Nile turning to blood, God sent a horde of frogs to cover the land; transformed the dust into tiny biting insects that attacked both people and animals; sent swarms of flies; a devastating disease that killed the animals; painful boils on the skin; a violent hailstorm, accompanied by thunder and lightning that destroyed most of the crops in the field; locusts that devoured those crops that remained; and three days of darkness that was so intense that no Egyptian could see anything or go anywhere. Finally God sent the tenth plague – the death of the firstborn of all Egypt. Pharaoh and the panic-stricken Egyptians urged the Israelites to leave so quickly that the people had to take their dough before it was leavened and bake unleavened cakes (matzot).

Moses and Jethro's daughters by Poussin. *France 2435 (1994)*

Burning Bush. *Brazil 902 (1959)*

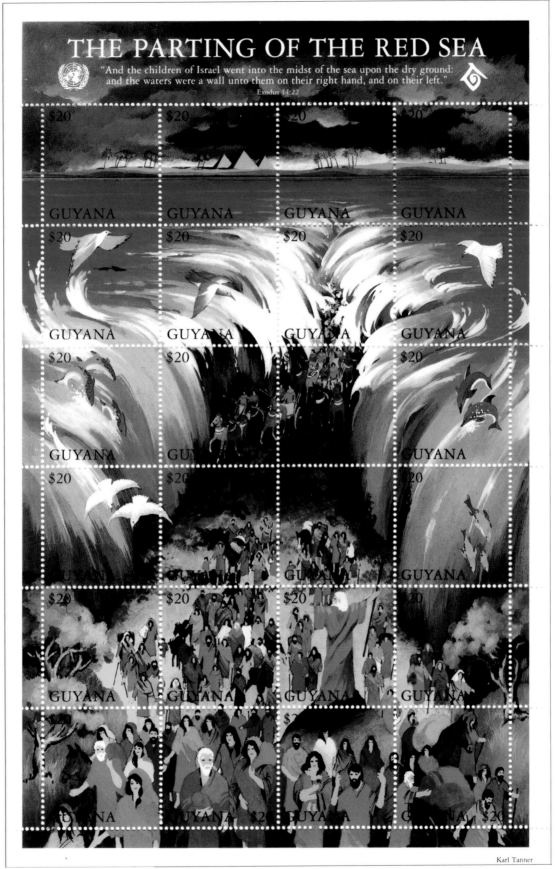

The Parting of the Red Sea. *Guyana 2835 (1994)*

Moses striking water from the rock by Tintoretto.
Uganda 1297 (1994)

Pharaoh soon regretted his rash decision to let the Israelites go, and he sent his army to bring back the former slaves. The Israelites were camped by the Sea of Reeds when the Egyptian forces appeared in the distance. God ordered Moses to stretch out his rod over the sea, and immediately a strong east wind blew apart the waters so that the Israelites were able to cross on dry ground, with a wall of water on either side of them. The Egyptians chased after the Israelites, but when they were halfway across the sea, the Almighty threw them into confusion, breaking the wheels of their chariots. God again commanded Moses to stretch out his hand over the sea, which crashed over the Egyptian army, covering the chariots and drowning all the soldiers while the Israelites watched safely from the opposite shore. Seeing the miraculous way in which God had saved them from the Egyptians, Moses and the people of Israel sang a hymn of glory to the Lord.

As they traveled in the wilderness, the people periodically complained about the lack of water and food, saying that it would have been better had they remained in Egypt. On several occasions, God commanded Moses to take his rod and strike a rock, from which water would flow to quench the people's thirst. He also caused the manna to fall from the sky to satisfy their hunger.

The Ten Commandments

On the first day of the third month after the Israelites had left Egypt, they camped near the foot of Mount Sinai. While the people waited below, Moses ascended the mountain. When Moses descended and reported God's words – "If you will obey My commands and keep My covenant, you shall be My special peoples, a kingdom of priests and a holy nation" – the Israelites replied as one, "All that the Lord has spoken, we will do."

On the morning of the third day, there was thunder and lightning, and a thick cloud covered the mountain. The sound of the shofar became exceedingly loud, and the people in the camp trembled. Moses led the people out of the camp to the foot of the mountain, so that they could meet with God. As God came down in a fire, Mount Sinai smoked like a furnace, and the whole mountain shook. The voice of the shofar sounded long and became increasingly louder; then Moses spoke and the voice of God answered him.

And God spoke all these ten phrases (commandments):

Moses and the Tablets of the Law by Rembrandt. *Nicaragua 890 (1971)*

I am the Lord your God.
You shall have no other gods before me (no graven image).
You shall not take the name of the Lord your God in vain.
Remember the Sabbath day, and keep it holy.
Honor your father and your mother.
You shall not murder.
You shall not commit adultery.
You shall not steal.
You shall not bear false witness against your neighbor.
You shall not covet anything that belongs to your neighbor.

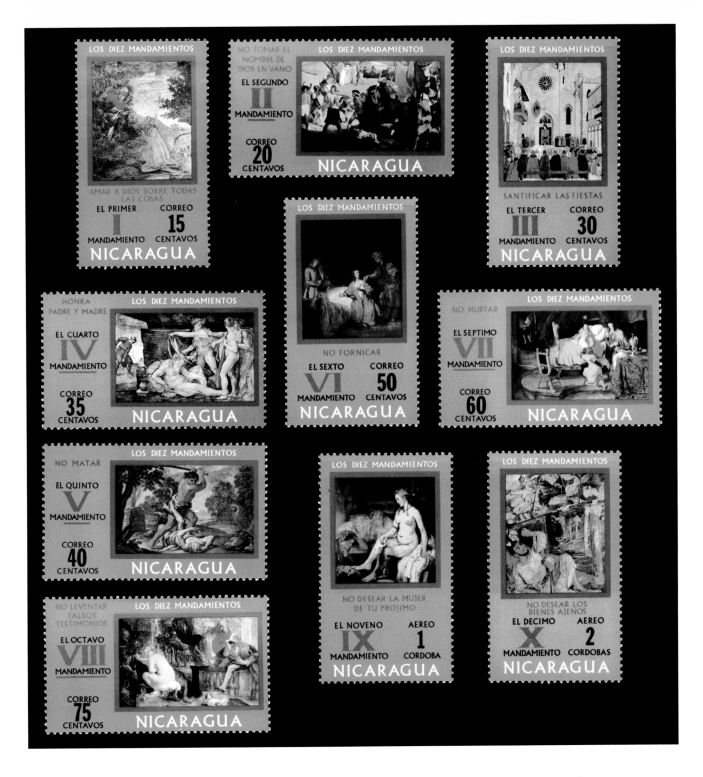

The Ten Commandments in World Masterpieces. *Nicaragua 891-898 (1994), C776-777 (1971)*

I. *Moses and the Burning Bush* by Botticelli.
II. *Jephthah's Daughter* by Degas.
III. *Preaching in Verona* by Morone.
IV. *Nakedness of Noah* by Michelangelo.
V. *Cain and Abel* by Francesco Trevisani.

VI. *Potiphar* by Rembrandt.
VII. *Isaac Blessing Jacob* by Eeckhout.
VIII. *Susanna and the Elders* by Rubens.
IX. *Bathsheba at Her Bath* by Rembrandt.
X. *Naboth's Vinyard* by Smetham.

Then Moses again ascended the mountain to receive the stones on which God would engrave these laws. As the glory of God blazed like a fire from the top of Mount Sinai, the Israelites watched Moses disappear into the clouds covering the mountain.

Fall of the Golden Calf.
Belgium 1545 (1994)

The Golden Calf

For forty days and forty nights, Moses remained on Mount Sinai. When the people saw that he was gone so long they became increasingly impatient and worried that the man who had led them out of Egypt would never return. They asked Aaron to make them a "god" to lead them, and he collected gold jewelry from the people, melted it down, and fashioned a molten calf. The next day the Israelites celebrated a wild festival, with eating, drinking, and frenzied dancing. Hearing the tumult below, Moses immediately descended from the mountain, carrying in his hand the two stone tablets on which God had personally written the Ten Commandments. When Moses saw the calf and the Israelites dancing with reckless abandon around it, he was so furious that he smashed the tablets to the ground, breaking them into many pieces. Moses grabbed the golden calf and threw it into the fire, until it melted. Then he ground the metal into powder, mixed it with water, and forced the Israelites to drink the potion. Moses again ascended the mountain and pleaded fervently for God to forgive the people. As a favor to Moses, God agreed and told Moses to cut two tablets of stone like the first ones he had broken and to write upon them the Ten Commandments. When Moses descended from Mount Sinai and returned to the camp, his face shone with the glory of God (mistranslated as horns, as in Michelangelo's famous statue). The people were afraid to come near him, and Moses wore a veil upon his face except when he was relating to them the word of God.

The Tabernacle

God commanded Moses to erect a *mishkan* ("tabernacle", literally "dwelling place"), a sanctuary that would be a symbol of God's presence among the Israelites. Explicit directions were given for the building of this portable structure. At the entrance to the Tabernacle stood the laver, a copper basin where the *Kohanim* (priests) washed before they brought sacrifices on the altar. The acacia-wood altar was overlaid with copper and had four horns. Within the Tabernacle stood the gilded wooden table, holding the twelve showbreads, and the menorah, the seven-branched candelabrum. The gilded incense altar was centered in front of the veil, which hung from four gilded pillars and hid the Holy of Holies, in which was kept the Ark of the Covenant and the stone tablets of the Ten Commandments. The Tabernacle was situated in the center of the camp; forming a living square around it marched the twelve tribes of Israel during their journey in the wilderness.

Moses by Michelangelo (detail). *Grenada 678 (1975)*

The Tabernacle: Ark, Table, Menorah, Incense Altar. *Israel 913-916 (1985)*

The Spies and Their Report

Spies with cluster of grapes.
Israel 87 (1954)

God told Moses to send twelve princes to spy out the land, its crops, and the number and military strength of its inhabitants. Reporting back to Moses and all the Israelites, the spies showed them the fruit of the land (including a huge cluster of grapes that required two men to carry), certifying that it surely flowed with milk and honey. However, when they related that the people of the land were strong and lived in walled cities, the Israelites feared they would not be powerful enough to conquer it. Caleb, one of the spies, tried to calm the people and urged that the Israelites go up to the land at once and possess it, since they had the power to do so. However, ten of the other spies disagreed, calling it "a land that eats up its inhabitants." They claimed that all the men they saw were of great stature, so that they felt as small as grasshoppers compared to them.

This report completely demoralized the Israelites, and they wept all night. Once again the people murmured against Moses and Aaron, wailing that it would have been better to have remained in Egypt than to die in the wilderness. As before, Moses had to plead with God not to destroy the Israelites. God reluctantly agreed, but swore that none of those who had provoked Him would ever see the Promised Land. Every Israelite twenty years and older (except for Caleb and Joshua) were condemned to die in the desert. And the entire people was fated to wander in the wilderness for forty years, one year for each day the spies had spent in the land.

The Brazen Serpent

On another occasion when the Israelites complained about the lack of bread and water, God sent venomous snakes whose bite caused many to die. When they admitted their sin and pleaded for Moses to intercede with God, the Lord responded to Moses' prayer by ordering him to make a venomous serpent of bronze and set it upon a pole; any person bitten by a snake who looked upon it would live.

The Brazen Serpent
by Tintoretto.
Uganda 1297 (1994)

Striking the Rock

After Miriam the sister of Moses died, water became scarce and yet again the people complained that it would have been better to remain in Egypt than to perish in the wilderness. As before, Moses and Aaron called to the Lord for help. God ordered Moses to take his rod and gather the people together and speak to the rock, which would then burst forth with water for the people and their animals to drink. Moses did as God had ordered, but impatiently castigated the people, calling them ungrateful rebels. Instead of merely speaking to the rock, Moses angrily struck it twice and it yielded abundant water to satisfy the thirst of man and beast alike.

However, this action of Moses aroused the wrath of God, Who wanted to demonstrate to the people how the Almighty would provide for them in time of need. The Divine punishment of Moses and Aaron was harsh: "Because you did not sanctify Me in the eyes of the people of Israel, therefore you shall not bring them into the Promised Land."

The Death of Moses

Nearing the end of their forty years of wandering in the wilderness, the Israelites approached the Jordan River. Across it lay Canaan, the land that God had promised to their ancestors. Moses assembled the people and laid his hands on Joshua, transferring the mantle of leadership to his Divinely chosen successor.

Moses then spoke directly to the Israelites, recounting what had happened to them during the forty difficult years since God had redeemed them from slavery in Egypt. He stressed the need for the people to strictly obey all of God's commandments, listing the blessings that they would receive in return. However, Moses also enumerated a much longer series of devastating curses that would befall the Israelites if they failed to heed the Divine law.

Finally, Moses climbed to the top of Mount Nebo, where God showed him the entire land of Canaan. And Moses died on Mount Nebo in his one hundred and twentieth year, still a strong man with an active mind. Never again has there been in Israel a prophet like Moses, whom the Lord knew face to face.

Prophets

Joshua and the Conquest of Canaan

After Moses died, God commanded Joshua to lead the Israelites across the Jordan into the Promised Land. The priests led the way, carrying the Ark of the Covenant containing the tablets on which the Ten Commandments were written. When the first priest set foot in the Jordan River, the waters stopped flowing and the Israelites crossed on dry ground.

God then explained to Joshua how the Israelites would conquer the walled city of Jericho. For six days, soldiers in full

Joshua's conquest of Canaan. From left: "Be strong and of good courage, for you will deliver the land;" "And Israel crossed the Jordan on dry land;" "And the people shouted and the wall fell;" "And the sun stood still in Gibeon, the moon in the valley of Ayalon." *Israel 820-823 (1982)*

battle dress marched once around the city, followed by seven priests carrying the Ark of the Covenant and shofars (ram's horns). On the seventh day, the army and the priests circled the city seven times. Then the priests blew a long blast with the ram's horns. As soon as the people heard the piercing sound of the shofar, they shouted as loud as they could and the great walls of Jericho came tumbling down. The Israelites rushed into the city and destroyed it, offering all the gold, silver, and other treasures to God in thanksgiving for this great victory.

Some time later, the five kings of the Amorites launched a war against Gibeon, which had made a treaty with the Israelites. Joshua rushed to help Gibeon, and God assured him of victory. As promised, the Israelites were defeating the Amorites but could not completely overcome them before the approaching darkness of evening. Then Joshua called out before the Israelites: "Sun, stand still upon Gibeon; and you, Moon, in the valley of Ayalon." These heavenly bodies heeded Joshua's call until the Israelites had time to avenge themselves upon their enemies. And there was never a day like that before or since, when the God listened to the voice of a man; for God fought for Israel.

The Time of the Judges

The Israelites successfully conquered all of the land of Canaan and lived there for many years. However, the people did evil in the sight of God, praying to the gods of the Canaanites and forsaking the God of their fathers Who had taken them out of Egypt. These actions provoked the wrath of God, Who angrily delivered the Israelites into the hands of enemies who ruled over them harshly. Repeatedly, God brought judges to save the Israelites from the hand of their oppressors. However, as soon as each judge died, the people quickly went astray, bowing in worship to other gods and becoming ever more corrupt. The best known of these judges were Deborah, Gideon, Jephthah, and Samson.

Deborah

Deborah was a prophetess and a judge in Israel when Jabin, the king of Hazor, and Sisera, the captain of his army, oppressed the Israelites. She summoned Barak to lead the tribes in the battle of Megiddo against the Canaanites. Deborah planned the strategy that brought Barak victory, even though the better-equipped enemy had "900 chariots of iron."

In thanksgiving for God's deliverance of her people, Deborah sang a glorious hymn of triumph to the Lord.

Deborah.
Israel 574 (1975)

Gideon

Gideon was the judge who decisively defeated the Midianites. With a force of only 300 men, Gideon set out to do battle with thousands of enemy soldiers. His men quietly surrounded the enemy camp, each carrying a shofar and an empty jar with a torch inside it. When Gideon blew his shofar, this was a sign for all the men to blow their shofars, smash their jars on the ground, and wave their torches wildly. The blare of the trumpets, the clatter of the broken pottery, and the flashing of the torchlights startled the enemy. Terrified and still half asleep, they ran off in all directions brandishing their weapons, attacking and killing one another in the mass confusion. In gratitude, the people offered to make Gideon king, but he immediately refused, saying: "I will not rule over you, neither shall my son. God shall rule over you."

Gideon.
Israel 573 (1975)

Jephthah

Jephthah the Gileadite was a mighty man of valor, but the son of a harlot, and his father's legitimate sons drove him away from home. However, some years later the elders of Gilead recalled Jephthah to repel an Ammonite invasion. Jephthah agreed to return on condition that he be appointed chief of the land after the victory.

When the time for battle arrived. Jephthah rashly vowed to sacrifice to the Lord whatever would first come out of his house to meet him upon his victorious return. To his horror, it was his only daughter who rushed out first to greet him,

Jephthah.
Israel 575 (1975)

but Jephthah felt obliged to fulfill his solemn vow. His daughter resigned herself to her fate, begging only that it be postponed for two months so that she might have time to mourn with her companions. At the end of this period she met her tragic fate. It then became customary for Israelite women to commemorate this event by an annual four-day mourning period.

Above: *Samson and Delilah* by Rubens. *Grenada Grenadines 1232 (1991).*
Left: *Samson brings down the temple* by Sert. *Spain 1342 (1966)*

Samson

Samson was a Nazirite, a man consecrated to God who was forbidden to partake of wine or strong drink and whose supernatural strength lay in his unshorn hair. Brave as well as powerful, Samson became the leader of the Israelites, and he served as judge over them for twenty years.

Hannah and Samuel.
Israel 885 (1984).

The Philistines tried unsuccessfully to capture and kill Samson. However, when they learned that the hero of Israel had fallen in love with the beautiful Delilah, they saw their opportunity. For a price, she agreed to ascertain the source of Samson's strength. After three unsuccessful attempts, Delilah finally induced Samson to divulge his secret. Telling the Philistines to lie in wait by her bedchamber, Delilah rocked Samson to sleep, with his head on her lap. Immediately, she called for a man to shave off all of Samson's hair. Deprived of his strength, Samson was then seized by the Philistines who blinded him and imprisoned him in Gaza, forcing him to grind corn by turning a huge millwheel like an animal.

Some time later, the Philistines gathered in their temple for a religious festival and led Samson out in chains, roaring with laughter at his misery. They did not realize that his hair had grown back, and with it his strength. Feigning weariness, Samson asked his guards for permission to lean against the temple pillars and rest for a few moments. Uttering a final prayer to the Lord for vengeance, Samson seized the pillars with all his might and bent them so that the roof came crashing down, killing himself and the 3,000 worshipers. So in his death Samson killed more Philistines than he had during his life.

The Prophet Samuel

Samuel was an Israelite judge and prophet in the 11th century B.C.E., standing at the close of one era and the beginning of another. He was instrumental in the painful, but necessary, transition from a loose confederation of Hebrew tribes to a centralized monarchy. Hannah, his long-barren mother, prayed for a child and promised to dedicate her son to a Nazirite life in the important sanctuary of Shiloh. After Samuel had served as a judge for many years, in his old age the people asked him to select a king to rule over them and lead them in battle to break the oppressive yoke of the Philistines. Samuel warned the people of the downside of a monarchy, arguing that a king would take their sons to fight his wars and their daughters to be his perfumers, cooks, and bakers; a king would expropriate the best of their crops, wine, and olive trees to feed his retainers, and ultimately would make everyone his slaves. However, the people were adamant, and Samuel reluctantly anointed Saul as the first king of Israel.

King Saul

As king, Saul was a brave warrior who fought many battles against the enemies of Israel and won numerous victories. One day, Samuel relayed God's command that Saul exterminate the Amalekites and completely destroy their possessions. However, Saul did not comply with this order, sparing Agag (the Amalekite king) and acceding to the people's request to save the best of the captured herds to make a sacrifice to the Lord. Furious, Samuel said to Saul: "Do you think God delights more in sacrifices than in obedience to God's words? … Because you have rejected God's word, God has also rejected you from being king."

King Saul.
Israel 184 (1960)

Publicly rebuked by the prophet, Saul was constantly troubled by an evil spirit. Recognizing the dramatic change in their master and convinced that his depression could be lifted by listening to beautiful music, the king's servants called for David (the youngest son of Jesse) who was an accomplished harpist. Saul was enchanted with David, who was also a fine warrior, and made the lad his armor bearer. When melancholia depressed Saul's spirit, David's music would refresh him. However, Saul envied David's increasing popularity with the people and eventually developed such a blind hatred for the younger man that David was forced to flee for his life. In Saul's last battle with the Philistines, the Israelite forces were badly defeated. With his sons slain by the enemy, Saul fell upon his sword and killed himself.

David and Goliath

The Philistines and Israelites again prepared for war, with the armies massed on two mountains on either side of a valley. One day, Goliath, the strongest of the Philistines, came down into the valley and stood before the Israelites. He was an imposing man, standing almost ten feet tall, wearing a bronze helmet and covered with a heavy coat of armor. He carried

DAVID AND GOLIATH

*And all this assembly shall know that
the Lord saveth not the sword and spear:
for the battle is the Lord's, and he
will give you into our hands.*

Samuel chapter 17 verse 47

David and Goliath. *Guyana 2651 (1992)*

David and Jonathan
by Rembrandt.
Russia 4513 (1976)

an iron-tipped spear that looked like the trunk of a tree. Goliath challenged the Israelites to choose their best warrior to fight him, with the people of the loser becoming the slaves of the winner. The poorly armed Israelite warriors were terrified, but David volunteered to fight the giant. Saul dressed David in his own armor and a helmet of bronze, but they were so heavy that David could barely move. So David took off the armor and went out to meet Goliath armed with only five smooth stones and a slingshot. As they faced off, David slung a stone that struck the Philistine giant in the forehead, and Goliath fell face down on the ground. David ran to Goliath, took the fallen warrior's sword, and chopped off his head. When the Philistines saw that their champion was dead, they fled in terror. With a great shout, the Israelites pursued the fleeing Philistines and destroyed the enemy camp.

David and Jonathan

Jonathan, Saul's son, was David's constant friend and companion. Even though he was heir to the throne, Jonathan recognized that David would succeed Saul as king. When Saul threatened to kill David, Jonathan arranged for David to escape his father's wrath. Hearing of the battlefield deaths of Saul and his sons, David wept bitterly and tore his clothes. However, his deepest grief was reserved for Jonathan, whom David eulogized as "dear and delightful you were to me; your love for me was wonderful, surpassing the love of women."

David meets Abigail by Rubens.
Grenada Grenadines 1234 (1991)

David and Abigail

When fleeing from Saul, David sent ten of his men to the wealthy Nabal to ask for food and drink to sustain the fugitives. However, the miserly Canaanite refused the request. Abigail, Nabal's beautiful and wise wife, heard what had transpired and

King David by Chagall.
Israel 399 (1969)

that the angry David was approaching with a large force of armed men. She rushed to take food and drink to the approaching soldiers and begged David to spare her worthless husband and his servants, lest he (the future king) shame himself by shedding blood without cause. David was impressed by Abigail's sagacity and, after Nabal's death ten days later, sent for Abigail and married her.

David, King of Israel

Long before Saul's death, the prophet Samuel had anointed David secretly. Now the elders assembled in Hebron anointed the thirty-year-old David as king over the house of Judah. David reigned in Hebron for seven years and six months, until he became king of both Israel and Judah in Jerusalem, where he reigned over the entire country for another thirty-three years. After capturing Jerusalem, David transformed it into a holy city. With music and rejoicing he brought the Ark of the Covenant to Jerusalem, which later became known as the City of David.

Anointing of David by Raphael.
Grenada Grenadines 538 (1983)

David and Bathsheba

One evening, David was walking on the roof of his house when he saw a beautiful woman bathing. Informed that she was Bathsheba, the wife of Uriah the Hittite, he ordered her brought to his palace. When David found out that Bathsheba was

The Jewish World in Stamps

pregnant with his child, he attempted to return Uriah to his house. Failing to do so, David ordered his military commander to station Uriah in the front line opposite the enemy where the battle was fiercest and then fall back, thus leaving Uriah to meet his death. After Bathsheba's period of mourning for her husband was completed, David called her to the palace and she became his wife.

David's actions displeased the Lord, and the prophet Nathan came to the palace to rebuke the king. Nathan related a parable about two men – a rich man with many flocks and herds, and a poor man who had nothing except for one little lamb. When a traveler came to the rich man's house, he took the poor man's only lamb to prepare a meal for his guest, since he was too miserly to use one of his own animals. When David expressed his anger against the rich man, Nathan told him that he was the man. David realized he had committed a grievous sin and repented for his actions. The child born to him from this union died, but the following year Bathsheba bore David a son and named him Solomon.

Bathsheba bathing by Rubens.
Hungary 2489 (1977)

Solomon

After ruling Israel for forty years, David died and his kingdom passed to his son Solomon, who was renowned for his great wisdom. One day, two women who had recently given birth came before the king, each claiming that the live baby was hers and the dead infant belonged to the other. Solomon called for his sword and ordered the living child divided in two; in that way, each woman would receive half so that both would be satisfied. "No!" shrieked the first woman, "Let her have the living child, but do not kill it." However, the second woman approved of Solomon's compromise, saying "Let it be neither mine nor yours, but divide it." The king promptly awarded the child to the first woman, certain that she was the true mother since she loved the baby so much she would rather part with him than have him killed.

Anointing of Solomon by Raphael.
Grenada Grenadines 537 (1983)

Judgment of Solomon by Poussin.
Yemen 427 (M)

In the fourth year of his reign, Solomon began building a temple for the Lord in Jerusalem. Constructed with the finest cedar wood from Lebanon and huge blocks of stone, it was decorated with gold and rich carvings and fronted by two great bronze pillars. After seven years the building was finished, and Solomon dedicated the imposing edifice as the House of God.

The price of Solomon's luxury was high taxation. His peace was earned at the cost of unrest, political conflict, and idol worship introduced by his foreign wives. After Solomon's death the kingdom split apart into two rival states – Israel (Ephraim) in the north and Judah in the south.

Solomon's Temple. *Israel 1341 (1998)*

Isaiah

First of the major prophets. Isaiah, son of Amoz, prophesied in Judah during the 8th century B.C.E. from the death of King Uzziah (c. 742) until the middle of the reign of King Hezekiah. Isaiah attacked the moral laxity and injustice of his time. In a passage read today in synagogues on Yom Kippur, Isaiah railed against those who piously fast and then oppress their neighbors, arguing that God is more interested in social justice for the weak and the poor than in the offerings of sacrifices in the Temple. Isaiah envisioned a messianic era of world peace at the end of days, when "the lion shall lie down with the lamb" and "nation shall not lift up sword against nation; neither shall they learn war any more."

Isaiah.
Israel 525 (1973)

Isaiah witnessed three major events that are reflected in his prophesies: the invasion of Judah by the armies of Israel and Damascus for the purpose of forcing King Ahaz into an anti-Assyrian alliance (734); the destruction of the kingdom of Israel by the Assyrians (721); and Sennacherib's invasion of Judah (701). Throughout this time, the small kingdom of Judah faced a dual danger – the risk of being swallowed up by neighboring empires, and spiritual destruction through the loss of its belief in one God. Isaiah's political wisdom impelled him to advise strict isolation for Judah and the avoidance of entangling alliances with foreign nations.

Isaiah by Michelangelo.
Vatican City 388 (1964)

Many scholars consider chapters 40-66 to be written by a different prophet ("Second Isaiah"), who lived during the time of the Babylonian exile. This prophet comforts the exiled, suffering, and despairing people, assuring them that God will send a "servant" who will lead Israel from darkness to light, and that Israel will become a "salvation" (or "light") unto the nations.

Isaiah's prophecies. Right: "Swords into plowshares." *Hungary 1462 (1962); Russia2305a (1967);* below, from left: *United Nations 177-178 (1967); Vatican City 768-769 (1986).*
"The wolf shall dwell with the lamb, and the leopard shall lie down with the kid." *Israel 225-227 (1962)*

Jeremiah

Jeremiah.
Israel 526 (1973)

Second of the major prophets. Son of Hilkiah, a priest of Anathoth, Jeremiah witnessed the tragic events that ended in the destruction of Jerusalem. Beginning his prophecy in the thirteenth year of King Josiah, Jeremiah severely castigated the people for forsaking God and the Torah and turning to idolatry. Using the relationship of husband and wife as an analogy to that between God and Israel, Jeremiah accused Israel of being unfaithful to God, like a wife betraying her husband for a lover. Therefore, he exhorted the people to repent and worship the Lord, stressing the responsibility of each individual for his or her own acts. Jeremiah's prophecies foretold the disaster that would befall his people as punishment for their sins, but they rejected his doom-laden words. Although a prophet of apocalypse, Jeremiah emphasized the temporary nature of the destruction. He consoled the people with the assurance that God would redeem them from captivity, enabling a righteous Israel to eventually dwell in safety in its own land.

Jeremiah by Michelangelo.
Vatican City 390 (1964)

Ezekiel

Ezekiel.
Israel 527 (1973)

Third of the major prophets. Son of Buzi, Ezekiel was a younger contemporary of Jeremiah who also witnessed the destruction of Jerusalem and went into exile to Babylon. Like Jeremiah, Ezekiel believed in each person's individual responsibility to God and called for personal repentance to avert the otherwise inevitable catastrophe. Ezekiel's prophesies have great poetic beauty and are often steeped in mystical images. His vision of the Divine Chariot (merkava) formed the basis of early mystical speculation. In his symbolic vision of a valley of dry bones that were resurrected and rise again, Ezekiel envisioned a mighty army that will herald the rebirth of Israel.

The Chariot Vision of Ezekiel by Raphael.
Antigua 735 (1983)

Ezekiel's vision of the dry bones by Collantes. *Turks and Caicos 989-990 (1992)*

Joel

Second of the minor prophets. The Book of Joel gives a vivid, graphic description of a plague of locusts of unprecedented severity that struck the land like a marauding enemy, leaving in its wake ravished fields and vineyards and depriving the people of food. It exhorts the priests, the elders, and all the people to seek God's mercy through repentance, fasting, and prayer, promising that at the end of days God will destroy the nations that oppressed Judah and will restore God's exiled people to their land.

Amos

Third of the minor prophets. A shepherd in the hills of Judah around 750 B.C.E., Amos went to sell his animals in nearby Bethel, the principal religious center of the northern kingdom of Israel. There he cried out against the injustice and poverty of the masses, sorrowfully predicting that the punishment of Israel would be its destruction by Assyria. Amos called for justice for all humanity and was the first to see God as the universal Lord of all the nations. Nevertheless, Amos charged Israel with living up to a unique standard of righteousness, in keeping with its role as God's chosen people.

Jonah

Fifth and most famous of the minor prophets. The son of Amitai, Jonah was commanded to go to Nineveh to announce to its inhabitants that God would destroy the city because of their wickedness. He attempted to flee by sea in the opposite direction, was cast overboard during a savage storm, and swallowed by a great fish (often mistranslated as a whale). After spending three days and nights in the fish's belly praying to God, Jonah was spewed out onto dry land. Finally Jonah obeyed God's will and went to Nineveh to prophesize its destruction. When the people repented and God renounced the planned punishment, Jonah was greatly displeased by this Divine forgiveness (since his prophesy of destruction did not come true) and petulantly asked God to take his life. While Jonah was sitting sweltering in the hot sun outside Nineveh, God caused a large plant to grow and provide welcome shade. On the following day, however, God sent a worm to attack the plant, which withered and died. As the heat of the day increased, Jonah became faint and asked for death. Then God said: "You cared about the plant, which you did not work for and which you did not grow, which appeared overnight and perished overnight. And should I not care about Nineveh, that great city, in which there are more than a hundred and twenty thousand persons who do not yet know their right hand from their left, and many beasts as well?" Because of its message of Divine forgiveness in response to true repentance, the entire Book of Jonah is read in the synagogue during the afternoon service on Yom Kippur.

Joel.
Brazil 872 (1958)

Amos.
Palau 396 (1996)

"And there was a mighty tempest... and Jonah was in the belly of the fish... the sun beat upon the head of Jonah ." *Israel 242-244 (1963)*

Now the Lord had prepared a great fish to swallow up Jonah.

Jonah 1:17

Jonah and the Whale

Jonah and the Whale. *Palau 321 (1993)*

Micah

Sixth of the minor prophets. A peasant from a tiny village in Judah (ca. 730-705 B.C.E.), Micah railed against the social corruption of the cities, the injustice of the rulers, and the oppression of the poor. He predicted the destruction of the Temple and the beloved city of Jerusalem. Reminding the people of God's love for Israel, Micah prophesied an era of universal justice at the end of days, when "they shall sit every man under his vine and under his fig tree, and none shall make them afraid."

Nahum
Brazil 988 (1964)

Micah's "End of Days"
prophecy. *Israel 704 (1978)*

Nahum

Seventh of the minor prophets. Nahum prophesied the coming of Divine vengeance on Nineveh and provides a vivid description of the city's destruction in 612 B.C.E.

Zechariah

Eleventh of the minor prophets. Zechariah lived in Jerusalem after the return from Babylonian exile (c. 520 B.C.E.). His writing is filled with mystic visions replete with symbolic figures. Zechariah called for rebuilding the Temple and prophesied the coming of the messianic age, when all the nations will recognize the universal kingdom of God in Jerusalem – "And the Lord shall be King over all the earth; in that day there shall be the Lord alone and His name alone" (also the concluding verse of the *Aleinu* prayer).

Zechariah.
Italy 823 (1961)

Elijah

Prophet of the Northern Kingdom during the reign of Ahab (874-853 B.C.E.), the king who "did what is evil in the eyes of the Lord." Ahab married the wicked Phoenician princess Jezebel and permitted her to build an idolatrous altar and sanctuary to Baal.

A gaunt figure clothed in goatskin, Elijah prophesied drought as punishment for idolatry and disappeared into the desert to be fed by ravens. When the people cried out for rain, Ahab still refused to forbid idol worship. In a dramatic confrontation on Mount Carmel, Elijah challenged the 450 priests of Baal to prove that their idol was the true god. After they vainly beseeched Baal for some response, the Lord answered Elijah's prayer by sending fire from heaven to consume the offering on the prophet's altar. Witnessing this awesome sight, all the people fell on their faces chanting, "The Lord He is God; the Lord He is God;" then a heavy rain fell and the drought ended.

According to tradition, Elijah did not die but was carried to heaven in a chariot pulled by horses of fire. The prophet is portrayed as eventually descending from heaven to usher in the messianic age. Indeed, when the Talmudic sages had a difference of opinion and could not arrive at a decision, they tabled the discussion by deferring it "until the appearance of Elijah the prophet." Elijah is described as the comforter of the poor and the suffering, appearing miraculously when the need is greatest. To this day, a special cup for Elijah is filled with wine at the Passover seder.

Elijah fed by the angels
by Tintoretto
Uganda 1294 (1994)

Elijah goes to heaven.
Sweden 640 (1964)

Because Elijah is said to appear at every circumcision to determine whether this child will be the long-awaited Messiah, a special chair is left for the prophet.

Elisha

Israelite prophet who was Elijah's devoted servant and outstanding disciple (late 9th century B.C.E.). Continuing his master's efforts to rid Israel of Baal worship, Elisha instigated a revolt against King Jehoram, son of Ahab, which succeeded in destroying him, his mother Jezebel (the idolatrous queen), and the priests of Baal. No other prophet in Israel is reputed

Elijah goes to heaven.
Vatican City C3 (1938)

IN OUR IMAGE · ELISHA
Guy Rowe (1894-1969)

PALAU   20¢

Elisha. *Palau 396 (1996)*

to have performed as many miracles as Elisha. He is said to have divided the waters of the Jordan, resurrected a child, and healed a Syrian captain of leprosy. The many stories of Elisha's miracle-working reflect the people's love for this prophet, who healed the sick and helped the poor.

Huldah

Only prophetess mentioned during the period of the monarchy. Huldah was consulted by King Josiah concerning the Book of the Law discovered during the restoration of the Temple (622 B.C.E.). She prophesied God's ultimate judgment upon the nation, but this was to be postponed until after Josiah's peaceful death because of the king's acts of repentance.

HULDAH חולדה

Huldah.
Israel 887 (1984)

Writings

Psalms verses: 150:5 and 33:3. *Marshall Islands 162-3 (1987)*; 19:4 and 121:4. *Israel 496 (1972), 642-644 (1992, 1977)*

Psalms

First book in the Writings. Most of the 150 psalms, known in Hebrew as *Tehilim* ("chants of praise"), are attributed to King David. Some are odes praising God, called Halleluyahs; others are poems of thanksgiving, pilgrim songs, or mournful elegies. Many of the psalms have been incorporated into the formal synagogue service. Psalms stressing God's mercy are frequently recited by persons gathered at the bedside of the dangerously ill and at houses of mourning.

Proverbs

Second book in the Writings. Composed according to tradition by King Solomon, Proverbs (together with Job and Ecclesiastes) constitutes the major Wisdom Literature of the Bible. The book contains a variety of pithy sayings that teach wise and moral conduct for everyday life.

Proverbs verses: 4:7, 22:6, 3:10. *Israel 475-476 (1972), 814 (1983)*

Job

Job.
Palau 396 (1996)

Third book in the Writings. The theme of Job is Divine justice, and the book delves into the timeless question of why do the righteous suffer. Job is a good and wealthy man who is blessed with a loving family of ten children. Satan (the accusing angel) argues that Job's piety is only the result of his good life; he bets God that if Job were deprived of all his riches, he would surely denounce the Lord to his face. In a series of calamities, Job loses his wealth and his children and becomes ill with a loathsome disease. Three friends visiting Job assume that his misfortunes have come as punishment for his sins, and they urge him to confess his guilt and accept his sufferings as God's righteous judgment. However, Job insists that he is innocent and pours out the bitterness of his soul. Finally, a fourth friend scolds Job for lacking trust in God. The book ends with Job realizing that humans cannot really understand the mystery of God's ways; God speaks to him "out of a whirlwind" and restores his health and happiness.

Song of Songs

Fourth book in the Writings and first of the *Megillot*, Song of Songs is read in the synagogue on Passover. According to tradition, King Solomon in his youth was the author of this series of beautiful love poems, which are viewed as an allegory symbolizing the mutual love of God and Israel.

Song of Songs 7:12
Israel 554 (1975)

Book of Ruth

Ruth and Boaz.
Israel 886 (1984)

Fifth book in the Writings and second of the five *megillot*, the Book of Ruth is read in the synagogue on Shavuot. It tells of Elimelech and Naomi of Bethlehem in Judah, who in a time of famine migrated to Moab where their two sons married local women (Orpah and Ruth). When her husband and two sons died, the grieving Naomi prepared to return home to Bethlehem and told her daughters-in-law to go back to their parents. Orpah obeyed sadly, but Ruth refused, loyally clinging to her mother-in-law and saying: "Wherever you go, I will go; wherever you lodge, I will lodge; your people shall be my people, and your God my God." Arriving in Bethlehem at the beginning of the grain harvest, Ruth took advantage of the privilege of gleaning for food, a custom accorded the poor. The field in which Ruth came to glean fortuitously belonged to a kind and prosperous farmer by the name of Boaz, who was a kinsman of Elimelech and thus also of Ruth's dead husband. According to the tradition of levirate marriage, once the one closer relative refused to marry Ruth and underwent the ritual of *chalitzah* (taking off the shoe), Boaz consented to marry Ruth, thus fulfilling the ancient duty of "establishing the name of the dead upon his inheritance." Ruth and Boaz had a child named Obed, who was the grandfather of King David.

Top, left to right: Ruth tells Naomi, "Wherever you go I shall go;" Ruth harvesting grain in the fields of Boaz.
Bottom, left to right: Ruth receives a man's sandal, finalizing sale of Naomi's field; Ruth with Naomi, Boaz and Oded (King David's grandfather). *Guyana 2833 (1994)*

Lamentations

Sixth book in the Writings and third of the *Megillot*, Lamentations is read in the synagogue on Tisha b'Av. Traditionally ascribed to the prophet Jeremiah, the book consists of five beautiful elegies, poems of mourning lamenting the fall of Jerusalem and the destruction of the First Temple.

Ecclesiastes

Seventh book in the Writings and fourth of the *Megillot*, Ecclesiastes is read in the synagogue on Sukkot. Also traditionally ascribed to Solomon, but actually written much later, Ecclesiastes views life as devoid of meaning, for the purposes of God cannot be fathomed. Since "all is vanity," there is nothing good for people except to be happy and live the best life they can.

Jeremiah by Michelangelo.
Italy 825 (1961)

Esther

Eighth book in the Writings and last of the five *megillot*, the Book of Esther is read in the synagogue on Purim. It tells the story of the beautiful Esther, whose Hebrew name was Hadassah (myrtle). She was an orphan who lived with her wise cousin Mordecai in the Persian capital of Shushan. When King Ahasuerus deposed Queen Vashti for insubordination, he sponsored a nationwide contest and selected Esther as her replacement. Neither the king nor his wicked minister Haman knew that Esther was Jewish. When Haman plotted to destroy all the Jews of Persia, Mordecai convinced Queen Esther to forgo her personal safety and plead with the king to save her people from destruction. She skillfully exposed Haman's nefarious plot at a banquet, and the evil minister was summarily hung on gallows that he had prepared for Mordecai. The joyous feast of Purim celebrates this deliverance of the Jewish people.

The story of Purim.
From right: King Ahasuerus' feast;
crowning of Esther; Haman leading Mordecai's
horse. *Israel 593-595 (1976)*

Esther, Haman and Ahasuerus *by Rembrandt*.
Russia 4516 (1976)

Esther before Ahasuerus by Rubens.
Grenada Grenadines 1227 (1991)

Daniel

Ninth book in the Writings, it relates the story of the prophet Daniel, who was taken captive to Babylon and trained for the king's service. At a great royal banquet, while a thousand Babylonian lords drank wine from gold and silver utensils from the vanquished Temple, a mysterious hand suddenly appeared and silently wrote four strange words across the palace wall: *Mene mene tekel upharsin.* Trembling with fright, King Belshazzar called his wise men to explain this eerie event, but none could interpret the words. When the queen remembered that Daniel had interpreted the visions of the king's late father, the young man was brought to the palace. He explained that the words foretold the downfall of the king, whose arrogant actions had earned the wrath of God.

Daniel in the Lions' Den by Rubens.
Grenada Grenadines 1235 (1991)

II Chronicles 30:5:
"Let the voice of Israel
be heard from Beer
Sheba to Dan. . ."
Israel 936 (1986)

That very night, Belshazzar was killed and Darius became king. Despite the enactment of a royal decree prohibiting anyone from presenting a petition to any god or man other than the king, Daniel continued to pray and give thanks to God three times a day. As punishment, Daniel was cast into the lion's den, but was miraculously saved from death.

The last half of the Book of Daniel, written in Hebrew (the rest is in Aramaic), contains mystical revelations about the end of days, the day of judgment in which the wicked world powers will be destroyed and the Jewish people restored to their home.

Chronicles

The first and second Books of Chronicles are the final books in the Writings. They retell the history of the Jewish people from Creation to the close of the Babylonian exile. Unlike the first and second Books of Kings, Chronicles omits the story of the northern Kingdom of Israel and concentrates on the history of Judah, stressing the priestly duties and Temple ritual.

Apocrypha

Book of Judith

Historical narrative dating from Second Temple times. Nebuchadnezzar, king of Assyria who reigned in Nineveh, sent Holofernes, his commander in chief, to subdue the Jews. He laid siege to Bethulia, a small fortified town that occupied a strategic position along a mountain pass. When famine and thirst undermined the courage of the defenders and they contemplated surrender, a widow named Judith said that she would deliver Bethulia from its enemy. Gaining the permission of the leaders of the town, Judith went down to the camp of Holofernes who, captivated by beauty, invited her to a feast. When, overcome by wine, Holofernes fell asleep, Judith took his dagger, cut off his head, and returned with her trophy. Deprived of their commander by Judith's courageous deed, the panic-stricken Assyrian soldiers fled when the Jews attacked.

Judith with the head of Holofernes by Titian. *Dominica 1114 (1988)*

Susanna and the Elders

Apocryphal work added at the end of the canonical Book of Daniel in ancient versions. The virtuous and beautiful wife of a prosperous Jew of Babylon, Susanna was unjustly accused by two Jewish elders of having committed adultery and was condemned to death. However, she was proved innocent when the elders, interrogated by Daniel, disagreed about the tree under which the adultery allegedly took place. In accord with biblical law that visits false witnesses with the punishment that the accused would have received, the elders were executed.

In the 16th to late 18th centuries, the image of the elders lasciviously watching Susanna bathing was popular among such masters as Veronese, Tintoretto, Rubens and Rembrandt.

Susanna in the bath by Rubens. *Paraguay 1710d (1977)*

Book of Tobit

In this book of the Apocrypha, Tobias travels to claim money lent by his father, Tobit, to a relative named Raguel. Raguel had an only daughter Sarah, who had already been married seven times; however, on each occasion, the bridegroom had died on the wedding night. According to the law of the Torah, Sarah was obligated to marry her young kinsman Tobias rather than a stranger. After magically driving away Ashmedai, the demon who slew the grooms, Tobias married Sarah. When his father-in-law saw that Tobias had survived, he doubled the duration of the wedding banquets from seven to 14 days.

Wedding of Tobias by Guardi. *Antigua 2118 (1997)*

Salome

Salome by Titian. *Dominica 1117 (1988)*

Daughter of Herod and Herodias and, through the latter's remarriage, stepdaughter of the tetrarch Herod Antipas, the youngest son of Herod the Great. In celebration of the birthday of Herod Antipas, Salome danced before the ruler and his assembled guests. To signify his pleasure, the tetrarch offered to give Salome whatever she asked of him, "unto half of my kingdom." Salome consulted her mother Herodias who, infuriated by John the Baptist's condemnation of her marriage to Herod (which was against Jewish law), suggested that Salome demand the preacher's head. With extreme reluctance, Herod ordered the execution of John, whom he had confined in prison. John's head was brought out on a platter, a grisly relic that Salome presented to her mother.

The Jewish World in Stamps

The Jewish Diaspora

Exiled to a strange land and with their Temple in ruins, the Jews in Babylon wept bitterly over their fate, longing for a return to Zion. In time, however, they developed their own traditions and institutions. The Babylonian rulers gave them autonomy in religious and spiritual matters, while allowing them to engage freely in agriculture and trade.

When Cyrus of Persia defeated the Babylonians in 538 B.C.E., he fulfilled Isaiah's prophecy by permit-

The Babylonian Exile by Lilien. ("By the rivers of Babylon there we sat down, yea, we wept, as we remembered Zion.") Israel 625 (1977)

ting the exiled Israelites to return to Judea and rebuild the Temple in Jerusalem. However, the majority of Jews remained in their adopted land, where they had maintained their religious identity while reaching a standard of living never known in Israel. This vibrant community was critical to Jewish survival during subsequent eras when few Jews remained in the Land of Israel..

Above: Cylinder of Cyrus. *Romania 2293 (1971)*. Below: Tomb of Cyrus. *Turkey 1898 (1971)*

Alexander the Great. *Greece 404 (1937)*

Under the leadership of Ezra and Nehemiah, those who returned rebuilt the Temple and the walls of Jerusalem. During the following period, high priests ruled instead of kings, scribes replaced prophets as the teachers of the people, and the synagogue developed into a permanent institution. Judea came under Greek rule when Alexander the Great (356-323 B.C.E.) conquered the Persian Empire. After his death, his empire was divided; Judea first came under the control of the Ptolemies of Egypt, and then was ruled by the Seleucids of Syria. Tensions between Greek culture and Jewish traditions reached a boiling point during the reign of Antiochus IV (Epiphanes), who defiled the Temple altar and turned the building into a shrine to Zeus. The infuriated Judeans launched a revolt led by Judah Maccabee, whose greatly outnumbered forces ousted the Syrians from the land in 165 B.C.E. and rededicated the Temple (see Chanukah). His descendants, the priestly family known as Hasmoneans, established a free commonwealth. However, the Hasmoneans soon forgot the lesson of religious freedom and forcibly converted the entire population of Idumea when they conquered this southern land. This came back to haunt the Jews when Roman legions invaded Judea in 63 B.C.E. The Romans gave control of the country to an Idumean family, who though officially Jewish were really pagans who had little respect for Judaism or the Jews. The most famous of these rulers was Herod the Great (73-4 B.C.E.), who imposed heavy taxes to pay for his

Judah Maccabee. *Israel 209 (1961)*

King Herod.
Finland 581 (1975)

massive building projects and lavish decoration of the Temple. After more than 100 years of rule by members of the Herodian line, the Jews rebelled once again but were crushed by the Roman legions. In 70 C.E., Jerusalem fell and the Temple was destroyed by Titus. This victory was later commemorated in Rome by the erection of an arch on which a bas-relief depicts the Temple vessels carried as spoils in a triumphal procession. The fires of rebellion were kindled again in the Bar Kochba revolt of 132-135 C.E., which was violently suppressed. The Romans renamed the land Palestine to erase all Jewish associations; Jerusalem was rebuilt as a soldiers' colony and renamed Aelia Capitolina.

Herod's Temple .
Antigua 2012 (1996)

Yet Jewish life in the land was not extinguished. Two years before the fall of the Temple, the aged Rabbi Yochanan ben Zakkai asked a pair of his students, Joshua ben Hananiah and Eliezer ben Hyrcanus, to pretend that he had died and carry him in a coffin out of the besieged city of Jerusalem. Once past the armed guards, ben Zakkai went directly to the Roman general Vespasian and requested permission to gather a small community of sages and organize a school at Yavneh, south of Jaffa. When Jerusalem fell, the Academy of Yavneh became the site of a new Jewish High Court (Sanhedrin) and the seat of Jewish scholarship and culture. It retained this position until the unsuccessful Bar Kochba revolt, when the major focus of Jewish activity moved north to Tiberias. There, in about 200 C.E., Judah the Prince (Judah ha-Nasi) supervised the completion of the Mishnah, the systematic code of law that represented the authoritative version of the verbal tradition that had been handed down through the generations. Over the next several hundred years, sages in Palestine and Babylon engaged in exten-

Arch of Titus. *Italy 749 (1958)*

sive discussions (Gemara) concerning how to apply the rules and precepts of the Mishnah to the practical issues of the day. This produced the Talmud, the massive work that became the lifeblood of Jewish thought. There are actually two Talmuds: the Palestinian, completed about 400 C.E., and the more authoritative Babylonian, which was finally edited in the 6th century.

Ashkenazim and Sephardim

After the Muslim conquests of the 7th and 8th centuries, the rule of Islam extended

Talmudic sages and heroes (left to right): Rabbi Joshua ben Hananiah. *Israel 730 (1979)*;
Bar Kochba. *Israel 210 (1961)*; Rabbi Johanan Ha'Sandlar. *Israel 732 (1979)*

from India to the Mediterranean. For four centuries, the Babylonian community ruled much of the intellectual and spiritual life of world Jewry. Its customs and traditions were adopted by Jews as far away as Spain, which gradually became the most important Jewish center in Europe, and those who followed these traditions became known as Sephardim. Living in a huge territory with a magnificent culture, the Sephardim of this "Golden Age" participated in all aspects of society, rising to the highest ranks of government, prospering in business, and gaining fame in the professions, especially in medicine. They produced outstanding Jewish literature, unrivaled Hebrew poetry, and the greatest of all Jewish philosophers, Maimonides. The intrepid Benjamin of Tudela (12th century), often called the "Jewish Marco Polo," spent 13 years traveling throughout the known world, writing vivid and detailed descriptions of Jewish life and customs in Europe, Asia, and North Africa.

Golden Age of Spain (left to right): Toledo Synagogue; Benjamin of Tudela.
Spain 2972, 2969 (1998)

Rashi.
Israel 732 (1979)

Meanwhile, the Jews of Central and Eastern Europe who preserved the Palestinian traditions became known as Ashkenazim. After the fall of the Roman Empire, the area in which they lived became a battleground for Germanic tribes who fought each other and against the Christian Church. City life collapsed, schools closed, and education was all but unknown during these so-called Dark Ages. Nevertheless, the Jews preserved a high level of literacy, with all males learning to read the Bible, Talmud, and prayer book. The Ashkenazim also produced great sages, most notably the preeminent biblical and talmudic commentator, Rashi. An acronym for Rabbi Shlomo Yitzchak, Rashi (1040–1105) founded a famed Talmudic academy in his native Troyes (France) that attracted students from far and wide. Convinced of the lack of good commentaries to facilitate study of the Torah and Talmud, Rashi undertook the task of providing one. His clear and explicit explanations, incorporating both literal and midrashic interpretations and written in a

Jews who helped Columbus discover America (clockwise): Abravanel, fundraiser; Santangel, fundraiser; de Torres, translator; Zacuto, astronomer.
Sierra Leone 909-912 (1992)

lucid Hebrew style using his own unique script, have become the standard guide for every student to this day.

Unlike the Sephardim, who flourished under the generally tolerant rulers of the Muslim Empire, the Ashkenazim faced unremitting persecution by the Roman Catholic Church. The Jews were falsely accused of a litany of crimes, even including the "ritual murder" of Christian children for the purpose of using their blood in making matzah for Passover. Many Ashkenazi Jews were massacred; others were expelled from England, France, and many parts of Germany.

For several centuries, Spanish Jews escaped the worst of these horrors. However, when the Catholics gained control of Spain they forcibly converted tens of thousands of Jews to Christianity. Many of these continued to practice Judaism in secret, but those "Conversos" or "Marranos" who were caught by the Inquisition were ruthlessly tortured and then burned at the stake. Finally, in 1492 the ruling monarchs Ferdinand and Isabella signed an edict expelling all Jews from Spain. The decree was made effective on Tisha b'Av, the fast day commemorating the destruction of the First and Second Temples. Ironically, on the same day three

The two events of 1492: above, Ferdinand and Isabella, who expelled Spanish Jewry. *Anguilla 704 (1986)*; below, the discovery of America. *Israel 1112 (1992)*

Maimonides - "The 'Moses' of the Diaspora"

Maimonides (Rambam, acronym of Rabbi Moses ben Maimon; 1135-1204)

Jewish philosopher, religious thinker, codifier and royal physician. The most illustrious figure in Judaism in the post-talmudic era, and one of the greatest of all time, Maimonides was born in Cordova, Spain, where his father was the religious head (dayan) of the community. After being forced to flee first to Fez (Morocco) and finally to Egypt, Maimonides settled in Fostat near Cairo. Though he served as both court physician and head of the Jewish community, Maimonides still devoted much time to study.

Among his voluminous writings are two major literary efforts. The *Mishneh Torah*, his only work written in Hebrew, was composed for the believing Jew untroubled by the apparent contradictions between revealed law and current philosophy, and its aim was to instruct him in the proper conduct so as to live according to the law. Divided into 14 books, the *Mishneh Torah* embraces the entire field of Jewish law. It is a model of logical sequence and studied method, with each chapter and each paragraph coming in natural sequence to its preceding one. As an introduction to this massive tome, Maimonides wrote the *Sefer ha-Mitzvot*. Deeming all previous attempts at enumerating the traditional 613 commandments unsatisfactory, Maimonides gave his own listing of the 248 positive and the 365 negative commandments, along with extensive comments. His *Guide for the Perplexed* was designed for the Jew who was firm in his religious beliefs and practices but, having studied philosophy, was perplexed by the literal meaning of biblical anthropomorphisms and needed an explanation of how to harmonize philosophy with religion. Maimonides is also known for his famous formulation of 13 Principles of Faith, which in his view every member of the Jewish community is bound to accept. Maimonides' death led to universal expressions of grief, and three days of public mourning was ordained throughout the Jewish world. His remains were taken to Tiberias for burial, and Maimonides' grave is still an object of pilgrimage.

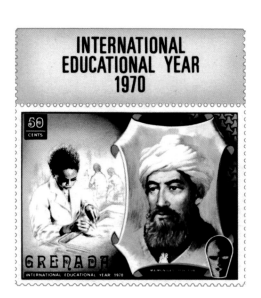
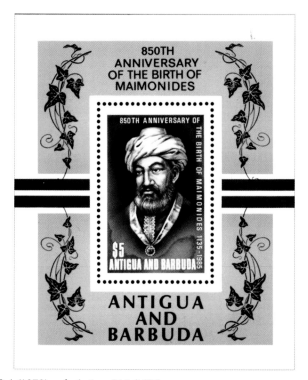

Moses Maimonides. *Grenada 402A (1970)* and *Antigua 816 (1985)*

Left: Don Isaac Abravanel. *Grenada Grenadines 1405 (1992)*. Right: Jews from Spain settle in Turkey. *Turkey 2526 (1997)*

500th anniversary of Jewish life in America. *Uruguay 1430 (1992)*

small ships sailed from the Spanish port of Cadiz on an expedition largely supported by Jews and Marranos – the voyage of Christopher Columbus to the land that would one day be the home of the largest Jewish community in the world.

In the early 1500's, the Jews of Germany and Italy were moved into ghettos, special walled sections of the towns in which they lived. As the ghettos became increasingly crowded and Christian rulers imposed heavier taxes, the Jews were reduced to desperate poverty. Although the Jews of Eastern Europe were not locked in ghettos, they also lived in poor conditions apart from their Christian neighbors. According to tradition, the Jewish community of Prague had to resort to a Golem fashioned by the Maharal (Judah ben Bezalel Loew; c. 1515-1609) to save itself from persecution.

Left: Maharal's tomb. *Czechoslovakia 3010 (1997)*. Right: *Shulchan Aruch. Israel 340 (1967)*

Nevertheless, some Jewish communities flourished during this time. The Turks, who had welcomed the Jewish exiles from Spain, conquered the Holy Land and permitted the revival of Jewish settlement there. The mystical city of Safed in the Galilee, where the first Hebrew printing press in Israel was established in 1577, became home to the two most illustrious figures of the age – Joseph Caro and Isaac Luria. Caro (1488-1575) compiled the *Shulchan Aruch* ("Set Table"), which until this day is the authoritative code of Jewish law. Originally intended for young students not yet prepared to weigh the complex decisions of the authorities, the *Shulchan Aruch* provided such a methodical and easily accessible arrangement of the various laws that it became the most popular handbook for both scholars and laypersons. Caro's code was accepted immediately by Sephardic Jewry, but was only adopted by Ashkenazim when Moses Isserles (the Rema) added many of their customs and practices in his gloss, the *Mapa* ("Tablecloth"). Isaac ben Solomon Luria (1534–1572), known as Ha-Ari (an acronym meaning "the [sacred] lion", taken from the initials of the Hebrew phrase Ha-Elohi Rabbi Yitzchaki, "the Divine Rabbi"), was the most influential teacher of Kabbalah. In brief, Luria described a concept in which the present world has arisen out of three great dramatic cosmic events – the contraction of God (*Tzimtzum*) to allow space for the creation of a finite world, the breaking of the vessels (in which Holy Sparks flew off in all directions, to be trapped in shells of impurity), and the human task of repairing the world (*Tikkun Olam*). Since all things and actions in the world, no matter how seemingly trivial, are saturated with Holy Sparks, the task of the Jew is to observe the commandments and practice good deeds so as to elevate these sparks to their state of pre-creation unity.

Isaac Luria's synagogue. *Israel 495 (1972)*

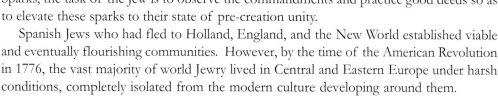

Seal of an Austrian ghetto. *Austria 985 (1974)*

Spanish Jews who had fled to Holland, England, and the New World established viable and eventually flourishing communities. However, by the time of the American Revolution in 1776, the vast majority of world Jewry lived in Central and Eastern Europe under harsh conditions, completely isolated from the modern culture developing around them.

Enlightenment and Emancipation

The Enlightenment was an era of great social and cultural changes that began in Western Europe in the 18th century. An age of rationalism and unparalleled scientific advancement, it led to philosophers in England and France questioning the existing authority of Church and State and the prevailing social order. They introduced new concepts of freedom, religious tolerance, equality, and reliance on reason rather than tradition. These concepts led to the Emancipation, which began with the French Revolution (1789) and eventually resulted in the removal of some political and civic restrictions from Jews. Both of these processes allowed Jews in Western Europe and the New World to become more active participants in the

Emancipation, 150th anniversary.
Italy 2197 (1995)

Moses Mendelssohn.
Germany 9N429 (1979)

general life of their communities. A prime example was Moses Mendelssohn (1729-1786), the preeminent philosopher of the German Enlightenment and spiritual leader of German Jewry. A master of secular culture and considered the embodiment of the humanist ideal, Mendelssohn wanted Jews to learn the German language as a gateway to the knowledge of the outside world. His translation of the Pentateuch and Psalms into German (in Hebrew letters printed by the side of the original Hebrew text) allowed many advanced Jewish students to learn the German language and become immersed in the study of general European culture. Mendelssohn's masterwork, *Jerusalem*, outlined the ideals of religious and political toleration, separation of Church and State, and equality of all citizens. At the same time, however, Mendelssohn pleaded with Jews to maintain their "particularism" and the absolute authority of Jewish laws. Nevertheless, the Enlightenment and Emancipation had little effect on the masses of Jews trapped in Eastern Europe, many of whom remained in cultural and physical isolation until their destruction in the Holocaust.

A natural result of the Enlightenment and Emancipation was assimilation. Throughout Jewish history, although Jews have tended to adopt the language, manners, and customs of their neighbors, they continued to live a full and traditional Jewish life. Protected from outside influences in the ghettos of Central Europe and the shtetls of Eastern Europe, the bulk of the Jewish people retained their identity. However, as Jews of Western Europe became aware of the vibrant life around them, many decided that success in this new world required them to renounce their Jewish

The French Revolution (with text of the law "Relative to the Jews"). *Israel 1027 (1989)*

The Jewish World in Stamps

The Baal Shem Tov's synagogue.
Israel 211 (1961)

customs and completely adopt the culture of their neighbors. For many Jews, being baptized as Christians was their ticket to societal advancement in the arts and the professions. Others attempted to retain their Jewish traditions while at the same time becoming active participants in the secular culture around them. However, the pogroms in Russia and anti-Semitic events like the Dreyfus Affair in France clearly indicated that Europe was not ready to accept the Jews fully, whether assimilated or not, and led to the rise of Zionism. This lesson was given tragic validation during the Holocaust, when the official policy of the Nazi occupation of Europe was the physical extermination of all Jews, even those who had assimilated. With the birth of Israel and the coming of age of American Jewry, Jews are finally free to live a full Jewish life or to assimilate completely. Except in the Orthodox community, today an alarming number of Jews outside Israel assimilate by lack of Jewish education and intermarriage, issues that have been labeled as crises by rabbis and community leaders who have so far been powerless to solve them.

Hasidism, Reform, and Orthodoxy

Although the Enlightenment and Emancipation led many Jews to assimilation, this period also saw the development of two important new approaches to Judaism, both of which were met with harsh opposition from traditionalists. In 18th century

Vilna Gaon.
Israel 1304 (1997)

Poland, the charismatic Baal Shem Tov (Israel ben Eliezer; c. 1700-1760) founded the Hasidic movement, which appealed to the religious needs of the poor, unlearned, and neglected masses. The Baal Shem Tov (literally, "master of the good name" or "miracle worker"), popularly known by the acronym "Besht," found his true religious feeling in the marvels of the natural world and stressed devotion to God and dedicated prayer. He taught that joyful and enthusiastic worship, even that of an ignorant man, finds more favor in the eyes of God than cold scholarship and knowledge of the Law. These teaching had great popular appeal, and this new Hasidism spread like wildfire throughout East European Jewry.

Chatam Sofer
Slovakia 196 (1994)

The major figure of the Mitnagdim ("opposition" [to Hasidism]), was the Vilna Gaon (Elijah ben Solomon; 1720–1797). A semi-legendary intellectual giant, he towered over Lithuanian ("Litvak") Jewish culture, whose achievements attained their pinnacle of expression in the 19th century in many celebrated yeshivot. The Vilna Gaon strenuously objected to the singing of wordless melodies (nigunim) in prayer services and other new customs of the Hasidim, attacking their stress on emotions rather than traditional scholarship and their giving Kabbalah precedence over halachic studies.

The Reform movement in the 19th century tried to combat assimilation by modernizing Judaism to adapt to the popular tenets of the Enlightenment. In an effort to make their services more understandable and enjoyable, they eliminated some rituals deemed no longer meaningful and introduced new ones, such as using an organ during services and reciting some prayers in the vernacular. The success of Reform Judaism led to two different approaches by traditionalists. The Chatam Sofer (Moses Sofer; 1762–1839), head of the prestigious yeshivah of Pressburg, declared total war with no concessions in the battle against modernity, arguing that any innovation, even though unimportant from the point of view of halachah, was strictly forbidden simply because it was an innovation. Samson Raphael Hirsch, the leader of Neo-Orthodoxy, understood the need for change in Jewish life and accepted the value of secular culture, but steadfastly maintained that the Jews must keep their unique identity through observance of the mitzvot as taught in the Torah and interpreted in the Talmud.

Statue of Liberty with Emma Lazarus' poem,
The New Colossus. Antigua & Barbuda 834 (1985)

From 1880 to 1914, Western Europe enjoyed the world's highest standard of living and ruled most of the peoples of the earth through a vast network of colonies on all continents. In Russia, vicious pogroms terrorized the Jewish population and were the catalyst for a mass exodus of Jews. Indeed, between 1880-1920, about two million Jews (20% of the world Jewish population) emigrated from Eastern Europe to the United States, heeding Emma Lazarus' call to "give me your tired, your poor, your huddled masses yearning to breathe free." They established vibrant communities, especially in the Lower East Side of Manhattan, where nearly three-quarters of the Jewish immigrants settled. Distressed by hordes of penniless immigrants flooding their community, the wealthier Jews moved to better homes and neighborhoods uptown. Soon there were two separate Jewish populations in New York – the prosperous, Americanized, assimilated or predominantly Reform Jews of primarily German origin and the poor Eastern European Jews who spoke Yiddish and were traditional if not rigidly Orthodox. Life was hard in the slums and sweatshops of New York and other American port cities where Jews congregated, but they received much-needed help from the established Jewish community.

Dramatic changes throughout the globe were brought about by World War I, the first major European conflict in forty years. Lasting from 1914 to 1918, the war left nearly 10 million soldiers dead and another 20 million wounded. The Austro-Hungarian and Ottoman Empires collapsed. In the midst of the fighting, the Russian czar was overthrown and a new government was established by the Communists based on the economic and political theories developed by Karl Marx in his *Das Kapital*. The map of Europe was dramatically changed as new or recreated states were carved out of territory taken from the defeated powers and Russia. In the wake of the Versailles Peace Conference, millions of Jews found themselves as citizens of Poland, Lithuania, Romania, Czechoslovakia, Austria, Yugoslavia, or Hungary. In the Middle East, new states of Turkey, Syria, Lebanon, and Iraq were established, and the Land of Israel became part of the British Mandate of Palestine.

The treaties that ended World War I played a major role in creating the conditions that led to the rise of the Nazis in Germany and World War II. The victorious Allies forced Germany to pay huge amounts in war reparations that wreaked economic havoc on the country. Many of the new states were created artificially, rather than based on national culture; thus, a large number of German-speaking people suddenly found themselves in the new Czechoslovakia. Despite President Woodrow Wilson's call for complete world disarmament and the establishment of a League of Nations to keep the peace, the Western democracies forced Germany to relinquish its weapons while keeping their own armed forces. Moreover, the League of Nations was weak and ineffective; Germany was not permitted to join until 1926, Russia did not become a member until 1934, and the United States itself never even joined at all. For the next decade, Western Europe and the United States reveled in prosperity. Business was booming, and America celebrated the frivolity of the "Roaring Twenties." Germany, however, experienced a far different fate. Inflation was so great that paper money became all but worthless. Finally, in 1929 the world economy collapsed in the Great Depression. The American stock market crashed and fortunes were wiped out almost overnight. Business activity in America and Western Europe ground to a halt and millions lost their jobs. In 1933, new leaders emerged in both the United States and Germany. Franklin Delano Roosevelt campaigned on the promise of a New Deal that would revitalize the American economy. In Germany, Adolf Hitler called for a return to military glory. In his 1924 book *Mein Kampf* ("My Struggle"), written while in prison, Hitler clearly called for the domination of Europe by the pure Aryan race and eastward expansion to provide sufficient "living room" for the German people, as well as the subjugation of "inferior races" such as Jews and Slavs. Although *Mein Kampf* was ignored or ridiculed in the Western democracies, it proved a blueprint for the bloodiest decade in world history – World War II and the Holocaust.

Jews Who Shaped the Twentieth Century

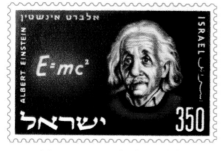

Albert Einstein shed new light on the physical universe.
Israel 117 (1956)

Sigmund Freud illuminated the dark recesses of the human mind. *Mali 345 (1979)*

Theodor Herzl helped the Jewish people return to the stage of history.
Israel 695(1978)

Karl Marx sought a new social order with his book
Das Kapital. Russia 3360 (1967)

The Holocaust

Holocaust refers to the deliberate international murder of two thirds of European Jewry by the Nazis and their collaborators during World War II. Since this Greek word, which means "wholly burnt offering/sacrifice," has become cheapened by being misapplied to other situations, many now use the Hebrew term "Shoah" ("catastrophic destruction").

The Nationalist Socialist Party under Adolf Hitler gained power in Germany in 1933 and immediately made racism and anti-Semitism central components of its regime. During its first months in power, the Nazi Party instigated anti-Semitic riots and campaigns of terror, climaxing in a nationwide boycott of Jewish-owned shops. Jews were deprived of their economic rights and means of survival. Civil servants, professors, doctors, and scientists were summarily dismissed from their places of employment. The infamous 1935 Nuremberg Laws deprived German Jews of their citizenship and formalized barriers between Jews and Germans, forbidding intermarriage between Jews and "Aryans." In 1938 Jews were barred from the medical and legal professions and were forced to register their property as a preliminary measure for its confiscation and forcible sale to Germans at only a fraction of the property's true value. After Germany annexed Austria in March of that year, all the same anti-Semitic measures were implemented there. By this time, two-thirds of German Jews had left the country, and 60% of those who stayed had lost their livelihood.

Kristallnacht's 50th anniversary.
Israel 999 (1988)

Kristallnacht

Kristallnacht.
GDR 732 (1979)

These anti-Semitic actions culminated in the Kristallnacht ("night of [broken] glass") pogrom, which occurred all over Germany and Austria on the night of November 9, 1938. During that night, Nazi mobs murdered more than 100 Jews and beat hundreds more; demolished 76 synagogues and set fire to 191 more; and destroyed and looted 7,500 shops and businesses owned by Jews. The authorities arrested 30,000 Jews and sent them to concentration camps. Two days later, top Nazi leaders decided that the Jews of Germany should bear the cost of the destruction regardless of insurance coverage. The Kristallnacht pogrom marked a crucial milestone in the Nazis' actions against the Jews, for it was the first occasion in the modern era in which widespread violence was directed against Jews in a western European country.

Ghettos

In a speech to the Reichstag on January 30, 1939, Hitler announced his ultimate goal as "the annihilation of Jewish race in Europe." When World War II broke out in September of that year and the German army overran Poland, the Jews were physically isolated in ghettos where they were ordered to set up Jewish councils that would carry out German orders. They were also forced to wear a yellow Star of David on their clothing and to perform forced labor. Severe overcrowding, lack of proper sanitation and health services, and meager food rations resulted in a high mortality rate among the inhabitants of the ghettos. Although Nazi leaders explained

Commemorating November 1938. *GDR 2712 (1988)*

"Protective Detention."
Czechoslovakia 1801 (1972)

Left: Deportation Monument. *Luxembourg 682 (1982)*

Deportation of Italian Jews from Rome to the concentration camps. *Italy 1948 (1993)*

From left: Deportation of French Jews. *France 2492 (1995)*; Memorial to the deportation of French Jews. *France 786 (1956)*

that they were only reviving the old medieval tradition of providing separate living areas for the Jewish population, heavily armed patrols and the electrified barbed wire surrounding the ghetto walls told a different story. Unlike the medieval ghettos, where Jews had unrestricted movement outside of the ghetto walls by day, the penalty for leaving a Polish ghetto without permission at any time was instant death.

The Final Solution

An early phase of the Final Solution was the formation of *Einsatzgruppen,* mobile S. S. units assigned to combat the civilian enemy in Poland and Russia by various methods including the mass murder of about one million Je ws. Strenuous efforts were made to keep these operations secret to prevent them from being used for anti-Nazi propaganda in the West. In 1941 at Babi Yar, a ravine on the outskirts of Kiev, more than 33,000 Jew were machine-gunned to death, an event that has come to symbolize Jewish martyrdom at the hands of the Nazis in the Soviet Union. The massacre at Babi Yar was memorialized in an impassioned poem by Yevgeni Yevtushenko, which was later set to music by Dmitri Shostakovich in his 13th Symphony.

Maidanek death camp in Poland. *Poland B45 (1946)*

As early as autumn1939, the Nazis had experimented with exterminating those with serious mental and physical disabilities by gassing them in specially sealed vans. Although Hitler ordered this euthanasia program discontinued because it was causing public disquiet, the experience acquired was used in the program of killing all the Jews of occupied Europe, known euphemistically as the "final solution". The Nazis decided to deport all Jews from occupied Europe by train in sealed boxcars to the east, to be methodically gassed and then cremated in specially constructed death-factories such as Auschwitz, Treblinka, Sobibor, and Maidanek. Some of the concentration camps also had forced labor facilities, where Jews were abused until they died from starvation or disease.

The Nazis employed camouflage and deception to convince the Jews of Western Europe to go quietly to what were called "resettlement colonies" in the East. The infamous death camp at Auschwitz was disguised as a labor facility with numerous factories and workshops. Over the entrance gate was emblazoned the slogan, "Freedom through work." The gas chambers with crematoria ovens were disguised as public showers for the purposes of disinfection.

Buchenwald memorial. *GDR 2702 (1988)*

Babi Yar - The Last Way by Yosef Kuzkovski. *Israel 843 (1983)*

Theresienstadt "showcase" concentration camp. From left: memorial to victims from 23 countries; children's drawings from the camp: Jew and guard; butterflies; flowerpot. *Czechoslovakia 2670 (1987), 1566-1568 (1968)*

The Nazis also established Theresienstad (Terezin) in Czechoslovakian as a "model settlement" to conceal from the free world the fact that European Jewry was being exterminated. The deportees to Theresienstadt included many artists, writers, and scholars, who organized there an intensive cultural life including several orchestras, an operatic and theatrical troupe, lecture series, and satirical entertainment. In late 1943, when information on the extermination camps began to filter through to the free world, the German authorities decided to show off Theresienstadt to an investigation committee of the International Red Cross. To improve the appearance of the ghetto, a bank, false shops, a café, kindergartens, and schools were set up and the town was adorned with flower gardens. Overcrowding was lessened by additional deportations to Auschwitz. The visit of the committee, all of whose meetings with inmates were carefully prepared in advance, was followed by the filming of a Nazi propaganda film on the "new life of the Jews under the protection of the Third Reich." When the filming was finished, most of the actors, including almost all the members of the autonomous administration and most of the children, were sent to the gas chambers.

Jewish Resistance Against the Nazis

Resistance in Nazi-occupied Europe was limited, since the Jews were completely disarmed and the Nazis went to great lengths to convince people that they were merely being deported to work camps. Moreover, the resistance of Jews was made more difficult because the local population often did not support them, whether out of anti-Semitism, fear of Nazi retribution, or callous indifference. Jews who managed to escape joined the partisans (the anti-Nazi resistance movement) in the forests.

Dramatic examples of Jewish resistance despite overwhelming odds were the armed uprisings that erupted in several ghettos. The most noteworthy of these insurrections was the April 1943 revolt in the Warsaw ghetto, which was sparked when the Germans ordered its complete evacuation. Only lightly armed, the remaining Jews of the ghetto put up a gallant struggle against the heavily armed Germans sent to destroy them. Led by young commander-in-chief Mordecai Anielewicz, the Jewish resistance fought to the last, holding out until September. Even in the death

Remembering the ghetto fighters. From right: Mordechai Anilewicz, Warsaw Ghetto; Yosef Glazman, Vilna Ghetto. *Israel 841 (1983)*

The Jewish World in Stamps

Images of the struggle against the Nazis. Top, from left: Warsaw Ghetto Memorial (detail). *Israel 1163 (1993)*; fighter and ruins of the ghetto; Heroes Monument by Natan Rappaport. *Poland 1132 (1963), 2572 (1983)*; Joint Polish-Israeli stamp for the 50th anniversary of the Warsaw Ghetto uprising. *Israel 1163 (1993)*. Middle, from left: Warsaw Ghetto uprising's 40th and 5th anniversaries. *Poland 2635 (1984), 418 (1949)*; Yitzhak Zuckerman and Zivia Lubatkin, resistance heroes of the Warsaw Ghetto. *Israel 906 (1985)*. Bottom, from left: Havivah Reik and Enzo Sereni (Jewish parachutists). *Israel 994-995 (1988)*

camps of Sobibor, Treblinka, and Auschwitz, revolts broke out among the Jewish prisoners. In the occupied countries of Western Europe, Jews joined all the national resistance organizations, concentrating their efforts on hiding Jewish children and smuggling Jews across borders to find refuge in neutral countries such as Switzerland and Spain.

In Palestine, the Haganah established a paratroop unit of European-born volunteers who jumped into occupied territories to rescue Jewish survivors and to organize Jewish youth in German-occupied territory for resistance against the Nazis. Most of these valiant heroes were captured and executed, including Havivah Reik (Slovakian; 1914-1944); Enzo Chaim Sereni (Italian; 1905-1944); and Hannah Senesch (Hungarian; 1921-1944), who is famed for her poems *Blessed is the Match* and *Eli, Eli* ("My God, My God").

Some Jews demonstrated resistance to the Nazis by heroically going to their deaths while comforting others. When Janusz Korczak (c. 1878-1942), the physician director of an orphanage in the Warsaw Ghetto, received the Nazi deportation order he suppressed the truth, telling his children that they were going on a picnic in the country. As he and the 200 orphans reached the cattle trucks waiting to ship them to Treblinka, Korczak refused a last-minute offer of his freedom in return for abandoning his charges and went with them to his death, creating a legend of heroism and martyrdom.

Responses of non-Jews and other nations

The roundup of Jews for deportation to the death camps elicited remarkably few protests from church dignitaries. Indeed, the silence of Pope Pius XII was deafening, even when the Jews of Rome were deported. One notable exception was Martin Niemoller (1892-1984), a German Lutheran pastor whose anti-Nazi activities made him a symbolic figure in the church's struggle against Hitler. Incarcerated in various concentration camps until the end of the war, Niemoller later spoke about the apathy or fear that prevented his fellow Germans from speaking out against the Nazi atrocities: "First they came for the communists, but I wasn't one and I said nothing; then they came for the trade unionists, but I was not a worker and said nothing; then they came for the Jews, but I was not a Jew and I said nothing; finally they came for me, and there was no one left to say anything."

Janusz Korczak.
Israel 230 (1962)

European nations demonstrated various responses to their Jewish citizens. In German-occupied areas, Jews were sent to the death camps regardless of the attitudes of the local population. In Estonia, Latvia, and Lithuania, thousands joined the Nazi killers voluntarily. Although Italy had a fascist government and was allied with Hitler, anti-Semitism was rare among Italians and they did not turn over many Jews to the Nazis. The most generous response to the desperate plight of the Jews occurred in Denmark. When the Germans ordered every Jew to be identified by a yellow arm band bearing a Star of David, King Christian X announced that he would be the first to don the badge of Judaism. Just as the Gestapo had completed their plans for dealing with the Jews without local assistance, the Danes secretly smuggled 95% of the Jews (more than 6,000) into Sweden using a special rescue fleet of small Danish fishing ships.

Martin Niemoller.
Germany 1698 (1992)

A relatively small number of men and women risked their lives to help persecuted Jews. Some 18,000 of them have been honored by the state of Israel with the title of "Righteous Among the Nations." Prominent among these are Swedish diplomat Raoul Wallenberg, who issued protection passports for thousands of Hungarian Jews, and German industrialist Oskar Schindler, who saved the lives of some 1,200 Jews working in his factory in Poland.

Diplomats who risked their lives to save Jews during the Holocaust. From left: Giorgio Perlasca (Italy), Aristides de Sousa Mendes (Portugal), Carl Lutz (Switzerland), Sempo Sugihara (Japan), Selahattin Ulkumen (Turkey). *Israel 1333 (1998)*

The Jewish World in Stamps

Liberation of the camps

As the war drew to a close, the Allied armies finally seized the death camps, some of which functioned at full capacity to the last. Troops from the United States, Great Britain, and the Soviet Union freed the survivors, many of whom were on the brink of death. With the liberation of the concentration camps, the Holocaust had finally ended.

Raoul Wallenberg.
Dominica 1134 (1988)

Memorials to the victims of the Holocaust

By the end of World War II in 1945, the entire Jewish secular and religious culture in Europe had been obliterated. Approximately 6 million Jews had been exterminated, about 1.5 million of the victims being children. Memorials and museums concerning the Holocaust have been established all over the world. In Germany and the European countries that were under Nazi occu-

Rescue of the Jews of Denmark. *Israel 529 (1988)*

Liberation of the camps. *Israel 1228 (1965), Belgium 772-773 (1965), Israel 292 (1965)*

Right: Liberated camp inmates; peace dove and broken barbed wire fence. *Greece 1810-1811 (1995)*. Below, from left: Soldier helping an inmate. *Czechoslovakia 981 (1960)*; reaching for freedom. *France 1282 (1970)*; liberation. *Cyprus 863 (1995)*; Liberation's 50th anniversary. *Canada 1590 (1995)*

pation, remnants of many concentration camps and killing centers have been converted into museums and memorials. Israel established Yad Vashem, not only as a memorial for those who perished but also as a research center for scholarly activity and for conferences attempting to ensure that such a horror never occur again. In the United States, the Holocaust Museum in Washington and the Museum of Tolerance in Los Angeles were opened in 1993. In 1995, many countries issued stamps commemorating the 50th anniversary of World War II and of the liberation of the concentration camps.

Memorial monuments at former camps. From left: Buchenwald, Maidanek,
Mauthausen, Treblinka. Far right: Auschwitz-Birkenau international memorial.
GDR 1687 (1975), 2128 (1980), 1943 (1978), 660 (1963), 2294 (1982)

From left: Pincas Synagogue memorial to camp victims. *Czechoslovakia 1478 (1967).*
Plasgow (site of Oskar Schindler's camp). *Poland 1366 (1965).* Monument to the
Holocaust of the Jewish People. *Uruguay 1590 (1995)*

Major figures of the Holocaust

Frank, Anne (1929–1945)

Jewish-Dutch teenaged author of a diary composed while hiding from the Nazis. For more than two years, Anne and her family (together with four other Jews) remained in rooms at the back of her father's business, kept alive by friendly gentiles.

An act of betrayal resulted in their discovery by the German police, and the Franks were transferred to a series of concentration camps. Anne died in Bergen-Belsen, one month before the end of World War II.

Anne Frank's diary is the best known Jewish book written during the Holocaust. It vividly portrays the all-pervading fear and desolate life of the incarcerated Jews. Since the initial edition appeared in 1947, the work has been translated into more than 50 languages and millions of copies have been sold. The author has become the symbol of the persecuted Jewish child, and her house in Amsterdam now serves as a museum and meeting place for youth to further the aims of peace.

Anne Frank and the Amsterdam house where she was hidden.
Israel 985 (1988)

Wallenberg, Raoul (1912-1947?)

Swedish diplomat who became a legend through his work to save Hungarian Jews scheduled to be deported to the death camps at the end of World War II. As a member of the staff of the Swedish embassy in Budapest, Wallenberg distributed Swedish certificates of protection to thousands of Jews and later established an "international ghetto" in which about 33,000 Jews found refuge in houses flying the flags of neutral countries. Wallenberg was last definitely seen on January 17, 1945, when he was arrested by the Russians after they liberated Budapest. Although the Russians claim that Wallenberg died in his cell of a sudden heart attack in 1947, his fate has never been clear. Subsequent to this date, there have been numerous reported sightings of questionable validity. Raoul Wallenberg has been made an honorary citizen of the United States and Israel, and the United States Holocaust Museum in Washington is located on a street named after him.

Top: Anne Frank (35th anniversary of the Liberation).
Netherlands 598 (1980).
Bottom: 50th anniversary of her birth.
Germany 1293 (1979)

Raoul Wallenberg with Jewish refugees and forged documents. From left: *Sweden 1643 (1987)*; *U.S.A. 3135 (1997)*; *Argentina (1998)*

The Holocaust Memorial: Yad Vashem

Literally meaning "Monument and Memorial," Yad Vashem is Israel's memorial to the Jewish communities and individuals who perished in the Holocaust. Located on a ridge called Mount of Remembrance, the monument is reached by the Avenue of the Righteous Among the Nations, which is lined with trees planted in tribute to each individual gentile who helped save Jewish lives during the Nazi era. The heavy entrance gate to the Hall of Remembrance, designed by two of Israel's leading sculptors, Bezalel Schatz and David Palombo, is an abstract tapestry of jagged, twisted steel. Inside is a huge stone crypt-like room in which an eternal flame sheds an eerie light over plaques on the floor listing the major concentration camps. Other memorials include a 20-foot high monument dedicated to the 1.5 million Jewish soldiers among the allied armies, partisans, and ghetto fighters; the Valley of the Destroyed Communities that commemorates the 5,000 Eastern European communities that disappeared during World War II; and the most recent memorial to the Children of the Holocaust, in honor of the more than 1.5 million murdered youth. Yad Vashem also contains an extensive library and the Hall of Names, which holds more than 3 million pages of testimony as well as the names, photographs, and personal details of as many as possible of those who perished in the Holocaust.

Holocaust Heroes and Martyrs Memorial Day in Israel. From left: the eternal flame; the yellow star and the six candles; Gate to the Hall of Remembrance by David Palombo; prison clothes, hand. *Israel 220-221 (1962), 1224 (1995), 523 (1973)*

Jews in World Culture

Art

Agam, Yaacov (1928–   ). Internationally renowned Israeli painter and one of the pioneers of contemporary optic and kinetic art. Born Yaacov Gipstein, the son of a rabbi in Rishon le-Zion, Agam studied painting at the Bezalel School in Jerusalem and at the Academy of Abstract Art in Paris. To introduce the dimension of time into his art, Agam created relief pictures, whose colors and shapes constantly change either by moving the picture or by the movement of the spectator. Agam utilized a wide range of media, including sound, light, and water. He combined these elements in the musical fountain he created for the business development of La Defense in Paris. Many of Agam's works are based on Jewish ritual objects and traditional Jewish themes, providing a visual continuation of his father's quest for spirituality.

Message of Peace by Agam. *France 1713 (1980)*

Alechinsky, Pierre (1927–). Belgian painter. Uniting expressionism with surrealism, his works have been described as "explosive" and characterized by a sense of perpetual movement and flux in which incomplete forms appear and dissolve. Alechinsky progressively abandoned oils in favor of ink, which gave free rein to a sensitive and flowing style, and then started working with acrylic paint.

Brodsky, Isaac Israelevich (1884–1930). Russian painter. A native of St. Petersburg (Leningrad), Brodsky became Russia's most successful portrait painter under the Soviet regime. His portraits of Lenin and other popular Soviet leaders were widely reproduced.

Sauvagemont Maransart by Alechinsky. *Belgium 1585*

Portrait of Lenin by Brodsky. *Russia 3696 (1970)*

Chagall, Marc (1887-1985). Russian-French artist whose colorful, dreamlike works made him one of the most popular painters of the 20th century. Born Marc Segal in Vitebsk, Belorussia, Chagall settled in Paris soon after the Bolshevik Revolution. Drawn with a bold imagination and little concern for realistic detail, many of Chagall's paintings are like strange dreams in which all objects appear topsy-turvy, without concern for logic or perspective. Chagall's work treats subjects in a vein of whimsy and fantasy that draws deeply on the resources of the unconscious, and he uses floating figures as a personal symbol for the liberation of the spirit through love or art. His personal and unique imagery is filled with poetic inspiration and profoundly influenced by his Jewish and Russian heritage. Many of his works are vivid recollections of Russian-Jewish village scenes and incidents in his private life. In Nazi Germany, however, many of Chagall's paintings were confiscated from public collections,

Chagall, 100th anniversary of his birth. *Monaco 1599 (1987)*

and some were held up for ridicule in the "Degenerate Art" exhibition at Munich in 1937. Fearing persecution by the Nazis when they invaded France, Chagall escaped to the United States in 1941, where he stayed for seven years before returning to Paris.

In addition to painting, Chagall designed the stained glass windows for the cathedral in Metz and the synagogue of the Hadassah Medical Center in Jerusalem, as well as glass panels for the entrance to the UN Secretariat in New York and the audience hall in the Vatican. He painted a new ceiling for the opera in Paris, murals for the New York Metropolitan Opera House, and contributed a mural, floor mosaics, and designs for the curtains for the Knesset in Jerusalem. In 1973, the Museum of the Marc Chagall Biblical Message was officially opened at Cimiez, just outside Nice, not far from his permanent residence at Saint-Paul de Vence. France conferred the Grand Cross of the Legion of Honor on Chagall in 1977, and in that same year he was given an exhibition at the Louvre, an honor never before granted to a living artist.

Chagall's paintings and stained glass windows.
Top, from left: *Promenade*; *Man over Vitebsk*. *Belarus 52, 53 (1993)*;
The Married Couple of the Eiffel Tower. *France 1076 (1963)*
Below: Memorial Window. *United Nations 179 (1967)*

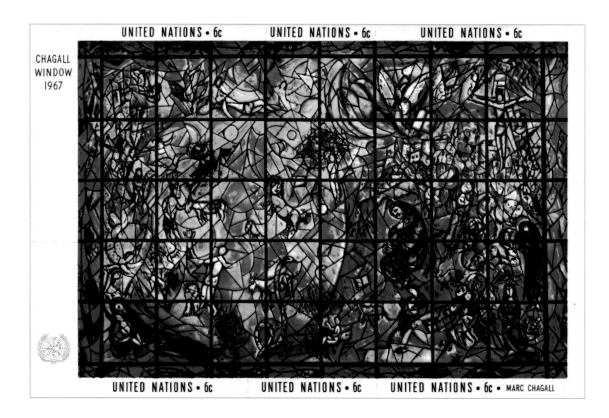

The Jewish World in Stamps

Guggenheims. Wealthy and powerful American family active in a wide spectrum of philanthropic causes. The progenitor of the American branch of the family was Meyer Guggenheim (1828-1905), who immigrated to the United States in 1848. Solomon Guggenheim (1861-1949), the fourth son commissioned Frank Lloyd Wright to design the spiral-shaped museum on Fifth Ave to house his modern art collection. Peggy Guggenheim (1898-1979), the daughter of Meyer's fifth son Benjamin (1865-1912), spent most of her life in Europe, and aided the modern art movement, especially American abstract expressionism. She was instrumental in rescuing artists from Vichy France, including her future husband Max Ernst.

From left: Frank Lloyd Wright (architect) *U.S.A. 1280 (1965);* The Guggenheim Museum. *Grenada 2113 (1992)*

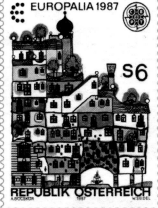

Hundertwasser (1928-2000). Austrian painter and architect who was a major influence in the Vienna postwar art scene until his death. Born Friedrich Stowasser, his mother was Jewish but his father was not; if not for his "mixed" background, he would not have survived the Holocaust, for virtually everyone on his mother's side of the family perished. Hundertwasser was known for his use of vivid primary colors, especially phosphorescent red and green. His buildings were characterized by irregular shapes, and his landscapes and human forms tended to be transformed into abstract dynamic spirals.

Kisling, Moise (1891–1953). French painter. Born in Cracow, Kisling moved to Paris in 1910 and lived there in poverty until an anonymous benefactor offered him a year's allowance. A close friend of Modigliani, Kisling found refuge in the United States during World War II. Kisling's many portraits, landscapes, flower still lifes, and nudes are characterized by a particular sensitivity and melancholy, with figures carefully painted in cool, restrained colors.

Hundertwasser's paintings.
Top, from left: *The Spiral Tree; Hundertwasser House. Austria 1029 (1975), 1389 (1987);* Middle, from left: *Social Summit,* Copenhagen. *United Nations 656 (1995); France (Council of Europe) 1051 (1994);* Bottom: *Vapor. Cape Verde 487 (1986)*

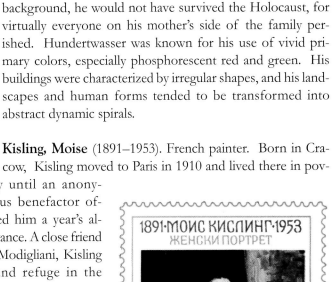

Painting by Kisling. *Bulgaria 3525 (1990)*

I. I. Levitan. *Russia 1528 (1950)*

Levitan Landscapes. Top: *March. Russia 2374 (1960);* bottom: *Golden Autumn. Russia 1527*

Levitan, Isaac Ilitch (1861–1900). Russian artist often called the father of Russian landscape painting. Born in Lithuania, Levitan was one of the first Russian artists to understand the achievement of the Barbizon painters and the Impressionists. Thus he was equipped to become the major interpreter of the Russian landscape, with its vastness and brooding melancholy. In 1896, Levitan was appointed professor of landscape painting at the Moscow Art Academy, where he taught until his death.

Max, Peter (1937-). American psychedelic artist. Born in Germany and raised in Israel and America, his vibrant colors and clean, cartoonish lines were wildly popular in the '60s. Each design bore Max's bold trademark: his name in an oval cartouche, written in sloping Art Nouveau calligraphy

Cosmic Jupitar by Peter Max. U.S.A. 1527 (1974)

Modigliani, Amedeo (1884-1920). Italian painter and sculptor. Born in Leghorn and raised in a Jewish ghetto where he suffered serious illnesses as a boy, Modigliani studied art in Florence and in 1906 moved to Paris, where he became associated with the avant-garde artists living there. Modigliani led a reckless, dissipated life with many love affairs, excesses of drunkenness, and frequent lapses into illness aggravated by poverty. Nevertheless, during his relatively short career Modigliani managed to produce a substantial body of work. He usually painted single figures with backgrounds only vaguely defined. Many of his portraits look as if Modigliani had caught the sitter in a moment of utter fatigue, lonely and devoid of glamour or gaiety. The heads of his subjects are inclined and their eyes look listlessly and unseeing, as though staring from another world. Modigliani's women seem to be constructed of almond shapes connected by trademark long and cylindrical necks to larger ovoids formed by the rounded shoulders of the upper body.

Modigliani's portraits. From left: *Paul Guillaume. Italy 1579 (1984)*; *Woman with Blue Eyes. France 1693 (1980)*; *Portrait of Alice. Wallis and Fortuna C135 (1984)*

Pascin, Jules (Julius Mordecai Pincus; 1885–1930). Born in Bulgaria, the son of a Sephardic grain merchant, Pascin arrived in Paris in 1905 after stays in Vienna, Berlin, and Munich, where he worked as an illustrator and cartoonist. Dressed as a dandy, he became a notorious figure in Montparnasse and Montmartre. Despite a life of dissipation, Pascin produced about 500 oils as well as drawings, prints, watercolors, and a few small sculptures. Though most of his work depicts women singly or in groups, Pascin also drew or painted children at play, circus artists, and nightclub scenes. Pascin was fascinated by figures from folklore and the Bible, including the Prodigal Son, Salome, and Bathsheba.

The Party. by Pascin. *Cuba 2255 (1979)*

Pissarro, Camille Jacob (1830-1903). French Impressionist painter whose friendship and support provided encouragement for many of his younger colleagues. Born into a Sephardic family that had migrated from Bordeaux to Saint Thomas in the Virgin Islands, Pissarro moved to Paris in 1855 where he lived for many years in poverty. Toward the end of his life, he became recognized as an outstanding painter of quiet rural landscapes, river scenes, and street scenes in Paris, Le Havre, and London. His sympathetic portrayal of peasants pushing wheelbarrows, digging potatoes, or tending geese, or farm workers in coarse garments with backs bowed by labor and limbs gnarled by rheumatism reflected his understanding of the poor. A painter of sunshine and the scintillating play of life, Pissarro was an original member of the Impressionists and participated in all eight of their group shows. An excellent teacher, he counted among his pupils Paul Gauguin, Paul Cezanne, and the American Mary Cassatt. With his socialist-anarchist convictions, Pissarro regarded himself a citizen of the world, with no particular religious or national ties. He was shocked and hurt by the Dreyfus case, but more as a man of progressive political ideals than as a Jew.

Portrait of Jeanne by Pissarro. *Romania 2471 (1974)*

Top: *The Foot Path* by Pissarro. *France 1729 (1981)*. Below: *Orchard in Bloom* by Pissarro. *Romania 2470 (1974)*

Segall, Lasar (1891–1957). Brazilian artist. Born in Vilna, Lithuania, one of eight children of a Torah scribe, Segall spent his childhood immersed in the traditions of Orthodox Judaism. Segall studied art in Germany and settled there, becoming one of the country's leading Expressionist painters. After an initial visit to Brazil in 1913, Segall returned to live in Sao Paulo ten years later. He became an influential figure, infusing Brazilian modernism with the color, psychological intensity, and spatial distortion characteristic of the German tradition. Between 1936 and 1949, Segall repeatedly painted large compositions based on the terrible events of the period, such as *Emigrants' Ship, War, Concentration Camp, The Survivors*, and *Exodus*.

Segall. *Brazil 2339 (1991)*

Soutine, Chaim (1893–1943). Russian-French painter. Born in Lithuania, Soutine was obsessed with drawing and at age fourteen he ran away, first to Minsk and then to Vilna, where he enrolled at the School of Fine Arts. Arriving in Paris, Soutine was befriended by Amedeo Modigliani. At one time, he and Modigliani shared a garret in Montmartre that contained only one cot, on which they took turns sleeping. Always impoverished and once contemplating suicide, Soutine's fortunes improved after American art collector Albert C. Barnes visited his studio and bought more than fifty of his pictures. Soutine was an Expressionist who rendered in violent color all the agony that he felt in the people, places, and scenes around him. His colors, even more than his technique, betrayed his troubled mind. Soutine's canvases often remind one of bleeding, tortured flesh; everything is broken, twisted, and distorted. Even in his landscapes, there is a continuous cataclysmic movement. When World War II broke out, Soutine refused opportunities to go to the United States. Forced into hiding after the Nazi invasion of France, the constant threat of being discovered made him ill with ulcers that led to his death.

Girl in Blue by Soutine.
Israel 539 (1974)

Other Art Forms

Thoreau by Baskin.
U.S.A. 1327 (1967)

Baskin, Leonard (1922–2000). American painter and sculptor. Son of a leading orthodox rabbi in New Jersey, Baskin taught printmaking and sculpture at Smith College, made numerous pen-and-ink drawings, and also was the honored illustrator of colorful children's books. Baskin's most prominent public commissions included sculptures for the Franklin Delano Roosevelt and Woodrow Wilson Memorials in Washington D.C., and the Holocaust Memorial in Ann Arbor, MI.

Breuer, Marcel (Lajos; 1902–1981). Hungarian-born American architect. After studying at the Bauhaus and later becoming director of the school's furniture department, this inventor of the tubular steel chair became famous as the designer of the modern, functional homes of wealthy Americans following World War II. In 1952, Breuer shared the commission for designing the UNESCO Headquarters in Paris. Other major projects included the American Embassy in The Hague, the IBM Research Center in France, and the Whitney Museum of American Art in New York. Breuer's combination of clear-cut architectural forms with an ever-present play of sun and shadow-rhythm influenced a whole generation of American architects.

UNESCO Headquarters
by Breuer.
Ecuador 649 (1958)

Portrait of John Steinbeck
by Halsman.
U.S.A. 1773 (1979)

Halsman, Philippe (1906–1979). American photographer. Born in Latvia, Halsman opened a photo studio in Paris and soon gained a reputation as a portrait and fashion photographer. The coming of the Nazis to France forced him to flee to the U.S. By 1956 his work was appearing on the cover of *Life*, which sent him on several assignments around the world. He received international acclaim for his portraits, including those of Albert Einstein, John Steinbeck, and Adlai Stevenson, which were engraved on American postage stamps.

Steinman, David Bernard (1887–1960). Eminent American bridge builder. Among many engineering projects, Steinman designed the Mackinac Bridge in Michigan and was in charge of the major rehabilitation of the Brooklyn Bridge. Steinman also was the founder of the National Society of Professional Engineers.

Mackinac Bridge,
designed by Steinman.
U.S.A 1109 (1958)

Literature, Scholarship, and Journalism

Arendt, Hannah (1906-1975). German-American political and social philosopher. Arendt believed that anti-Semitism contributed to totalitarianism, which she saw as connected with the fall of the nation state and change in the social structure. In her view, the dehumanizing process of modern times led away from genuine freedom to the evils of totalitarianism. After covering the Eichmann trial for the New Yorker magazine, Arendt subsequently published her account as a book *Eichmann in Jerusalem: a Report on the Banality of Evil* (1963), which aroused violent controversy. In it she claimed that the leadership of European Jewry had failed, that the victims of the Holocaust were partly responsible for the slaughter by not resisting, and that Eichmann represented the "banality of evil."

Hannah Arendt.
Germany 1489 (1986-91)

Azulai, Chaim Joseph David (1724–1806). Halachist, kabbalist, emissary, and bibliographer. Born in Jerusalem and known by the acronym Hida, Azulai traveled extensively throughout Europe collecting funds for the upkeep of the academies and scholars in the Holy Land. Visiting famous libraries wherever he went, Azulai gathered material for his book *Shem Ha-Gedolim* ("Name of the Great"), in which he listed 1,500 scholars and authors and more than 2,000 books written from Talmudic times to his own day.

Azulai.
Israel 1110 (1992)

Baeck, Leo (1873–1956). German rabbi, religious thinker, and theologian of Progressive (Reform) Judaism. Although declaring in 1933 that the "thousand-year" history of the German Jews had come to an end, Baeck courageously stayed in Berlin as head of the besieged Jewish community. He refused numerous invitations to serve as a rabbi or professor abroad, declaring that he would remain with the last Jews in Germany as long as possible. Deported to Theresienstadt in 1943, Baeck survived the war and then emigrated to London, where he became chairman of the World Union for Progressive Judaism.

Leo Baeck.
Germany 777 (1957)

In his major book, *The Essence of Judaism* (1936), Baeck stressed the essence of Judaism as "ethical monotheism," arguing that piety is achieved by the fulfillment of duties toward other human beings and that even ritual observances are directed toward this ethical aim. Despite his liberal outlook, Baeck was far from spiritual assimilation, maintaining that ethics must be supported by faith in God. Baeck had a sympathetic, although somewhat ambivalent attitude toward Zionism, viewing the building of Palestine as a valuable prospect for embodying the spirit of Judaism, but not a guarantee that it would be realized.

Vicki Baum.
Maldives 1161 (1986)

Baum, Vicki (1888-1960). Austrian novelist who later immigrated to the U.S. She began her career as a harpist, but her success as a short story writer led her to leave music. Of her 25 novels, the best known is *Grand Hotel*, which became a worldwide best seller and popular film

Berdyczewski (later, Bin-Gorion)**, Micha Josef (**1865–1921). Hebrew writer and thinker. Born in Medzibezh, Berdyczewski was the descendant of a line of Hasidic rabbis. Beginning to read Haskalah writers in his adolescence, the ensuing struggle between modern ideas and the concepts and forces of traditional Judaism

M. J. Berdyczewski.
Israel 1296a (1996)

was to animate his writings throughout his life. Berdyczewski attacked the limited scope of much of Hebrew literature, the inadequacies of the Haskalah and the Love of Zion movement, and he opposed both Herzl and Ahad Ha-Am, with whom he had a famous debate in *Ha-Shilo'ah* (1897). Berdyczewski wrote more than 150 stories, many in Yiddish and most highly autobiographical, dealing with two central subjects: life in the Jewish towns of Eastern Europe in the last decades of the 19th century, and the life of Eastern European Jewish students in the cities of Central and Western Europe.

Georg Brandes.
Denmark 486 (1971)

Brandes, Georg (Morris Cohen; 1842–1927). Danish literary critic and writer. Born into an assimilated family that had retained some nominal ties with the Copenhagen Jewish community, Brandes opposed romanticism and demanded that literature should stimulate the discussion of modern problems. His Danish article on the then unknown Friedrich Nietzsche (1888) marked the starting point of the German philosopher's world fame. Brandes wrote books on major political and artistic figures such as Shakespeare, Voltaire, Julius Caesar, and Michelangelo and lengthy essays on Swinburne, Garibaldi, and Napoleon.

Martin Buber.
Germany 1268 (1978)

Buber, Martin (1878-1965). Jewish philosopher and theologian, who exerted great influence on Jewish and Zionist thought in Western Europe. Buber was a leader of those Zionists who advocated a Jewish cultural renaissance, as opposed to the purely political Zionism of Herzl. In 1916, Buber founded and for eight years edited *Der Jude*, which became the leading voice of German-speaking Jewry and the major organ of the Jewish renaissance movement in Central Europe. Buber delved deeply into Jewish mysticism and published collections of Hasidic tales, in which he showed the beauty and light of this movement. With Franz Rosenzweig, Buber translated the Bible into German. After the rise of Nazism forced him to leave his university position, Buber settled in Palestine and was appointed professor of social philosophy at the Hebrew University. In 1960, Buber was chosen as the first president of the Israel Academy of Sciences and Humanities.

Buber is best known for his philosophy of dialogue, in which he viewed all human existence in terms of two fundamentally different kinds of relations: I-It and I-Thou. An I-It relation is the normal everyday way in which a human being relates towards the things surrounding him. Most of the time, a person also considers his fellows as an "It", viewing them from a distance, like a thing and as a part of the environment. Radically different is the I-Thou relationship, which the human being enters into with his innermost and whole being, with both partners engaging in a real dialogue. For Buber, I-Thou relationships are a reflection of the human meeting with God.

Egon Friedell.
Austria 1072 (1978)

Friedell, Egon (pseudonym of Egon Friedmann; 1878–1938). Austrian playwright and cultural historian. Born in Vienna, Friedell was a witty and versatile bohemian who not only wrote plays but often acted in them, particularly at Max Reinhardt's theaters in Berlin and Vienna. His magnum opus was *A Cultural History of the Modern Age*, a highly original three-volume work that is a brilliant, aphoristic, and sometimes ironic survey of world history and culture from the Reformation. Although only a "marginal" Jew, Friedell committed suicide to escape Nazi persecution.

Gordon, Judah Leib (Leon; 1831–1892). Hebrew poet, writer, and critic. Born in Vilna, Gordon was one of the outstanding poets of the 19th century. Gordon was also a witty, incisive journalist who courageously fought against the ills in Jewish society. A fiery exponent of the Haskalah, Gordon believed that the basic problem of Russian Jewry was the intransigence of the rabbis and their rigid adherence to old customs and *halachah*. The only solution was for Jews to leave their narrow, confined existence and adapt to the wider environment. This would

J. L. Gordon.
Israel 1269e (1996)

The Jewish World in Stamps

require them to stop speaking Yiddish and adopt the Russian language, pursue a general education, and engage in more productive occupations, such as crafts, industry, and agriculture. Gordon later became an ardent advocate for the revival of Hebrew and supported the Zionist cause.

Hakham, Simon (1843–1910). Author and Bible translator. Born in Bukhara, the son of a scholarly Baghdad emissary, Hakham came to Jerusalem in 1890. Active as an editor, publisher, and author, his translation of the Bible into the Judeo-Persian of the Bukharan Jews was a monumental achievement.

Simon Hakham.
Israel 1087(1991)

Heijermans, Herman (1864–1924). Dutch playwright and novelist. One of the most important Dutch dramatists of his generation and a writer of the naturalistic school, Heijermans' work displayed both his socialist leanings and his struggle with his Jewish identity. Heijermans' concern for the fate of Jewry first appeared in *Ahasverus* (1893), a play about a Russian pogrom. However, in two novels, *Sabbath* (1903) and *Diamond City* (1904) and the play *Ghetto* (1899), Heijermans contrasted the narrowmindedness of the Amsterdam Ghetto with the nobility of Dutch Christians. His highly successful drama *The Good Hope* (1900), which movingly described the miseries of Dutch fishermen, was subsequently staged by Abraham Shlonsky and the Ohel theater company in a Hebrew version, *Dayyagim* ("The Fishermen"; 1927).

Character in a
Heijermans play.
Netherlands B504 (1974)

Heine, Heinrich (1797-1856). One of the greatest lyric poets in the German language and Germany's outstanding Jewish writer. Because the profession of law was prohibited to Jews in Germany at that time, in 1825 Heine converted to Christianity (adopting the Christian name of Heinrich instead of his original Harry, or Chaim) in order to obtain a law degree and pursue a career as a civil servant or academic. Unfortunately, Heine was sadly mistaken, for doors remained closed to him – to Jews he was a renegade; to Christians an insincere turncoat or dangerous radical. Although Heine spoke of the baptismal certificate as an "admission ticket to European culture," it brought him no advantages and he always writhed under the stigma of a convert. Much of the bitterness and self-punishing irony of Heine's later writing derives from this sorely regretted piece of opportunism.

Herman Heijermans..
Netherlands B503 (1974)

Heine was known for his liberal political opinions and extolling of the virtues of ordinary Germans, but he savagely and satirical attacked the monarchy, church, and German nationalism. His writings and controversial activities brought him into disfavor with the German elite, but made him famous and widely applauded elsewhere in Europe. German and Austrian composers have made thousands of musical settings of his poems. Heine's work influenced Wagner's *Flying Dutchman* and *Tannhauser* and inspired countless subsequent writers. Even the Nazis who burned his books could not erase the love of these poems from the people. Since the Germans persisted in singing *Die Lorelei*, it was re-

Heinrich Heine *("His heart quivered at the word Jerusalem.")*
Israel 1460 (2001)

From top: Heinrich Heine.
Germany 1098 (1972), 1984 (1997)

printed as a "folksong" without the author's name.

Heschel, Abraham Joshua (1907–1972). American rabbi, scholar, philosopher, and theologian. He descended on his father's side from Dov Baer (The Maggid of Mezhirech) and on his mother's side from the Hasidic master Levi Yitchak of Berdichev. After traditional Jewish studies in Talmud and Kabbalah, at age 20 Heschel earned a doctorate in philosophy at the University of Berlin. In 1938 Heschel began teaching at the Hebrew Union College in Cincinnati, and from 1945 until his death he was professor of Jewish ethics and mysticism at the Jewish Theological Seminary in New York. A prolific writer known for his evocative presentation of Jewish mysticism, Hasidism, and prophecy, Heschel became one of the most influential modern philosophers of religion, recognized in both Jewish and Christian circles. Heschel expressed his religious-ethical concerns through participation in the American civil rights and antiwar movements (he marched with Martin Luther King in Alabama), as well as in extensive interfaith activities. Among his many books are *The Sabbath* (1951), *Man's Quest for God* (1954), *God in Search of Man* (1956), and *The Prophets* (1962).

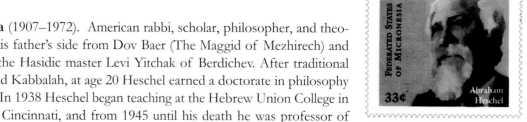

Abraham Joshua Heschel. *Micronesia 370L (2000)*

Joseph Hayyim ben Elijah. *Israel 1111 (1992)*

Joseph Hayyim ben Elijah (1833 or 1835–1909). Baghdad rabbi and halachic authority. Author of some 60 works on all aspects of Torah, only a few of which have been published, he is best known for his *Ben Ish Hai* (1898), a set of homilies blended with halachah and Kabbalah. This work achieved immense popularity, particularly in oriental communities, where it is studied extensively. He also was a prolific composer of piyyutim, many of which are incorporated in the liturgy of Iraqi Jewry.

Kafka, Franz (1883-1924). Czech-born German novelist whose disturbing symbolic fiction prefigured the oppression and despair of the late 20th century. He was one of the most significant figures in modern world literature, and the term "Kafkaesque" has become an international word to describe the anxious feeling of being trapped in a maze of grotesque occurrences. After studying law in Prague, Kafka took a civil service post and wrote in his spare time. The strain of this dual life added to his anxiety and depression; Kafka contracted tuberculosis and spent most of his last years in a sanitarium. Kafka deposited his manuscripts with his close friend and eventual biographer, Max Brod, leaving instructions that they were to be burnt upon his death. However, Brod was fully aware of the importance of Kafka's work and had them published posthumously (including his most famous novels, *The Trial* [1937], *The Castle* [1930], and *America* [1938]).

The action in most of Kafka's books is centered on the hero's unremitting search for identity – the loneliness, frustration, and oppressive guilt of an individual threatened by anonymous forces beyond his comprehension or control. Kafka blended reality with fantasy and ironic humor to create a nightmarish claustrophobic effect, as in "The Metamorphosis" (1915), in which a hardworking insurance agent awakens to find that he has turned into an enormous insect, is rejected by his family, and left to die alone.

From left: Kafka with view of Jewish cemetery in Prague. *Czechoslovakia 1633 (1969)*; Franz Kafka. *Israel 1330a (1998)*

Kafka's house in Prague. *Czechoslovakia 1471 (1967)*

Kraus, Karl (1874–1936). Austrian satirist and poet. Born in Bohemia, Kraus was a vitriolic critic of the liberal culture of pre-Nazi Austria.

A convert to Catholicism as a young man, Kraus blamed Jews themselves for the existence of anti-Semitism. His most important drama, the gigantic *Die letzten Tage der Menschheit* (1919), was estimated to take ten evenings to perform. It is a massive diatribe on the collapse of civilization in World War I and consists largely of verbatim extracts from the newspapers of the period.

Karl Kraus.
Austria 986 (1974)

Lazarus, Emma (1849-1887). American poet best remembered for her sonnet engraved on the Statue of Liberty. Born in New York to an affluent Sephardic family, her interest in Jewish problems was awakened by George Eliot's novel, *Daniel Deronda,* with its call for a Jewish national revival, and was reinforced by the Russian pogroms of 1881–82. Impressed by the Russian-Jewish refugees whom she encountered when she joined relief workers on Ward's Island, Lazarus energetically defended these "foreigners" against their detractors (who included some assimilated American Jews). In a magazine essay, she replied to anti-Semitic attacks by praising her fellow Jews as pioneers of progress, expressing her joy in belonging to a people that was the victim of massacres rather than their perpetrator. Lazarus is primarily known as the author of *The New Colossus*, a sonnet expressing her belief in the United States as the welcoming haven of Europe's "huddled masses yearning to breathe free." Composed in 1883, its was engraved on a memorial plaque and affixed to the pedestal of the Statue of Liberty in 1903.

Statue of Liberty.
U.S.A. 899 (1940)

Walter Lippman.
U.S.A. 1849 (1980)

Lippman, Walter (1889–1974). Leading American social and political commentator of the 20th century. Born in New York, Lippman wrote a column on public affairs for the New York Herald-Tribune, which was syndicated to more than 250 papers in 25 countries and earned him two Pulitzer prizes (1958, 1962).

Mapu, Abraham (1808-1867). Creator of the modern Hebrew novel. A principal exponent of the Haskalah (Enlightenment) movement in Eastern Europe, Mapu is best known for his first and most successful novel *Ahavat Zion* (The Love of Zion; 1853), which represents a turning point in the development of modern Hebrew literature. As the first Hebrew novel, it opened the prospect of a free and independent life to a people hopelessly fettered by political, social, and economic restrictions. Mapu's vivid descriptions of heroism and action, the free expression of emotion, and especially the colorful scenes of a people living unrestricted in its own land, inflamed the imagination of a life-starved generation. By fostering pride in the national past and focusing attention on the land of Israel, Mapu provided an emotional stimulus for generations of young readers.

Abraham Mapu.
Israel 378 (1968)

Marshak, Samuel Yakovlevich (1887–1964). Russian poet and Zionist. Born in Voronezh, Marshak is best known as the founder of Soviet children's literature. His nursery rhymes, songs, and verse formed part of the Soviet kindergarten and school curriculum, and his plays were among the mainstays of Soviet children's theater. There were few ideological elements in his verse, in which he usually exhorted children to be truthful, obey their parents, study diligently, and be kind to animals. Among his poems for adults is *Palestina* (1916), which contrasts the Jewish plight in Russia during World War I to the elation he experienced on a visit to the Land of Israel. His poem *Jerusalem*, which depicts his journey to the Holy City, was included in a Russian-language anthology of Jewish poetry.

Samuel Y. Marshak.
Russia 5612 (1987)

Mendele Mokher Seforim.
Israel 1269n (1996)

Mendele Mokher Seforim (1835–1917). "Mendele the Book Seller," pseudonym of Shalom Jacob Abramowitsch, Yiddish and Hebrew writer. Born in Belorussia, he was instrumental in the founding of modern literary Yiddish. He also exerted a profound effect on Hebrew literature, which he believed should be actively involved in current problems of the Jewish community and influence and inspire Jewish life. His book *Benjamin the Third* is a classic satirical picture of the narrow, daydreaming life of the ghetto.

Adolph Ochs.
U.S.A. 1700 (1976)

Ochs, Adolph Simon (1858-1935). Most distinguished member of a family of American newspaper publishers. Born in Tennessee, Ochs moved to New York in 1896 to take over the bankrupt *New York Times*. Adopting the slogan "All the News That's Fit to Print", he followed a policy of thorough, non-partisan, and non-sensational coverage of the news, in contrast to the "yellow journalism" prevailing at the other New York City papers. Ochs introduced the rotogravure printing of newspaper photographs, raised the standard of advertising, and brought responsible journalism to a high level, appealing to intelligent readers with trustworthy and comprehensive coverage. During his 39 years as its publisher, Ochs strengthened all aspects of the *New York Times*, which led to a dramatic rise in both its circulation and prestige.

I. L. Peretz.
Israel 1269g (1996)

Peretz, Isaac Leib (1852–1915). Yiddish and Hebrew poet and author. A child of the Enlightenment, Peretz considered Yiddish and Hebrew as only temporary media for educating the Jewish masses until they would learn the languages of their native countries. After the 1881 pogroms, however, his attitude toward Yiddish became more positive. Since three million Jews understood Yiddish, he argued that there must be a literature in that language. With Mendele Mokher Seforim and Shalom Aleichem, Peretz was one of the founders of modern Yiddish literature. However, Peretz also continued to write in Hebrew since he believed that Jews should also know this language as well as that of their country of birth. Despite his love for the Hebrew language and his persistent fight for Jewish national revival, Peretz himself did not join the Zionist movement. Doubting whether an ancient tongue and an ancient country could be revived, Peretz saw the future of the Jews in the Diaspora with Yiddish as their language.

Proust, Marcel (1871-1922). French writer and creator of *A la Recherche du Temps Perdu* (Remembrance of Things Past), a massive set of seven novels considered one of the greatest achievements in world literature. Although always in delicate health, Proust's wealth and personal qualities allowed him to mingle in the elegant high society that was to form the background of his literary works. During the last 17 years of his life, Proust was an invalid, spending most of his time locked up in his Paris apartment and feverishly working on his masterpiece. Although raised as a Catholic, Proust alluded to his Jewish ancestry in his writings, describing his mother and maternal grandparents and mentioning his grandfather's practice of placing a pebble on his parents' grave.

Marcel Proust.
France B369 (1966)

Pulitzer, Joseph (1847-1911). Hungarian-born American editor and publisher who bought declining newspapers and restored them to national influence. The son of a Jewish father and a Roman Catholic mother, Pulitzer immigrated to the U.S. at age 17 to serve in the Union Army during the Civil War. In 1878, Pulitzer took his first big step toward creating a newspaper empire when he bought the *St. Louis Dispatch* at auction and merged it with the *St. Louis Post* into the *Post-Dispatch*. Five years later, he left for New York to buy *The World* (and to develop its sister paper, *The Evening World*). These newspapers succeeded on a formula of vigorous promotion, exposes, sensationalism, crusades against corruption, sympathy with labor and the underdog, and new typographic techniques. Pulitzer also introduced such innovations as sports pages, sections dealing with women's fashions, comics, and illustrations. The competition between Pulitzer and William Randolph Hearst, who owned the *New York Morning Journal,* was especially fierce, and the sensational coverage they used to attract readers was dubbed "yellow journalism." Pulitzer's will provided for the establishment of the Pulitzer Prizes for journalism, literature, and music (awarded since 1917), and designated $1 million to endow a school of journalism at Columbia University.

Joseph Pulitzer.
U.S.A. 946 (1947)

Queen, Ellery. Pseudonym of two American Jewish writers, cousins Frederic Dannay (1905-1982) and Manfred B. Lee (1905-1971), who collaborated in creating the highly popular fictional detective.

Ellery Queen detective stories. *San Marino 949 (1979)*

Rand, Ayn (1905-1982). American novelist. Her extreme libertarianism, which championed individualism over collectivism and egoism over altruism, established her as a controversial figure in 20th-century literary and philosophical debate. Born Alissa Rosenbaum in St. Petersburg, Russia, Rand immigrated to the United States in 1926. Her first two novels, *We the Living* (1936) and *Anthem* (1938), portrayed the dangers of monolithic sociopolitical systems such as Communism and Fascism. Rand's best-known work is *The Fountainhead*, the story of architect and formidable egoist Howard Roark, who fought against his entire profession to preserve his own artistic vision. He exemplified Rand's philosophy of objectivism, which encouraged individuals to pursue their rational self-interests. She firmly believed that human beings must live for themselves, neither sacrificing any part of their natures or goals to other people, nor bending the wills of others to their own. Love can be achieved fully only by those individuals who possess the highest self-esteem, which is exhibited in the form of clearly defined and uncompromising values. Rand's other large and popular novel is *Atlas Shrugged* (1957), which describes five characters in a fictional America moving toward a bizarre form of socialism.

Ayn Rand.
U.S.A. 3308 (1999)

Richler, Mordecai (1931- 2001). Canadian novelist. Many of his books deal realistically with the urban environment in which he grew up in Montreal. Richler frequently wrote about a rootless individual who tries to browbeat an indifferent society into making some response.. His most famous novel, *The Apprenticeship of Duddy Kravitz* (1959), a satirical look at the transformation of a Canadian Jewish boy into a calculating businessman, was made into a successful film.

Salten, Felix (1869-1945). Austrian novelist, playwright, and critic who created *Bambi.* Born Siegmund Salzmann in Budapest, Salten became a writer of feuilletons for the Neue Freie Presse, continuing the high standard of his friend and predecessor, Theodor Herzl. As a dramatic critic, Salten made and unmade literary and stage reputations; however, his own plays had no lasting success. Salten's international fame rests on his animal story, *Bambi* (1923), about a deer's life in the forest. Bambi became a juvenile classic and was filmed by Walt Disney.

Clip from the movie based on Richler's novel.
Canada 1616b (1996)

Bambi, Salten's famous character.
Grenada Grenadines 419 (1980)

Arthur Schnitzler.
Austria 1396 (1987)

Schnitzler, Arthur (1862–1931). Austrian playwright and author. A physician and medical editor, Schnitzler's plays were among those most often performed on the German and Austrian stage before World War I. In his works, Schnitzler often expressed his views on the place of the Jew in modern life, holding that anti-Semitism was the natural outcome of the Jews' historical position as a minority group in every land. He believed that no amount of Jewish or Christian sentimentality would eradicate anti-Jewish prejudice, but retained a positive outlook on the issue of Jewish survival and derided those Jews who hid their origin.

Shabazi, Shalem (1618-1680). Yemenite Jewish poet. He wrote in Hebrew, Aramaic, and Arabic, always putting his name in acrostic form either at the beginning of the stanzas or in the poem itself. Living in a period of persecutions and messianic anticipations for Yemenite Jewry, Shabazi gave faithful poetic expression to the suffering and yearning of his generation and became its national poet. A legendary miracle worker, his tomb was considered holy and became a shrine where both Jews and Muslims prayed for relief from sickness and misery.

Shalom Aleichem (1859-1916). Pen name of the Yiddish writer and humorist Shalom Rabinowitz. Born in the Ukraine, as a young child Rabinowitz moved to Voronkov (or Voronka), which later served as a model for the fictitious town of Kasrilevke described in his work. His earliest compositions were in Hebrew, but he switched to Yiddish after marrying in 1883 and soon adopted the pseudonym "Shalom Aleichem." He wrote hundreds of stories, novels, and plays depicting Jewish life in the small towns of Eastern Europe at a time of great historical transition from the old order of traditional life to modern times. His tales reflected the wisdom and wit of his people, for whom Shalom Aleichem became their favorite writer. Among his unforgettable characters were Tevyeh, the milkman (the inspiration for the blockbuster movie, *Fiddler on the Roof*); Menachem Mendel, the luckless broker; and Motel, the cantor's son, whose escapades are especially endearing to young readers. Universally admired, Shalom Aleichem was given rousing receptions on his visits to the Jewish centers in Russia. It is said that a half million people came to his funeral when he died in New York.

Shabazi manuscript.
Israel 1357 (1999)

Spinoza, Baruch (1632-1677). Dutch rationalist philosopher and religious thinker. Born in Amsterdam to a family of Marrano refugees from the Portuguese Inquisition, Spinoza was steeped in classical Jewish sources of Bible and Talmud. In 1656, Spinoza began to attract attention for his heretical opinions, questioning, among other matters, whether Moses wrote the Pentateuch, Adam was the first man, Mosaic law took precedence over natural law, and the soul was truly immortal. When he refused to recant his views and withdrew from the synagogue, Spinoza was excommunicated. Since this forbade all in the Jewish community to be in contact with him, Spinoza was effectively banished from Amsterdam. He changed his name to Benedictus (the Latin equivalent of Baruch) and settled on the outskirts of the city, earning his living grinding optical lenses. After the appearance of several notorious philosophical works, in 1673 Spinoza was offered the chair of philosophy at the University of Heidelberg and promised freedom to philosophize provided that he would not disturb the estab-

Shalom Aleichem. Top: *Romania 1268 (1959)*. Bottom: *Russia 2164 (1959)*

Shalom Aleichem.
Israel 154 (1959)

lished religion. Spinoza declined the post, saying that he preferred his quiet life of philosophical research to teaching, and that he could not control the occurrence of religious dissension.

Spinoza rejected ceremonial Judaism and scriptural authority, insisting that religious tenets should be judged only on the basis of reason. He philosophy was based on the pantheistic idea that God is the universe, and everything in it is a manifestation of Him. Consequently, Spinoza denied the possibility of any supernatural event, providential action or revealed knowledge, thus eliminating the basic ingredients of both Jewish and Christian cosmology. Spinoza argued that the books of the Bible must be interpreted on their own terms, which required an analysis of the Hebrew language; the life, conduct, and pursuits of the each author; the time when it was written; and for whom and in what language the author wrote it – effectively laying the groundwork for modern biblical criticism.

Baruch Spinoza.
Netherlands 567 (1977)

Gertrude Stein.
Uganda 1186 (1993)

Stein, Gertrude (1874-1946). American author, critic, and patron of the arts. Born in Allegheny, Pennsylvania, Stein lived in Paris, where her apartment became a center of artistic life and a place of pilgrimage for aspiring American writers such as F. Scott Fitzgerald and Ernest Hemingway. *The Autobiography of Alice B. Toklas* (1933), ostensibly written by her secretary and companion, told the history of her salon and of her relationship with the new literature and art.

Superman. Cartoon hero created by Jerry Siegel (1914-1996) and Joe Shuster (1914-1992), two Jewish teenagers from Cleveland. Born on the eve of World War II as a symbol of "truth, justice and the American Way," Superman made his debut in the first issue of Action Comics in June, 1938. Displaying his Jewish roots, the Man of Steel's real last name on the planet Krypton was "El," a Hebrew name for God.

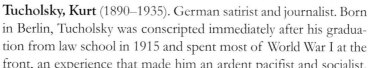

Superman.
Canada 1579 (1995)

Kurt Tucholsky.
Germany 9N506 (1985)

Tucholsky, Kurt (1890–1935). German satirist and journalist. Born in Berlin, Tucholsky was conscripted immediately after his graduation from law school in 1915 and spent most of World War I at the front, an experience that made him an ardent pacifist and socialist. A man of the left, an ardent European, and an anti-nationalist, Tucholsky's satire was aimed at militarism, injustice, entrenched privilege, deep-rooted flaws in the German national character, stupidity, and greed.

Werfel, Franz (1890-1945). Austrian novelist, playwright, and poet who later became a successful author in the United States. Three years in the Austrian army on the Russian Front made Werfel a confirmed pacifist, and his anti-war poems of 1919 voiced a longing for the rejuvenation of a blood-drenched world through love and universal brotherhood. Werfel's marriage in 1918 to Alma Mahler, the widow of composer Gustav Mahler, established him in Viennese society. In *The Eternal Road* (1937), a biblical play set to synagogue music by Kurt Weill, Werfel revealed his spiritual homelessness and the tragic ambiguity of his religious position. In 1938, Werfel escaped to France; when the German army invaded France in 1940, he fled

100th anniversary of Werfel's birth.
Germany 1904 (1990)

Franz Werfel.
Austria 1516 (1990)

once more and managed to reach the United States. Werfel spent his last years in California, where he completed *Das Lied von Bernadette* (1941), an account of the visionary of Lourdes who was elevated to sainthood. This work became famous in the English-speaking world as *The Song of Bernadette* (1942), which was later made into a popular motion picture.

Zamenhof, Ludwig Lazar (1859–1917). Polish linguist and creator of Esperanto. Born in Bialystok, Zamenhof studied medicine and specialized in ophthalmology. Intent on solving the problem of national conflicts, Zamenhof sought to develop a simple international language that would advance relations and mutual understanding between nations. In 1878, he completed the writing of the first pamphlet detailing the fundamentals of the new language, which used all the letters of the Roman alphabet except Q, W, X, and Y. It contained only 900 root words and a grammar with 16 rules. The work was published under the title *Lingvo Internacia* (International Language) in 1887, the year considered the beginning of the movement. Zamenhof signed the pamphlet with the pseudonym "Doktoro Esperanto" ("Dr. Hopeful"), which became the name of the language. Esperanto is spelled as pronounced, its rules have no exceptions, and its guiding principle is to use roots common to the main languages of Europe. At first Zamenhof encountered opposition and mockery; however, he succeeded in gaining numerous enthusiastic supporters in every country and more than 10,000 publications have appeared in Esperanto.

L. L. Zamenhof.
GDR 2617 (1987)

Zweig, Arnold (1887-1968). German novelist and playwright. Unlike the vast majority of German-Jewish writers, Zweig turned to Jewish nationalism and wrote extensively about Jews and Zionism. When the Nazis came to power, Zweig left Germany and lived in Haifa. However, he never felt at home in Palestine, being unable to adapt himself to a Hebrew-speaking milieu. After the declaration of Israel's independence, Zweig, now more sympathetic to Communism, made a much-publicized return to East Germany, where he became president of the Academy of Arts and won the International Lenin Peace Prize in 1958. Toward the end of his life, Zweig evidently reassessed his views on Zionism and courageously refused to sign a statement of East German intellectuals condemning Israel's "aggression" against the Arab states in the Six-Day War of 1967.

Arnold Zweig.
GDR 2604 (1987)

Zweig, Stefan (1881-1942). Austrian playwright, essayist, and biographer. Following the outbreak of World War I, Zweig became an ardent pacifist. His first major work, the dramatic poem *Jeremiah* (1917), passionately denounced what he regarded as the supreme madness of war.

Zweig was best known for his biographies, in which he often grouped three people of similar interests in one volume and attempted to find a common spiritual denominator. For example, *Three Masters* (1920) contains biographical studies of Balzac, Dickens, and Dostoevsky.

Stefan Zweig.
Austria 1119 (1981)

Opposite page: Esperanto stamps around the world

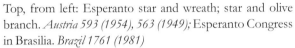

Top, from left: Esperanto star and wreath; star and olive branch. *Austria 593 (1954), 563 (1949);* Esperanto Congress in Brasilia. *Brazil 1761 (1981)*

Right: 100th anniversary of Zamenhof's birth; Esperanto Congress in Rio de Janeiro. *Brazil 905 (1960), C61 (1945).*

Below, from left: 100th anniversary of the Esperanto language movement; 100th anniversary of the movement in Bulgaria. *Bulgaria 3231 (1987), 3522 (1990)*; 100th anniversary. *China 2103 (1987)*

Above, from left: Zamenhof with Russian stamp inset. *Cuba 2926 (1987);* map of Europe. *Hungary 1436 (1962)*; Esperanto's 100th anniversary. *Malta 701 (1987)*

Right: Zamenhof; star, globe and flag; 100th anniversary of Esperanto. *Poland 859-860 (1959), 2811 (1987)*

Music

Adam, Adolphe (1803-1856). French composer. Born in Paris, Adam won popular success with his many compositions for the stage, especially the score for the ballet, *Giselle*. He also wrote the music for the popular Christmas carol, "O Holy Night."

Giselle. *Cuba C309 (1978)*

Leo Ascher.
Austria 1160 (1980)

Ascher, Leo (1880-1942). Austrian composer. A lawyer by profession, Ascher became a successful composer of more than thirty operettas, as well as popular songs and motion picture scores. Forced to leave Austria just prior to the Nazi annexation of his country in 1938, Ascher moved to New York City, where he composed musicals, patriotic songs, and educational pieces for children.

Benatsky, Ralph (1884–1957). Czech composer. Born in southern Moravia, Benatsky composed about 5000 songs and 92 operettas. Immigrating to the United States in 1938 but later returning to Europe and settling in Zurich, Benatsky wrote the scores for about 250 films.

Bernstein, Leonard (1918-1990). American composer, pianist, and conductor (see page 94).

Bloch, Ernest (1880-1959). Swiss-American composer. Among his major works are Three Jewish Poems for orchestra, the Israel Symphony for orchestra and five solo voices, *Schelomo*, a "Hebrew rhapsody" for cello and orchestra, and the *Baal Shem Suite* for violin and orchestra. After several visits to the United States as a guest conductor, in 1920 Bloch founded and organized the Cleveland Institute of Music. Five years later, he left to become director of the San Francisco Conservatory of Music. Returning to Switzerland, Bloch spent three years in seclusion composing one of his most important works, the *Sacred Service* for Sabbath morning, scored for baritone, mixed chorus, and orchestra. From 1940-1952 he was professor of music at the University of California at Berkeley. According to most critics, Bloch's finest compositions are those based on or expressing the idioms and emotional qualities of the Jewish soul. As he once stated: "I do not propose or desire to attempt a reconstruction of the music of the Jews. . . It is rather the Jewish soul that interests me—the complex, ardent, agitated soul that I feel vibrating throughout the Bible; the vigor and ingenuousness of the Patriarchs, the violence that is evident in the books of the Prophets, the Jew's burning love of justice, the desperation of the preachers of Jerusalem, the sorrow and grandeur of the Book of Job, the sensuality of the Song of Songs. All this is in us, all this is in me, and is the better part of me. This it is which I seek to feel within me and to translate in my music—the sacred race-emotion that lies dormant in our souls."

Ralph Benatsky.
Austria 1280 (1980)

Leonard Bernstein.
U.S.A. (2002)

Ernest Bloch. *Israel 1225 (1995)*

Giselle (first ballet performed in Seychelles).
Seychelles 591 (1986)

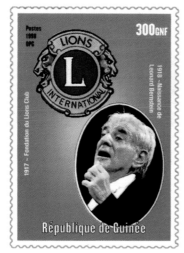

Leonard Bernstein.
Guinea (1999)

Bernstein conducting Symphony # 1
(*Jeremiah*). *Israel 1226 (1995)*

Rene Blum. *Monaco 636 (1966)*

Blum, Rene (1878–1944). French ballet impresario. When Diaghilev died in 1929, Blum was chosen to succeed him as director of the Ballet of the Monte Carlo Opera, a post he held until the German invasion of France in 1940. Refusing to leave for the free zone of France, Blum was interned with some 1000 French-Jewish intellectuals and was sent to Auschwitz, where he died.

Copland, Aaron (1900-1990). American composer. A dominant presence in United States music of the 20th century, Copland experimented with aggressive jazz rhythms in his earliest works before turning to a simpler, more melodic and lyrical style, frequently drawing on elements of American folk music. His best works of the 1940s (*A Lincoln Portrait* and the ballets *Billy the Kid*, *Rodeo*, and *Appalachian Spring*) express distinctly American themes, using native melodies and rhythms to capture the flavor of early American life. Copland employed Jewish motifs in such works as *Vitebsk*, *A Study on a Jewish Melody*, and *In the Beginning*, a choral setting on the theme of Creation. Copland composed for several movies, winning the 1949 Academy Award for best dramatic film score for *The Heiress*. A distinguished teacher, for 25 years Copland was head of the composition department at the Berkshire Music Center in Tanglewood.

Aaron Copland. *Grenada Grenadines 1865g (1996)*

Don Juan. *Monaco 1603(1978).*

Da Ponte, Lorenzo (1749–1838). Italian poet and librettist. Best remembered for his collaboration with Mozart, Da Ponte was born Emanuel Conegliano and given the family name of his sponsor, the bishop of Ceneda, upon his family's baptism in 1763. He was educated for the priesthood and ordained, taught briefly, and embarked upon a writer's career. Banished from Venice after a period of dissipation and scandal, Da Ponte reached Vienna in 1783 and was appointed librettist to the Imperial Opera, where he wrote the libretti for three great Mozart operas – *The Marriage of Figaro* (1784), *Don Giovanni* (1787), and *Cosi Lan Tutte* (1789). *Don Giovanni*, although based on previous stage works, at least owes a spiritual debt to Da Ponte's friendship with Casanova, whom he had known in Venice. Da Ponte later abandoned his clerical status by marrying Nancy (Anne Celestine) Grahl, the daughter of a German-English merchant, in a ceremony that one report stated was held "according to the Jewish rite." After moving to New York, Da Ponte became the first professor of Italian at Columbia University.

Figaro. *France 690 (1953)*

Paul Dukas. *France B387 (1965)*

Dukas, Paul Abraham (1865-1935). French composer. Dukas studied at the Paris Conservatory and taught there from 1909 until his death. In French music, his style formed a bridge between the school of Cesar Franck and that of Claude Debussy. He achieved fame in 1897 with his orchestral scherzo *The Sorcerer's Apprentice*, a brilliant piece of program music based on a ballad by the German poet, Goethe, and popularized in the Walt Disney movie, *Fantasia*. Dukas is also known for *Ariane and Bluebeard* (1907), considered one of the most important of modern French operas.

Fall, Leo (1873–1925). Czech composer. Born in Moravia to a military bandmaster, Fall studied at the Vienna Conservatory and became a highly successful composer of operettas, notably *Die Rose von Stambul* (1916) and *Madame Pompadour* (1922). Fall's music was distinguished for its swinging melodies, rhythmic irregularities, and clever orchestration.

Leo Fall. Austria *1021 (1975)*

Top: Scene from *The Marriage of Figaro*. Ghana 1501 (1992)
Middle: *Turkish March* from *The Marriage of Figaro*. Gambia 1342 (1992)
Bottom: *The Three Masked Revelers* from *Don Giovanni*. Nevis 739 (1992)

Fiedler, Arthur (1894-1979). Conductor of the Boston Pops Orchestra. Born in Boston, he was the scion of several generations of violinists, or "fiedlers." His engaging programs in an informal setting contained a mixture of standard classics and sophisticated arrangements of popular tunes, which when combined with his buoyant personality, made Fiedler and the Pops an American institution.

Gershwin, George (1898-1937). American composer and pianist (see page 94).

Arthur Fiedler. *U.S.A. 3159 (1997)*

From left: opening bars of *Raphsody in Blue; Sportin' Life, Porgy and Bess;* Gershwin.
Monaco 2092 (1998), U.S.A. 1484 (1973), Grenada Grenadines 1865c (1996)

Goodman, Benny (1909-86). American jazz clarinetist and bandleader. Born Benjamin David Goodman, he learned to play the clarinet as a child in Chicago in a music program fostered by a local synagogue. Goodman organized his own orchestra in 1934, and with weekly radio broadcasts it soon became one of the most popular jazz groups in the United States. One of the founders of the "swing" style prevalent in the 1930s, Goodman was known as "The King of Swing." His was the first jazz ensemble in which both white and black musicians played together. Goodman's virtuosity allowed him to also appear with symphony orchestras and chamber ensembles. Bartok dedicated his clarinet trio *Contrasts* to Goodman in 1938, and Hindemith (1947) and Copland (1948) each wrote a clarinet concerto for him.

Benny Goodman. From left: *Dominica 1861 (1996), St. Vincent 1144 (1989), U.S.A. 3099 (1996)*

The Jewish World in Stamps

Gottschalk, Louis Moreau (1829-1869). American pianist and composer. Born in New Orleans, Gottschalk was a child prodigy who toured Europe as a virtuoso pianist while still a teenager. The sole support of his six younger siblings after the death of his father, Gottschalk was forced to play hundreds of concerts per year until his health and mental stamina faltered. After withdrawing from the concert stage, Gottschalk composed easy salon pieces to meet the growing market for piano music. His youthful exposure to the French and African-tinged Caribbean folk music that characterized the music of the Creoles had a profound influence on his more serious works. The ability to create memorable and catchy tunes, combined with a flair for unusual orchestration, enabled Gottschalk to be a fresh and often uninhibited voice on the American musical scene.

Louis Gottschalk.
U.S.A. 3165 (1997)

Halévy, Ludovic (1834–1908). French librettist. In collaboration with Henri Meilhac, Halévy wrote the text for Bizet's opera *Carmen* (1875). He also penned the librettos for several operettas by Jacques Offenbach, including *Orpheus in the Underworld* (1858) and *La Vie Parisienne* (1866). Halévy was the nephew of Jacques Francois Fromental Halévy (1799–1862), who is best known for his grand opera *La Juive* ("The Jewess"; 1835).

Scenes from the opera *Carmen*. Clockwise: Prologue. *Monaco 964 (1975)*;
Carmen and Don Jose. *Hungary 1852 (1967)*; Carmen at the tavern; Carmen
with the smugglers; Carmen at the bull ring. *Monaco 965-967 (1975)*

Huberman, Bronislaw (1882-1947). Violinist and founder of the Israel Philharmonic Orchestra. Born in Poland, Huberman was a child prodigy in Warsaw. At age ten, he played before emperor Francis Joseph in Vienna and became a frequent soloist in the concert halls of Europe. When Hitler introduced restrictive measures against Jews in 1933, the German conductor Furtwaengler nevertheless invited Huberman to appear with him. Huberman refused, later explaining to an English newspaper that he accused the German intellectuals of having silently acquiesced in the actions of the Nazis. When visiting the Land of Israel in 1936, Huberman conceived of the idea of founding a Palestine Orchestra (forerunner of the Israel Philharmonic Orchestra). He assembled in Tel Aviv a number of experienced refugee musicians and raised the financial backing, thus creating the basis for a full-fledged concert life in Israel. Arturo Toscanini agreed to conduct the opening concerts, and the orchestra immediately acquired international standing.

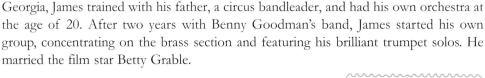

Bronislaw Huberman.
Israel 954 (1986)

James, Harry (1916–1983). American trumpet player and bandleader. Born in Albany, Georgia, James trained with his father, a circus bandleader, and had his own orchestra at the age of 20. After two years with Benny Goodman's band, James started his own group, concentrating on the brass section and featuring his brilliant trumpet solos. He married the film star Betty Grable.

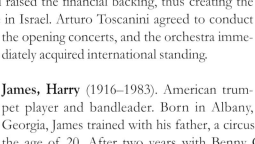

Harry James.
Dominica 1863 (1996)

Joachim, Joseph (1831–1907). Slovakian violinist. A musical prodigy, Joachim concertized widely throughout Europe and was considered the most notable violinist of his generation (and its most distinguished teacher), an artist in whom technique, taste, intellect, and emotion were combined to a rare degree. Joachim's friendships with the great composers and performers of his time are an important factor in the history of 19th century music, especially his association with Mendelssohn, Liszt, Robert and Clara Schumann, and Brahms. Although Joachim converted to Protestantism in 1855, he resigned from his position as concertmaster and conductor of the Royal Hanoverian Orchestra when the violinist J. M. Gruen was refused tenure as a Jew (a principle that had not been observed in Joachim's case). In 1866, Joachim became director of the newly founded *Hochschule fuer Musik* (Music Academy) in Berlin, where one of his prize students was Leopold Auer.

Joseph Joachim.
Germany 9N280 (1969)

Kalman, Emmerich (Imre; 1882–1953). Hungarian composer. A practicing lawyer, Kalman was drawn to the field of operetta with the success of cabaret songs he had written under a pseudonym. His works were based on the melodic idiom of urban Hungarian folk and entertainment music, including the gypsy element. Kalman's operettas, which he orchestrated himself, were popular for their melodic richness that ranges from sentimental pathos to dashing gaiety.

Emmerich Kalman.
Austria 1226 (1982)

Klemperer, Otto (1885–1973). Polish-born conductor who is often considered the last in the grand German tradition. Klemperer converted to Catholicism before the Nazi takeover and raised his children in that faith. However, he formally returned to Judaism a few years before his death. After emigrating to the United States in 1933, Klemperer became director of the Los Angeles Philharmonic, later re-

Otto Klemperer.
Germany 9N502 (1985)

organized the Pittsburgh Symphony Orchestra, and undertook tours to various countries. Illness and accidents interrupted his career, but he returned to the podium despite increasing bodily handicaps that obliged him to conduct while seated.

Lehar, Franz (1870-1948). Hungarian operetta composer. The eldest son of a bandmaster in the Austro-Hungarian army, Lehar studied violin and composition at the Prague Conservatory of Music, where he was said to have been advised by no less a figure than Dvorak to "Hang up your fiddle, my boy, and write music!" Lehar is most famous as the composer of more than 30 operettas, especially *The Merry Widow*. Although definitely of Jewish ancestry, Lehar remained in Austria after the German takeover in 1938 and was left unmolested, presumably because *The Merry Widow* was one of Hitler's favorite works.

From left: Lehar and his home at Bad Ischl; *The Merry Widow*; The People's Opera in Vienna. *Austria 1084 (1978), 875 (1970), 1767 (1998)*

Lewandowski, Louis (1821-1894). Choral director and composer. Conductor of the choir at the Old Synagogue in Berlin and, after 1866, at the New Synagogue, Lewandowski was the most significant composer of synagogue music after Solomon Sulzer. He reproduced the traditional Jewish melodies in a more classical form and treated the organ accompaniment with greater freedom than did his predecessor. Lewandowski's style appealed to a wide public, and the adaptable musical and instrumental settings of his works allow them to be utilized by both small ensembles and professional synagogue choirs with grand organs and musically trained cantors. Lewandowski's style was early adopted by Conservative and Reform congregations in urban communities of the United States.

Louis Lewandowski. *GDR 2845 (1990)*

Mahler, Gustav (1860-1911). Austrian composer and conductor. In 1897, Mahler converted to Catholicism to secure the prestigious position of director of the Imperial Opera in Vienna, which he succeeded in raising to a previously unknown level of artistic achievement. Although today one of the most revered symphonic composers, during his lifetime Mahler's compositions were overshadowed by his successes as a conductor. Employing vast orchestral resources, Mahler's works mark the culmination of the post-romantic development of the symphony and were a major influence on such 20th-century composers as fellow countrymen Arnold

Gustav Mahler. Left: *Israel 1275 (1996)*; right: *Austria 654 (1960)*

Schoenberg and Alban Berg. Mahler's use of Jewish musical motifs, including hints of klezmer, testified to his continued allegiance to his Jewish roots. Expressing the same sense of rootlessness in his personal life as he felt in his artistic pursuits, Mahler noted: "I am thrice homeless. As a Bohemian born in Austria. As an Austrian among Germans. And as a Jew throughout the world."

Mahler with pardessus de viole, kettle drum, double horn. *Hungary 2942 (1985)*

Mahler. *Czech Republic 3119 (2000)*

Mehta, Zubin (1936-). Indian-American conductor of the Israel Philharmonic Orchestra. Known for his passionate and flamboyant style, during his meteoric career Mehta has been the chief conductor of the Los Angeles, Montreal, and New York Philharmonic Orchestras. Though not Jewish, Mehta plays an important role in the musical life of Israel and has been Music Director of the Israel Philharmonic Orchestra since 1977. During both the Six-Day and Yom Kippur Wars, Mehta canceled all engagements and hastened to Israel to conduct special concerts and generally identify himself with the country.

Zubin Mehta. *Maldive Islands 1821 (1992)*

Mendelssohn-Bartholdy, Felix (1809-1849). German composer and leading figure of early 19th century European romanticism. The grandson of famed Jewish philosopher Moses Mendelssohn, Felix (born Jakob Ludwig Felix) was converted to Christianity as a child to spare him from anti-Jewish discrimination. To further conceal his son's Jewish origin, his father added the name Bartholdy (after a property that had belonged to his wife's brother) to the family name; however, Felix generally dropped it from his signature.

A child prodigy, Mendelssohn's masterful overture to *A Midsummer Night's Dream* was composed at age 17 (though the famous "Wedding March" and the rest of the incidental music to the play were not written until 17 years later). Mendelssohn appeared as a pianist and conductor throughout Europe, making frequent trips to England where he was especially popular. Some of his most important programmatic works reflect impressions of a three-year grand tour of Europe – the *Hebrides Overture* and the *Italian* and *Scotch symphonies*. One of Mendelssohn's greatest achievements was his rediscovery of the music of Bach, which initiated a revival of the Baroque composer's works. Mendelssohn also founded the Leipzig Conservatory, which became the most renowned institution of its kind in Germany in the 19th century. Unfortunately, Mendelssohn's

From left: Score of *Song without Words*; Felix Mendelssohn.
GDR 2393 (1984), Israel 1274 (1996)

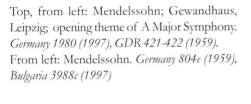

Top, from left: Mendelssohn; Gewandhaus, Leipzig; opening theme of A Major Symphony. *Germany 1980 (1997), GDR 421-422 (1959).* From left: Mendelssohn. *Germany 804e (1959), Bulgaria 3988c (1997)*

strenuous existence as pianist, conductor, composer, and pedagogue wore him out prematurely. The sudden death of his beloved sister Fanny (Zipporah) in 1847 was a shock to his already weakened system, and he died six months later.

Milhaud, Darius (1892-1974). French composer. He was descended from an old Jewish family that claimed to have been among the first settlers in southern France after the fall of Jerusalem. In Paris, Milhaud joined a group of progressive artists, the musicians of which formed an inner circle later known as "Les Six" (The Six). A versatile and prolific composer, Milhaud wrote vocal and orchestral music for concert, stage, and screen. South American rhythms, American jazz, Jewish synagogue traditions (especially those of his native region), 12-tone music, and polytonality (simultaneous use of several keys) all merge in his works, yet the mixture is always unmistakably his own. Among the best known of his compositions on Jewish themes are his *Sacred Service* (1947) and two song cycles with piano accompaniment. Milhaud also wrote musical settings of Psalms for solo voices and chorus; the ballet *La Creation du Monde* (1923); a piano suite, *Le Candelabre a Sept Branches* (1951); and music for various festival prayers. When France collapsed in 1940 in the face of the German onslaught, Milhaud moved to the United States and became a professor at Mills College in Oakland, California.

Darius Milhaud. *Israel 1232 (1995)*

Milhaud.
France 1975 (1985)

Offenbach, Jacques (1819-80). German-born French composer of witty and satiric comic operas and operettas. Besides cello studies at the Paris Conservatoire, Offenbach began basic instruction in composition from Jacques Halévy (1799-1862), whose grand opera *La Juive* (The Jewess) is one of the few works on an explicitly Jewish theme that has been a cornerstone of the operatic repertory. In 1835, Offenbach began writing short, sentimental pieces, although he attracted attention more because of his eccentric behavior than the quality of his music, and his first theatrical works met with little success. The 1855 Paris World Fair proved a turning point in Offenbach's career, when he obtained the lease for a small theater on the Champs-Elysees. Opened under the name Les Bouffes Parisiens, its success surpassed his expectations. Offenbach took Paris by storm with his musical plays, and it was stated that, "All Europe sang his melodies and danced to his rhythms." By 1875, Offenbach had composed 90 operettas, many of them to librettos by Ludovic Halévy.

Among his most famous works are *Orpheus in the Underworld* (1858), *La Vie Parisienne* (1866), and *The Tales of Hoffman*, his grand opera masterpiece that was premiered posthumously and contains the popular "Barcarolle."

Top, from left: Scenes from *Orpheus in the Underworld* and *La Vie Parisienne. Benin 499-500 (1980).* Below, from left: Centennial of Offenbach's death. *France B536 (1981), Gabon C230 (1980), Congo C288 (1980)*

Ormandy, Eugene (1899-1985). Hungarian-American musician who was the long-time conductor of the Philadelphia Orchestra. Born Eugene Blau, violinist Ormandy was a child prodigy who moved to the United States in 1921. He became the associate conductor of the Philadelphia Orchestra (with Leopold Stokowski; 1936–1938) and then its permanent conductor. During his 42-year tenure as its music director, Ormandy raised the Philadelphia Orchestra to one of the world's major symphonies, renowned for its lush rich sound, particularly that produced by the strings.

Eugene Ormandy.
U.S.A. 3161 (1997)

Rubinstein, Arthur (1886-1982). Polish-born American piano virtuoso. At the outbreak of World War I, Rubinstein offered his services to the Polish Embassy in London and gave concerts for the Allied Forces. Seeing the results of German brutality among civilians, he decided never to appear again in Germany and settled in France. Rubinstein developed into a master pianist of deep insight, whose recitals (as many as 150 a year) drew both the general public and the connoisseurs. With the German occupation of France in 1940, Rubinstein moved to the United States and subsequently Americanized the spelling of his name (originally Artur). He became best known as an interpreter of the romantic composers, especially Chopin. A prolific solo recording artist, Rubinstein also appeared in memorable recordings of chamber music with Heifetz, Feuermann, and Piatigorsky. In 1963, the Israel Philharmonic Orchestra established the Artur Rubinstein Chair of Musicology at the Hebrew University, using the proceeds of his concerts in Israel for which he always refused payment. Awarded an honorary doctorate by the Weizmann Institute and appointed a Distinguished Citizen of Jerusalem, in 1978 Rubinstein was one of five recipients of the newly instituted Kennedy Center Honors. The prestigious Rubinstein International Piano Competition, established in his name, was first held in Israel in l974 and has become a regular triennial event.

Schoenberg, Arnold (1874–1951). Austrian-American composer whose twelve-tone system of musical composition exerted immense influence on 20th century music. Born to an Orthodox family in Vienna, Schoenberg converted to Christianity in 1898 under the influence of Gustav Mahler. Essentially self-taught and initially influenced by Brahms and Wagner, Schoenberg began to employ far-reaching harmonies that led to atonality. Premieres of his first two string quartets in 1905 and 1908 caused riots, experiences that made Schoenberg feel persecuted by a public that could not understand his music. Schoenberg is best known for his twelve-tone system, in which a basic row containing the twelve notes of the chromatic scale (in an order predetermined by the composer) serves as the foundation for an entire composition. In

Arthur Rubinstein *by Picasso*.
Israel 935 (1986)

Arnold Schoenberg.
Israel 1231 (1995)

1933, after being removed from his post at the Prussian Academy of Arts in Berlin on "racial" grounds, Schoenberg returned to Judaism at a formal religious ceremony in Paris where one of the witnesses was Marc Chagall. He immigrated to the United States and taught for many years at the University of Southern California and then at the University of California in Los Angeles, where the music school building bears his name.

A devoted Zionist, in 1951 Schoenberg accepted an invitation to head the newly established Rubin Academy for Music in Jerusalem, but his state of health prevented him from taking up the appointment. Schoenberg's Jewish loyalties, the Holocaust, and the establishment of the State of Israel are strongly reflected in several of his musical works. He focused on religious themes in his cantata *Die Jakobsleiter*, the cycle of *Modern Psalms*, and his opera *Moses and Aaron*, which was unfinished at his death but has been highly successful in its two-act form.

Arnold Schoenberg.
Austria 1001 (1974)

Shaw, Artie (1910-). Clarinetist and bandleader. Born Arthur Jacob Arshawsky, the son of Russian Jewish immigrants, Shaw formed the Gramercy Five, a band that became a leading exponent of the swing style of the 1940s. His autobiographical novel, *The Trouble with Cinderella* (1952), tells of his many marriages to, among others, film actresses Lana Turner and Ava Gardner.

Artie Shaw.
Dominica 1860 (1996)

Beverly Sills in *Daughter of the Regiment*. St. Vincent 2509f (1997)

Sills, Beverly (1929-). American soprano who won international popularity through her clear, pliant coloratura voice and sparkling personality. Born Belle Silverman in New York City, Sills made her first public appearance under her nickname "Bubbles," becoming a child radio star at age three. Since her debut with the Philadelphia Civic Opera in 1947, Sills has sung at virtually all the major American and world opera houses. Her most notable successes were in Italian operas, especially those of Donizetti. In 1955, Sills joined the New York City Opera, becoming its general director in 1979. In an effort to bring opera to wider audiences, Sills promoted live television broadcasts and productions of operas in English translation.

Straus, Oscar (1870–1954). Austrian operetta composer. In 1907, Straus composed the *A Waltz Dream*, the first of his international successes. This was followed the next year by a second popular operetta, *The Chocolate Soldier*, based on George Bernard Shaw's *Arms and the Man*. After his works were banned by the Nazi regime he lived in Switzerland, France, and in the United States, before returning to Europe after the war.

Johann Straus the Elder. *Austria 560 (1949)*

The Waltz Dream. *Austria 673 (1970)*

Strauss, Johann. Austrian father and son musicians, known as the "waltz kings" of Vienna in the 19th century. The father of the first Strauss was Jewish, but converted. Great efforts were made during the Nazi period to cover this up, including the destruction of baptismal records. The younger Strauss's wife and stepdaughter were Jewish.

Johann Strauss the Elder (1804-1849) organized his own orchestra in 1825 and toured Europe, popularizing the waltz. His son, Johann Strauss the Younger (1825-1899), made his first appearance conducting his own orchestra at the age of 19. After the death of the elder Strauss, he united his group with the orchestra his father had made famous. His many tours

Clockwise: *Blue Danube Waltz. Austria 786 (1967);* Strauss the Younger with dancers. *Monaco 998 (1975);* Strauss the Younger's 150th birthday. *Austria 1024 (1975); Die Fledermaus. Austria 872 (1970);* Dancers. *Germany 2045 (1999)*

The Jewish World in Stamps

throughout Europe and a visit to the United States in 1872 featured his own dance music, especially his waltzes. Strauss composed such famous waltzes as *The Blue Danube* (1867) and *Tales from the Vienna Woods* (1868). He also composed 16 stage works for Viennese theaters, of which the best known today are the operettas *Die Fledermaus* (The Bat, 1874) and *Der Zigeunerbaron* (The Gypsy Baron, 1885).

Sulzer, Solomon (1804–1890). Austrian cantor and reformer of liturgical music. Sulzer adopted a moderate path, seeking to "renovate" traditional *hazzanut* by taking into consideration the musical trends of the time. He purified many melodies of their excessive ornamentation, but also allowed some of his choral music to be dominated by the style of the 19th century Christian church. Though Sulzer's innovations aroused little sympathy among the cantors of Central and Eastern Europe, they were not considered as foreign or "un-Jewish" sounding as those of the Reform movement and thus were widely adopted in modern synagogues in the mid 19th century.

Solomon Sulzer.
Austria 1488 (1990)

George Szell.
U.S.A. 3160 (1997)

Szell, George (1897-1970). Hungarian-born American conductor and pianist. After immigrating to the United States in 1940, Szell became principal conductor of the Metropolitan Opera in New York (1942–45). Six years later, Szell was appointed permanent conductor of the Cleveland Orchestra, which he developed into one of the finest in the world.

Tucker, Richard (1914-1975). American operatic tenor who began his singing career as a cantor. Engaged by the Metropolitan Opera in 1941, Tucker continued officiating as hazzan at the Brooklyn Jewish Center until 1947. Tucker was known as one of the leading lyric tenors, specializing in French and Italian operas, and he performed in major opera houses throughout the world. Nevertheless, he continued to sing as a cantor in special appearances and in recordings.

Wieniawski, Henri (1834-1880). Polish violin virtuoso and composer. After touring Europe with his pianist brother Joseph, Wieniawski in 1850 was appointed solo violinist to the czar. Wieniawski's dazzling technique, combined with warmth and delicacy, gained him wide admiration. As with other virtuosos of the time, Wieniawski composed numerous works for his instrument, including two concertos and the popular *Legende*, which are noted for their Slavic coloring and bravura style.

Richard Tucker.
U.S.A. 3155 (1996)

Henri Wieniawski. From
left: *Poland 795 (1957),
2482 (1981)*

Irving Berlin's song "Oh How I Hate to Get Up in the Morning." *Gambia 2052 (1998)*

Berlin, Irving (1888-1989). American popular song writer. Born Israel Baline in Russia, the son of a cantor, Berlin moved to New York in 1893. Without formal musical education and unable to read music, Berlin nevertheless wrote more than 1,000 songs, including such American classics as "Alexander's Ragtime Band," "White Christmas," and "God Bless America." Berlin also wrote the songs for such films as *Top Hat* (1935); *Follow the Fleet* (1936); *On the Avenue* (1937); *Holiday Inn* (1942); and *Easter Parade* (1948), and for Broadway musicals *Annie Get Your Gun* (1946) and *Call Me Madam* (1950).

Bernstein, Leonard (1918-1990). Internationally renowned American composer, conductor, and pianist. As assistant conductor of the New York Philharmonic at age 25, Bernstein attracted national attention by acquitting himself brilliantly when called upon to conduct a difficult program at short notice in place of the indisposed Bruno Walter. In 1948, Bernstein became music director of the Israel Philharmonic Orchestra, conducting concerts for soldiers at the front during the War of Independence. Ten years later, he was appointed music director and conductor of the New York Philharmonic, the first American-born musician to occupy this post. Professor of music at Brandeis University and head of the conducting program at the Berkshire Music Center at Tanglewood, Bernstein retired in 1969 to devote himself to composing. Among his symphonic works are the *Jeremiah Symphony*, with a moving vocal solo in Hebrew based on the cantillation for the Book of Lamentations (1944); *Kaddish* (in Hebrew), an oratorio for narrator, chorus, and orchestra, which he conducted for the first time in Tel Aviv in 1963; and *Chichester Psalms* (also in Hebrew), for chorus and

Irving Berlin. *U.S.A. (2002)*

From left: "West Side Story;" Bernstein. *Gambia 2050g-h (1998)*

orchestra (1965). Bernstein had his greatest popular triumph with *West Side Story* (1957), and he also wrote the music to *On the Town* (1944), *Wonderful Town* (1953), and *Candide* (1956). Bernstein was a brilliant lecturer on music, and a collection of his talks from his exceptionally popular series of televised young people's concerts was published under the title *The Joy of Music* (1959).

Gershwin, George (1898-1937). American pianist and composer of musicals, popular songs, and classical works. Born to immigrant parents in Brooklyn, the 1918 success of his song "Swanee," sung by Al Jolson in the revue *Sinbad*, caused a sensation and established Gershwin as a Tin Pan Alley composer. The lyrics for nearly all of his songs were written by his brother Ira (1896-1983), his collaborator in a series of revues and musical comedies that included *Lady Be Good* (1924), *Funny Face* (1927), and *Of Thee I Sing* (1931), the first musical comedy to win a Pulitzer Prize. Gershwin's popular songs are marked by striking harmonic inventiveness and the rhythms and melodic twists of jazz. At the invitation of bandleader

George and Ira Gershwin. *U.S.A. 3345 (1999)*

Paul Whiteman, Gershwin was commissioned to compose a jazz symphony – *Rhapsody in Blue* for piano and orchestra – which was first performed in 1924 with the composer at the piano. This work profoundly influenced European and American composers to use jazz-derived melodies and rhythmic patterns and made jazz "respectable" for the American concert stage. Another masterpiece was his opera *Porgy and Bess* (1935), in which he skillfully blended the idioms of black folk music, jazz, Tin Pan Alley, and European classical music together with aspects of Jewish prayer chants.

From left: George Gershwin. *Malagasy 873 (1988)*; *Porgy and Bess* and its creator. *Gambia 2050e-d (1998)*

Hart, Lorenz (1895-1943). American popular lyricist. Born to Jewish immigrant parents, in 1918 Hart met Richard Rodgers, with whom he created some of the most successful musicals of the first half of the 20th century. Hart wrote the lyrics for such shows as *The Girl Friend* (1926), *A Connecticut Yankee* (1927), *Babes in Arms* (1936), and *Pal Joey* (1940); his most popular songs include "My Funny Valentine," "Where or When," and "The Lady is a Tramp."

Lorenz Hart.
U.S.A. 3347 (1999)

Herrmann, Bernard (1911–1975). American composer and conductor. Born in New York City, Herrmann became one of the world's most famous composers of film scores, notably for Orson Welles (*Citizen Kane* and *The Magnificent Ambersons*) and Alfred Hitchcock (*Psycho, Vertigo,* and *North by Northwest*). He won an Oscar for *The Devil and Daniel Webster.*

Bernard Herrmann
U.S.A. 3341 (1999)

Kern, Jerome (1885-1945). American composer for the Broadway stage. Among his most famous compositions were "Ol' Man River" (*Show Boat,* 1927), "Smoke Gets in Your Eyes" (*Roberta,* 1933), and "The Last Time I Saw Paris."

From left: *Show Boat*; Jerome Kern.
U.S.A. 2767 (1993), 2110 (1985)

Erich Korngold.
U.S.A. 3344 (1999)

Korngold, Erich Wolfgang (1897-1957). Austrian-American musician. Korngold composed classical works, such as a violin concerto for Jascha Heifetz, as well as motion picture scores. Known for his colorful, melodious, and sensuous style, the lush romantic "swashbuckling" sound of his film music is unmistakable. Korngold won two Academy Awards for best musical score, for *Anthony Adverse* and *The Adventures of Robin Hood*.

Lerner, Alan Jay (1918-1986). American lyricist and librettist, known for his musical comedies written in collaboration with composer Frederick Loewe. These include such Broadway successes as *Brigadoon* (1947), *Paint Your Wagon* (1951), *My Fair Lady* (1956), and *Camelot* (1960), and the Academy-Award winning movies *Gigi* (1958) and *My Fair Lady* (1964). Lerner also won an Academy Award for his screenplay for *An American in Paris* (1951).

Top: Lerner and Loewe. Bottom: *My Fair Lady. U.S.A. 3346 (1999), 2770 (1993)*

Loewe, Frederick (1904-88). American composer for the musical stage. Born in Vienna and beginning his career as a concert pianist, Loewe is best known for his musical comedies written in collaboration with lyricist and librettist Alan Jay Lerner. These include such Broadway successes as *Brigadoon* (1947), *Paint Your Wagon* (1951), *My Fair Lady* (1956), and *Camelot* (1960), and the Academy-Award winning movies *Gigi* (1958) and *My Fair Lady* (1964).

Loesser, Frank Henry (1910-69). American composer and lyricist. Loesser wrote the words and music for the film *Hans Christian Andersen* (1952) and the musicals *Guys and Dolls* (1950), *The Most Happy Fella* (1956), and the Pulitzer-Prize winning *How to Succeed in Business Without Really Trying* (1961).

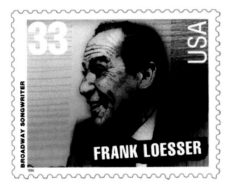

Top: Frank Loesser. *U.S.A. 3350 (1999).*
Right: H. C. Anderson fairy tales.
Israel 1393-1395 (2000)

Alfred Newman.
U.S.A. 3343 (1999)

Newman, Alfred (1901-70). American film composer. Born in New Haven, Newman composed the scores for more than two hundred movies. He received 45 Academy-Award nominations and won 9 Oscars, mostly for musicals that he arranged and supervised.

Rodgers (**Richard**; 1902-1979) and **Hammerstein** (**Oscar** II; 1895-1960). Composer and librettist who collaborated in revolutionizing the American musical theater. Among their Broadway and film hits were the Pulitzer-Prize winning *Oklahoma!* (1943) and *South Pacific* (1949), *Carousel* (1945), *The King and I* (1951), *Flower Drum Song* (1958), and *The Sound of Music* (1959). Composer Rodgers had previously joined with lyricist Lorenz Hart in such musical comedies as *The Girl Friend* (1926), A *Connecticut Yankee* (1927), *Babes in Arms* (1937), and *Pal Joey* (1940).). He also composed music for many films, including the documentary *Victory at Sea* (1952). Librettist Hammerstein had previously collaborated with Rudolf Friml in *Rose Marie* (1924), with Sigmund Romberg in *The Desert Song* (1926), and with Jerome Kern in *Show Boat* (1927).

Rodgers and Hammerstein.
U.S.A. 3348 (1999)

From left: Rodgers and Hammerstein; *The King and I.*
Gambia 2050e-f (1998)

The musical *Oklahoma.*
U.S.A. 2722 (1993)

Max Steiner. *U.S.A. 3339 (1991)*

Steiner, Max (1888-1971). Austrian-American film composer. Born in Vienna, Steiner studied with Gustav Mahler and composed scores for the Viennese concert hall and theater. After moving to the United States, Steiner scored more than 200 films. He received 18 Academy-Award nominations and won three Oscars, for *Now, Voyager, The Informer,* and *Since You Went Away.* Ironically, two of his most famous scores were nominated but did not win – *Casablanca* and *Gone with the Wind.*

Tiomkin, Dimitri (1879-1979). Hollywood film composer. Born in Russia, Tiomkin emigrated to the United States in 1925. Classically trained, Tiomkin was instrumental in introducing the music of Gershwin to Europe and also served a brief stint as the conductor of the Los Angeles Philharmonic. Turning to writing scores for films in the 1930s, Tiomkin received 18 Academy-Award nominations for best score and won three times – for *High Noon, The High and the Mighty,* and *The Old Man and the Sea.*

Dimitri Tiomkin.
U.S.A. 3340 (1999)

Waxman, Franz (1906-1967). Hollywood film composer. Born in Germany, Waxman wrote the music for many German films until forced to emigrate when the Nazis took control. Waxman wrote the scores for almost 200 movies, earning seven Academy-Award nominations and winning Oscars for *Sunset Boulevard* (1950) and *A Place in the Sun* (1951).

Franz Waxman. *U.S.A. 3342 (1999)*

Weill, Kurt (1900-1950). German-born American composer who initially wrote operas and symphonic and chamber music, but later turned to social satire in the theater. Weill was the son of a cantor and came from a family in which there had been many rabbis. In association with the German dramatist Bertolt Brecht, Weill composed his masterpiece *The Threepenny Opera,* which was an extraordinary success in Europe and the United States. After his works were termed subversive and banned in Nazi Germany, Weill and his non-Jewish wife, actress and singer Lotte Lenya, moved to Paris; before eventually settling in the U.S. in 1935. Unusually adaptable, Weill adjusted to the ways of the American theater and produced a number of successful musical comedies, a one-act American folk opera, *Down in the Valley* (1948), and the music for Ben Hecht's pageant in honor of the State of Israel, *A Flag is Born* (1948). In his music, Weill made liberal use of modern dance rhythms, particularly jazz, often combining these modern resources with nostalgic and even sentimental ballad forms. His most famous "Jewish" work was the opera *The Eternal Road*, from a story by the famous Austrian Jewish writer, Franz Werfel. Rarely staged due to its cost, the opera was revived in 2000 in honor of Weill's 100th birthday.

Kurt Weill with wife Lotte Lenya and instruments.
Grenada Grenadines 1119 (1989)

Theater, Motion Pictures, Entertainment

Abbott, Bud (1897-1974). Straight man of the famous comedy team of "Abbott and Costello." Born William Alexander Abbott in Asbury Park, N.J., he and Louis Francis Cristillo mastered the straight man/clown relationship, creating a magical chemistry that would take them from the burlesque stage to radio to Broadway, film, and finally television. They rocketed to stardom after an appearance on the Kate Smith Radio Hour, where they performed what would become known as their classic signature skit, "Who's On First."

Lauren Bacall with Humphrey Bogart.
Granada Grenadines 1778h (1995)

Bacall, Lauren (1924-). American film star who combined a sultry voice and provocative demeanor with cool sophistication. Born Betty Joan Perske in New York City, Bacall began her career as a model. Featured on the cover of Harper's Bazaar in 1943, she attracted the attention of director Howard Hawks, who promptly signed her to a long-term film contract. The next year Bacall co-starred in her first film (*To Have And Have Not*) with Humphrey Bogart, whom she married one year later (he was 46). They made three more classic films together — *The Big Sleep* (1946), *Dark Passage* (1947), and *Key Largo* (1948). After Bogart died in 1957, Bacall continued her career both in motion pictures and on the stage.

Top: Bud Abbott in *The Naughty Nineties. Gambia 1348d (1993)*. Bottom: Abbott and Costello. *U.S.A. 2566 (1991)*

Bara, Theda (1890-1955). Star of the silent screen, who was noted for her femme fatale roles. Born Theodosia Goodman in Cincinnati, Bara became known as the foremost "vamp" of the early days of motion pictures.

Theda Bara.
U.S.A. 2827 (1994)

Benny, Jack (1894-1974). American comedian who hosted long-running shows on both radio and television. Born Benny Kubelsky in Chicago, he began a successful career as a violinist in vaudeville at age 17. In 1932, he launched "The Jack Benny Show," which was a weekly fixture on radio for the next 23 years. Benny portrayed the beloved character of an acerbic penny pincher with a deadpan stare, who was a demanding boss and an atrocious fiddler. His co-star was his wife, Mary Livingston (nee Sadye Marks). Benny successfully transformed his show to television, where he appeared for another 10 years. Extremely generous in real life and a talented musician, Benny frequently appeared as a comic violin soloist with major American symphony orchestras in fund-raising concerts.

Jack Benny.
U.S.A. 2564 (1991)

Jack Benny.
Grenada 2550 (1996)

Berg, Gertrude (1900–1966). American actress. She wrote, directed, and starred as Molly Goldberg in the popular show "The Goldbergs," which was on radio for 17 years and later had a five-year run on television.

Gertrude Berg.
Grenada 2551 (1996)

Sarah Bernhardt.
Antigua 1567 (1992)

Bernhardt, Sarah (1844-1923). One of the best-known stage stars of her time. Born Rosine Bernard, she was the eldest of the three illegitimate daughters of Judith Van Hard, a high-class Dutch-Jewish courtesan in Paris. When ten years old, Sarah was sent to the convent of Versailles and baptized. Nevertheless, she remained proud of her Jewish heritage. When she vigorously supported Captain Dreyfus during his ordeal, Bernhardt was attacked as a Jew. After a series of personal triumphs throughout Europe and the United States, Bernhardt undertook the direction of a large Paris theater, which she renamed for herself. Here she presented *Hamlet*, in which she played the title role. Famed for her slim beauty and bell-like voice, Bernhardt was known as the "Divine Sarah." At age 70, complications resulting from a neglected knee injury forced her to have her right leg amputated. However, she refused to abandon the stage, continuing to appear in roles that permitted her to sit, and performing for troops at the front in World War I.

Bernhardt.
France B191 (1945)

Brice, Fanny (1891-1951). Leading American comedienne of stage, screen, and radio. Born Fanny Borach in New York, she achieved her first success in the 1910 Ziegfeld Follies and appeared in almost every annual production of the Follies until 1924. Brice had a gift for mime and satire, and she was noted for her moving versions of dramatic songs as well as her hilarious Yiddish dialect numbers sung with a Brooklyn accent. In 1936, Brice originated the part of a comic child character, Baby Snooks, on radio and played the role almost continuously until her death. Although a major star in the 1920s and 1930s, Brice would be largely forgotten today if not for the Barbra Streisand movies about her (*Funny Girl* and *Funny Lady*).

Fanny Brice.
U.S.A. 2565 (1991)

Burns, George (1896-1996). American comedian. Born Nathan Birnbaum in New York City, Burns began his 70-year career as a child in vaudeville. In 1923, Burns teamed up with his future wife, the Irish-Catholic Gracie Allen; they performed together for 35 years, making more than a dozen motion pictures. Initially Burns starred as the funny man, but later they exchanged roles. Their radio show ran for 17 years, and they appeared for another decade on television until Gracie retired. Burns continued on his own, taking on dramatic roles as well as comic ones. He won an Academy Award as Best Supporting Actor in 1975 for his appearance in *The Sunshine Boys*.

George Burns with wife Gracie Allen. *Grenada 2554 (1991)*

Cantor, Eddie (1892-1964). American comedian and vaudeville performer. Born Isidor Iskowitch on New York's Lower East Side, as a teenager Cantor won a music-hall amateur contest and began touring with a comedy blackface act. Cantor toured the music halls of Europe and was given top billing in the Ziegfeld Follies of 1917-1919. Songs associated with him were immediate hits on the radio. Cantor raised large sums for refugees from Nazi Germany and other Jewish causes and was a founder and president of the Screen Actors' Guild.

Eddie Cantor.
Grenada 2554 (1996)

Copperfield, David (1957-). American contemporary magician. Born David Seth Kotkin to Russian Jewish immigrants, Copperfield is a highly successful illusionist.

David Copperfield.
Grenada Grenadines 2239 (2000)

Cukor, George (1899-1983). American movie director known for his comedies and adaptations of literary classics. Cukor is often regarded as a "women's director", reflecting his ability to elicit outstanding performances from female actresses. Nominated for the Academy Award for best director four times, he finally won for *My Fair Lady* in 1964. Other notable films include *Dinner at Eight, David Copperfield, Little Women, The Philadelphia Story, A Star is Born,* and *Adam's Rib.*

George Cukor.
Hungary 3668 (1999)

Davis, Sammy Jr. (1925-1990). American actor, singer, impressionist, dancer. Born in Harlem, N.Y., Davis was an incredibly talented performer who broke ground in the entertainment industry for many other African-Americans. In 1954, following a serious auto accident, Davis converted to Judaism with his wife, Swedish actress Mai Britt.

Sammy Davis, Jr.
Malagasy 1055 (1992)

Douglas, Kirk (1916-). American actor. Born Issur Danielovich in New York, Douglas is credited with three milestones in the history of filmmaking. Douglas gave Stanley Kubrick his biggest break by selecting him as the director of *Paths of Glory*; helped destroy the McCarthy-inspired blacklist when he insisted that writer Dalton Trumbo get screenwriting credit for the blockbuster movie, *Spartacus*; and succeeded in convincing John Wayne to appear in the pro-Israel film, *Cast a Giant Shadow*, based on the exploits of Col. David (Mickey) Marcus, an American citizen who was a commander of Israeli forces on the Jerusalem front during its War of Independence in 1948.

Dylan, Bob (1941-). American singer and songwriter. Born Robert Zimmerman in Duluth, Minnesota, Dylan traveled throughout the country

Kirk Douglas in *Spartacus*.
Mali 693 (1994)

Katherine Hepburn and Spencer Tracy in *Adam's Rib*.
Grenada Grenadines 1778g (1995)

KIRK DOUGLAS

Kirk Douglas has been one of the world's most famous entertainers of the 20th century, having starred in over eighty motion pictures spanning more than fifty years. He is the recipient of numerous entertainment awards including the Golden Globe, Cecil B. DeMille Award, Academy Award (for lifetime achievement) and the Presidential Medal of Freedom. As an Actor and sometimes Producer, Douglas has starred in some of the most popular films of all time including Champion, The Bad and the Beautiful, Lust For Life and Spartacus. He has also penned two novels and a best selling autobiography.

Kirk Douglas in various movie roles.
Grenada 2136 (1999)

before settling in New York in 1961, where he sang in the coffee houses of Greenwich Village. Dylan began composing shortly afterward and immediately became a prominent figure in both the folk music revival of that period and the protest song movement that arose shortly afterward.

Eisenstein, Sergei Mikhailovich (1898-1948). Russian film director, who is generally recognized as one of the greatest innovators in movie history. Born in Riga, Latvia, of a Jewish father and a non-Jewish mother, Eisenstein's work was revolutionary both in technique and in subject matter. His 1925

Scene from Eisenstein's
Potemkin. Russia 4760
(1979)

Bob Dylan.
Gambia 1825 (1996)

film *Battleship Potemkin* had a profound and immediate impact on contemporary film making, utilizing such approaches as a dramatic handling of crowd scenes and the use of nonprofessional actors for greater realism. Unlike commercial movies of that and subsequent eras, Eisenstein's films were didactic, teaching a lesson instead of being mere entertainment. His signature technique was the montage style, in which he used editing to juxtapose apparently unrelated images and create rapid and dynamic shifts in rhythm. Under Stalin, the Soviet authorities attacked Eisenstein for having deviated from socialist realism and demanded that he adopt a more accessible style that depicted the lives of common people in sympathetic ways. Finding no alternative but to submit to governmental demands, Eisenstein was restored to favor and assigned to direct his first sound film, *Alexander Nevsky* (1938), an epic about a medieval Russian prince who defeated the Teutonic (German) tribes invading from Europe. Designed to boost morale in Russia, in anticipation of an attack by the German army, the movie contained a brilliant music score by composer Sergei Prokofiev.

Scene from the movie *Potemkin*. *Russia 3085 (1965)*

Douglas Fairbanks. *U.S.A. 2088 (1981)*

Fairbanks, Douglas (1883-1939). American film actor best known for his daring athletic feats and expert swordsmanship. In 1919, Fairbanks founded United Artists in association with his second wife (actress Mary Pickford), director D.W. Griffith, and actor-director-producer Charlie Chaplin.

Houdini, Harry (1874-1926). American magician. Born Ehrich Weiss in Budapest, Hungary, he came to the United States as an infant. He took his professional surname from that of the French magician Jean Eugène Robert-Houdin. Beginning his career as a trapeze performer at age 8, Houdini subsequently became world famous for his performances of feats of magic. He showed astounding ability in extricating himself from handcuffs, ropes, locked trunks, and bonds of any sort.

Jolson, Al (1886-1950). American singer and star of vaudeville and motion pictures. Born Asa Yoelson, as a child he sang in the synagogue where his father served as cantor. After working for years in circuses, vaudeville, and minstrel shows (singing in the blackface makeup that became his trademark), in 1911 Jolson was an instant success in his first Broadway show, *La Belle Paree*. In 1927 Jolson made screen history in *The Jazz Singer*, the first full-length movie with synchronized sound ("talking picture") made in America.

Houdini. *U.S.A. (2002)*

Clockwise: Jolson. *U.S.A. (2002)*; Jolson as the *Jazz Singer*. *Mali C536 (1987)*; First talking picture. *Tanzania 1480 (1996)*; 50th anniversary of the talking picture. *U.S.A. 1727 (1977)*

Danny Kaye. *Grenada 2089 (1992), Gambia 774 (1988)*

Kaye, Danny (1913-1987). American comedian, singer, and dancer who developed a highly individualistic style based on a sunny personality combined with the use of broad physical gestures and an uncanny ability to imitate speech accents. Born David Daniel Kominski in New York City, Kaye began his entertainment career on the "Borscht Circuit" of Catskill Mountain resorts. He first gained renown for his rapid delivery of complicated lyrics in the Broadway musical *Lady in the Dark* (1941). Among his major films were the title roles in *The Secret Life of Walter Mitty* (1947) and *Hans Christian Andersen* (1952). Kaye starred on his own television show during the 1960s, received two special Academy Awards, and served as ambassador at large for UNICEF.

Kubrick's *Space Odyssey. Nicaragua 2051k (1994)*

Kubrick, Stanley (1928-1999). American film director. His work includes such movies as the epic star-studded *Spartacus* (1960), *Lolita* (1962), the black comedy and anti-military-establishment *Dr. Strangelove* (1964), the landmark science fiction film *2001: A Space Odyssey* (1968), and the futuristic and violent *A Clockwork Orange* (1971).

Lahr, Bert (1895-1967). American comedian. Born Irving Lahrheim and the son of German immigrants, Lahr is best known for his film role as the cowardly lion in *The Wizard of Oz* (1939).

Lang, Fritz (1890-1976). Austrian film director and screenwriter who developed narrative and created atmosphere through expressionistic symbolic sets and lighting in such masterpieces as *Metropolis* (1926) and *M* (1931). Goebbels approached Lang with the proposition of putting him

The Cowardly Lion (Lahr). *Montserrat 722 (1989)*

Judy Garland in *The Wizard of Oz. Mali 728 (1994)*

Fritz Lang. *Dominica 944 (1986)*

Jerry Lewis (right) with Dean Martin.
Ghana 1909 (1996)

in charge of Nazi films. Fearing that his Jewish origin would become known, Lang fled that same evening to France and eventually came to the United States.

Lewis, Jerry (1926-). American movie actor and director, known for his screwball comedies. Born Joseph Levitch to a family of professional stage performers in Newark, New Jersey, Lewis is best known for his antics as the frantic and blundering sidekick of Dean Martin, who played the suave, romantic ladies' man. In addition to his comic performances, Lewis is an active campaigner for various charitable causes. In 1963, he began the "Jerry Lewis Telethon for Muscular Dystrophy," an annual Labor Day television fundraising campaign to benefit children suffering from this muscle-wasting disease.

The Marx Brothers. Zany and irreverent American theatrical comedy team, whose wild and impromptu humor appealed to lowbrows and intellectuals alike. Trained as musicians, there originally were five Marx Brothers who began their careers in vaudeville with their mother as the "Six Musical Mascots." When their mother left the act, they became "The Nightingales." The Marx Brothers were known by their professional names: Chico (Leonard; 1891–1961), Harpo (Adolph, later Arthur; 1893–1964), Gummo (Milton; 1894–1977, who was in the act only briefly), Groucho (Julius; 1895–1977), and Zeppo (Herbert; 1901–1979). Each brother developed a distinct persona with readily identifiable characteristics. Chico donned a pointed hat over a deadpan face, affected an Italian accent, and was an accomplished pianist who frequently broke the comedy with a turn at the keyboard. Harpo, with a battered hat over a frizzled wig of blond curls, never spoke during the act and communicated either by means of a bulb horn or a romantic harp. Groucho, at-

A Night at the Opera poster.
Guyana 2545 (1992)

Left from top: Groucho Marx. *Grenada 2663 (1996)*, *Ghana 1942 (1988)*.
Above: The Marx Brothers. *Gambia 776 (1988)*

tired in swallowtail coat, chewing a long cigar, and wearing a large black moustache, was master of the caustic insult. After the brothers' film career had ended, Groucho continued his entertainment career as master of ceremonies of the weekly television quiz show, "You Bet Your Life." Among the Marx Brothers' cinema classics were *Animal Crackers* (1930); *Duck Soup* (1933); *A Night at the Opera* (1935); and *A Night in Casablanca* (1946).

Matthau, Walter (1920-2000). American actor known for his gruff, yet lovable, character. Matthau starred in the movie versions of *The Odd Couple, Hello Dolly!, Cactus Flower,* and *Plaza Suite,* and received an Academy Award for best supporting actor for *The Fortune Cookie.*

The movie *Bad News Bears* with Matthau.
Gambia 1351b (1993)

Metro-Goldwyn-Mayer (MGM). Major movie production company. Samuel Goldwyn (1882-1974), born Samuel Goldfish in Warsaw, moved to the United States at age of 13 and entered the motion-picture industry in 1913 as an associate of his brother-in-law, Jesse L. Lasky, and Cecil B. de Mille. Two years later, Goldwyn joined Edgar and Archibald Selwyn to form the Goldwyn Pictures Corporation (using the first syllable of Goldfish and the last of Selwyn), adopting the name as his own. Louis Burt Mayer (1885–1957), was born in Russia and taken to Canada at the age of two. After several years as a theater owner in Massachusetts, Mayer moved to Hollywood in 1918 and established the Louis B. Mayer Pictures Corporation. In 1924, this company merged with Metro Studios and Goldwyn Pictures to form Metro-Goldwyn-Mayer, which became an enormously successful movie production company.

Movie poster for *Bacon Grabbers.*
Guyana 2544 (1992)

Midler, Bette (1945-). American actress and singer with a trademark brassy style. Born in Hawaii, she was named for one of her mother's favorite actresses, Bette Davis (who was not Jewish). Midler gained notoriety performing in a cabaret act at the Continental Baths, a meeting place for homosexuals, where she sang a wide range of popular music, spicing the songs with outrageous, bawdy comedy. Her first major role was in the original production of *Fiddler on the Roof,* in which she started out in the chorus and eventually played one of Tevye's daughters. Midler turned actress in *The Rose* (1981), a movie loosely based on the life of Janis Joplin.
Monroe, Marilyn (1926-1962). American actress and 50s sex goddess who personified Hollywood glamour.

Bette Midler. *Mali 730 (1995)*

Monroe, Marilyn (1926-1962). American actress and 50s sex goddess who personified Hollywood glamour. Born Norma Jean Baker, Monroe converted to Judaism in 1956 to marry playwright Arthur Miller. She starred in such films as *Gentlemen Prefer Blondes* (1953), *How to Marry a Millionaire* (1953), *Bus Stop* (1956), and *Some Like It Hot* (1959).

Images of Marilyn Monroe. Clockwise: *U.S.A. 2967 (1995), The River of No Return. Mali 696 (1994); Marshall Islands 592 (1995); Antigua 1041 (1987)*

Zero Mostel in *Fiddler on the Roof. Antigua 2037c (1995)*

Mostel, Zero (1915-1977). American actor who created the role of Tevye in the Broadway production of *Fiddler on the Roof* (1964). Born Samuel Joel Mostel in Brooklyn, he acquired the name "Zero" because of his poor marks at school. After a few film roles in which he generally portrayed corpulent villains, Mostel was blacklisted (he never belonged to any political party, but his Jewish ethical principles would not allow him to testify against others in what he regarded as a witch hunt). Only in 1958, when the political climate had changed, did Mostel resume full activity, starring in stage productions such as Ionesco's *Rhinoceros* (1961) and *A Funny Thing Happened on the Way to the Forum* (1962).

Nimoy and Shatner in *Star Trek*.
St. Vincent Grenadines 2244-2245 (1996)

Nimoy, Leonard (1931-). American actor who starred as the super-rational Mr. Spock on the classic science-fiction series *Star Trek*. His trademark was the Vulcan greeting with the fingers in the form of a "V," an ancient Jewish gesture used by the *kohanim* (priests) blessing the congregation. The symbol of two hands, fingers widespread, is traditionally carved on the tombs of Jews of priestly descent.

Shatner, William (1931-). Canadian actor who starred as Captain James T. Kirk, commander of the Starship Enterprise, on the enormously successful *Star Trek* series.

Reinhardt, Max (1873–1943). Austrian stage producer and director. Born Max Goldmann near Vienna, Reinhardt was a leading force in the theater during the first part of the 20th century. As director of the Salzburg State Theater, Reinhardt's goal was to have classic plays speak to

Max Reinhardt.
Austria 1952 (1973)

contemporary audiences, rather than having them acted as in the days when they were written. Reinhardt's methods were experimental and spectacular, and he used massive crowds and a projecting rostrum. For *A Midsummer Night's Dream* he introduced a revolving stage; and for *Hamlet*, he used modern dress. These technical innovations accompanied a revitalized concept of the theater that distinguished Reinhardt's productions and deeply influenced European stagecraft.

Robinson, Edward G. (1893-1973). Legendary screen tough guy. Born in Bucharest, Romania, as Emmanuel Goldenberg, he retained the initial "G" from his surname in his stage name. His family came to the United States in the wake of anti-Jewish riots. Robinson made more than 100 films, but was primarily associated with his gangster roles in 1930s films, most notably *Little Caesar*.

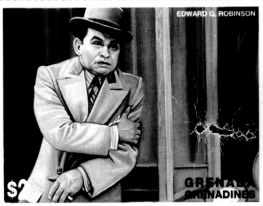

Edward G. Robinson.
Grenada Grenadines 2124c-d (2000)

Sellers, Peter (1925-1980). British comic actor, renowned for his versatile impersonations. Sellers discovered his talent for mimicry while entertaining the forces in India as a member of the Royal Air Force. He achieved his greatest fame as Inspector Clouseau, a bumbling French detective, in *The Pink Panther* (1963) and its many sequels, including *A Shot in the Dark* (1964). His genius for making radical character changes is evident in his assuming triple roles in two political satires, *The Mouse that Roared* (1959) and *Dr. Strangelove* (1964).

Peter Sellers.
Dominica 1845 (1996)

Shore, Dinah (1917-1994). American popular singer and television performer. Born Frances Rose Shore in Winchester, Tennessee, her sweet southern accent and folksy and unpretentious manner made her a symbol of grassroots America and a universal favorite. As a vocalist, she made numerous hit recordings and was extremely popular entertaining the troops during World War II. Her subsequent television career as a variety and talk show hostess spanned three decades and earned her eight Emmy Awards. Shore increased the popularity and acceptance of women's professional golf with her Dinah Shore Classic, a major Ladies Professional Golf Association (LPGA) tournament she hosted beginning in 1972.

Dinah Shore.
Grenada Grenadines 1419 (1992)

Signoret, Simone (1921-1985). French film actress. Born Simone Kaminker in Wiesbaden, Germany, the daughter of a Jewish officer in the French army, Signoret (her mother's name) was brought up in Paris. Signoret appeared in several productions with singer and actor Yves Montand, whom she married in 1951. Although Montand was not Jewish, he almost lost his life several times during World War II because his birth name of "Ivo Livi" made many people in German-occupied France assume he was Jewish. Signoret achieved international stardom and an Academy Award for her role in the British film *Room at the Top* (1959), and subsequently starred in such movies as *Diabolique* and *Madame Rosa*.

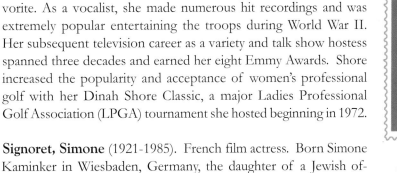

Simone Signoret.
France B685 (1998)

Silvers, Phil (1912-1985). American comedian. Born Philip Silversmith in Brooklyn, Silvers started in vaudeville and toured for five years with the Minsky Burlesque Troupe. A leading Broadway musical comedy star, in 1955 Silvers launched a long-running television series, "Sergeant Bilko," for which he won numerous awards. His most famous movie appearance was in *A Funny Thing Happened on the Way to the Forum* (1966).

Phil Silvers.
Grenada 2088 (1992)

Streisand, Barbra (1942-). American singer, actress, director, and producer. Born in Brooklyn, she worked as a switchboard operator and theater usher until she won a singing contest at a

Barbra Streisand.
St. Vincent Grenadines 2011 (1994)

Greenwich Village bar. After an initial Broadway success in the musical *I Can Get It For You Wholesale* (1962), Streisand starred as Fanny Brice in *Funny Girl* (1964), winning an Academy Award for her film debut in the same role. She has achieved legendary status in the American entertainment world, commanding huge sums for her rare live performances and earning several Grammy awards. Her subsequent films have included *Hello, Dolly!* (1969), *What's Up Doc?* (1972), *A Star Is Born* (1976), and *Yentl* (1983), which is based on a story by Isaac Bashevis Singer in which she played a girl disguised as a yeshivah student in pre-war Poland.

Taylor, Elizabeth (1932-). Internationally celebrated American actress. Born in London of American parents who returned to the United States in 1939, Taylor made her motion-picture debut in *There's One Born Every Minute* (1942) and signed a long-term contract with Metro-Goldwyn-Mayer (MGM) the next year. Among the many successful movies Taylor made as a child performer were *Lassie, Come Home* (1943), *Jane Eyre* (1944), *National Velvet* (1944), *Life with Father* (1947), and *Little Women* (1949). Classic young adult roles were *A Place in the Sun* (1951), *Ivanhoe* (1952), *The Last Time I Saw Paris* (1954), *Giant* (1956), and *Raintree County* (1957), and she starred in two film adaptations of plays by American playwright Tennessee Williams, *Cat on a Hot Tin Roof* (1958) and *Suddenly, Last Summer* (1959). Taylor won Academy Awards for *Butterfield 8* (1960) and *Who's Afraid of Virginia Woolf?* (1966). Taylor desired to convert to Judaism when she married her third husband, Jewish film producer Mike Todd; he told her to wait and be sure, but then died in a plane crash. Taylor finally did convert before marrying her fourth husband, entertainer Eddie Fisher.

Elizabeth Taylor in
Cleopatra. Mali 694 (1994)

Three Stooges.
Senegal (1999)

Three Stooges. American slapstick comedians. The original Three Stooges formed in the early 1930s and consisted of Larry Fine (Louis Fienberg; 1902-1975) and a pair of brothers—Moe Howard (Moses Horowitz; 1897-1975) and Curly Howard (Jerome Lester Horowitz; 1903-1952). When Curly was forced to retire because of illness, he was replaced by his brother Shemp Howard (Sam Horowitz; 1895-1975). After Shemp left the group, Joe Besser (1907-1989) joined for two years, before being replaced by Curly Joe DeRita (Joseph Wardell; 1909-1993).

Sports

Koufax, Sandy (1935–   ). American baseball player, considered by many as the greatest left-handed pitcher of all time. Born in Brooklyn, Koufax joined the Brooklyn Dodgers in 1955, but it was not until four years later (with the team now in Los Angeles) that he was able to control his blazing fastball and strike out 18 batters in a nine-inning game to equal a major league record. Koufax won 25 games three times, took five straight ERA titles (lowest earned run average), and pitched no-hitters in four consecutive seasons, culminating with a perfect game in 1965. The first pitcher to average more than one strikeout per inning in his career, Koufax led the Dodgers to three National League championships and two World Series triumphs. Troubled by arthritis, Koufax retired from baseball at the close of the 1966 season and became the youngest person elected to the Baseball Hall of Fame. Koufax won the admiration of Jews throughout the country by refusing to play on the High Holy Days.

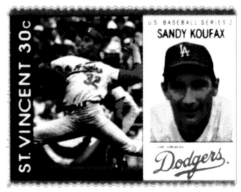

Sandy Koufax.
St. Vincent 2356 (1996)

Rosenfeld, Fanny (1903-1969). Canadian Olympic champion in track and field. Born in Russia, Fanny (nicknamed "Bobbie") came to Canada as an infant. Encouraged by her family to participate in all sports, Rosenfeld excelled in track-and-field events. In just one day at the 1925 Ontario Ladies Track and Field Championships, Rosenfeld won first place in two hurdle events, the long jump, the discus, and the shot put, and came in second in the 100-yard dash and javelin. At the 1928 Olympics in Amsterdam. Rosenfeld was a member of the record-setting Canadian 400-yard relay team. In a controversial decision, the judges placed her second in the 100-yard dash, as Rosenfeld and an American runner crossed the finish line in a virtual dead heat. Severe arthritis forced Rosenfeld into early retirement, and she wrote a sports column for twenty years. In 1949, Rosenfeld was named Canadian Woman Athlete for the Half-Century, and the Canadian Press still awards the Bobbie Rosenfeld trophy to Canada's Female Athlete of the Year.

Fanny Rosenfeld.
Canada 1610 (1996)

Spitz, Mark (1950–). United States Olympic champion, often called the best all-round swimmer in history. In his first international competition at age 15, Spitz represented the United States at the Maccabiah games in Israel, winning four gold medals. At the 1968 Olympic Games in Mexico City, Spitz took two gold medals as well as a silver and a bronze. During the next four years, Spitz won numerous national and collegiate titles, set many world records, and became the first Jewish winner of the AAU's James E. Sullivan Award as his nation's outstanding amateur athlete. Spitz completed his competitive swimming career with an unprecedented seven gold medals in the 1972 Olympic Games in Munich. His victories, all world records, were in the 100- and 200-meter freestyle, the 100- and 200-meter butterfly, and all the relay events.

Mark Spitz.
Grenada Grenadines 1695 (1994)

Chess

Fischer, Bobby ((Robert James; 1943-). American chess master. Born in New York of a Jewish father, he was a chess prodigy but high school dropout At age 15, Fischer became the youngest grandmaster up to that time. In 1972, Fischer won the world chess championship, becoming the only American to accomplish this feat, and he was generally regarded as the strongest chess player in history. For the next twenty years, Fischer did not play a single game of chess in public (turning down lucrative offers), forfeiting his world title in 1975 by refusing to play against Karpov. In 1992, he was indicted for participating in a match with Boris Spassky in Yugoslavia, a country against which the United States had imposed an economic boycott.

Bobby Fischer.
Cambodia 1555 (1996)

Antaloy Karpov.
Cambodia 1556 (1996)

Karpov, Anatoly Yevgenyevich (1951-). Russian chess master. In 1974, Karpov became the official challenger for the world championship title held by American grandmaster Bobby Fischer. When Fischer refused to play Karpov, the International Chess Federation named Karpov world champion by default. Karpov held the title until 1985, when he was defeated by Gary Kasparov.

Kasparov, Gary (1963-). Russian chess master, born Garri Weinstein in Baku. Following the death of his Jewish father when he was 12, he adopted his mother's maternal surname of Kasparov on the advice of his coach, who suggested that taking a "less Jewish name" would help his career. During the Soviet period, Kasparov was shunted aside in favor of non-Jewish players by the Soviet chess establishment. Kasparov became world champion in 1985 and held the title for 15 years. He has been a frequent visitor to Israel, and in 2000 the Gary Kasparov Chess Academy opened in Tel Aviv.

Gary Kasparov.
Cambodia 1557 (1996)

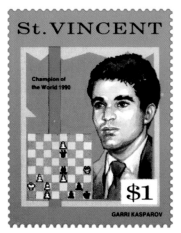

Below: Fischer, Karpov, Kasparov. *St. Vincent 1562f-h (1991)*

Lasker, Emanuel (1868–1941). German chess master. Born in Berlin, the grandson of a rabbi and son of a German cantor, in the early 1900s Lasker moved to New York City, where he published his own chess magazine and was chess editor of the *New York Evening Post*. Lasker won the world chess championship in 1894, beating Wilhelm Steinitz, and held the title for 27 years.

Spassky, Boris (1937–). Russian chess master. Born in Leningrad of a Jewish mother, in 1969 Spassky won the world championship by defeating Tigran Petrosian. Three years later, Spassky lost the title to the American chess giant Bobby Fischer.

Steinitz, Wilhelm (1836-1900). Czech-born American chess master. In 1886, Steinitz and Zukertort decided to play a match in which the winner would be considered officially "world champion," a title that did not exist until then. Steinitz was victorious and held the title until defeated by Emanuel Lasker in 1894.

Boris Spassky.
St. Vincent 1562e (1991)

From top: Emanuel Lasker.
Cambodia 1390 (1996), Laos 901E (1988)

Wilhelm Steinitz.
Laos 901D (1988), St. Vincent 1562c (1991)

Mikhail Tal.
Cambodia 1554 (1996)

Tal, Mikhail (1936–). Soviet chess master. Born in Latvia, Tal won the world championship in 1960 by beating Botvinnik but lost the subsequent year after suffering severe kidney disease. Although the illness hampered his playing career, Tal was an important commentator and coach.

Science and Industry

Einstein, Albert (1879-1955). Theoretical physicist, discoverer of the theory of relativity, and winner of the 1921 Nobel Prize in Physics. Generally considered the most outstanding scientist of modern times, Einstein was selected by Time Magazine as its "Man of the Millennium."

Born in the German town of Ulm, Einstein received his scientific education in Switzerland. Unable to obtain an instructorship at the Zurich Polytechnic Institute, from which he graduated at the age of 21, Einstein took a post at the patent office in Bern. This position left him ample time to carry on his own research, and in 1905 Einstein prepared three brilliant scientific papers that gained him international acclaim. In these Einstein introduced his famous $E = mc^2$ equation, showing that mass is convertible to energy. In 1916, Einstein published his general theory of relativity, which has been described as "the greatest intellectual revolution since Newton." With the rise of Hitler to power, in 1933 Einstein left Berlin and settled in the United States, where he became professor of theoretical physics at Princeton's Institute for Advanced Studies. During World War II, Einstein signed the letter to President Roosevelt that pointed out the feasibility of an atomic bomb and sparked the Manhattan Project. Ironically, although his own theories played a crucial role in unbinding the energies of the atom, Einstein joined many other prominent scientists in opposing the use of this explosive device.

Einstein dedicated considerable effort to the Zionist cause, especially to the development of the Hebrew University in Jerusalem, on whose Board of Governors he served until his death. After the death of Chaim Weizmann, Ben-Gurion asked Einstein to stand as a candidate for the presidency of the State of Israel. However, Einstein refused on the ground that he was "not suited for the position."

Albert Einsten. Left, from top: with his equation. *Mexico C592 (1979)*; with satellite gravity probe "B." *Comoro (1999); San Marino 947 (1979)*.
Middle, from top: *Israel 1220d (1998); Paraguay 875 (1979)*; with Galileo. *Italy 2048 (1995)*.
Right, from top: Photoelectric effect. *Germany 1299 (1979)*; with satellite. *Chad 718 (1997); Russia 4741 (1979)*

Top, from left: 100th birthday. *Swaziland 438 (1979)*; 60th anniversary of his Nobel Prize. *Sweden 1387 (1981)*; Einstein Observatory, Potsdam. *Togo 1021 (1979)*. Below: with J. R. MacDonald; sights and actuality diagram; playing the violin. *Togo C380-381 (1979)*

From left: atomic symbol and formula of relativity; portrait. *Togo C382-383 (1979)*; Einstein. *U.S.A. 1285 (1965)*

Top: Einstein's 100th birthday. *U.S.A. 1774 (1979)*.
Right: Einstein being offered the presidency of Israel by Prime Minister Ben-Gurion. *Ghana 2192 (2000)*

Albert Einstein, Man of the Century. *Mongolia 2451 (2000)*

Adler, Saul Aaron (1895-1966). Israel parasitologist who earned an international reputation for his pioneering research into Leishmaniasis and its carrier, the sandfly. Born in Russia, Adler was taken to England at age 5. After serving as a doctor with the British army in the Middle East during World War I, Adler moved to Palestine in 1924. Four years later, he was appointed the director of the Parasitological Institute of the Hebrew University Medical School.

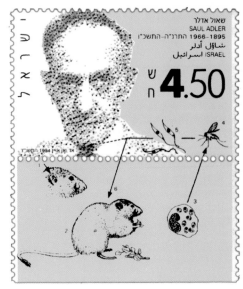

Saul Adler. *Israel 1202 (1994)*

Citroen, Andre Gustave (1878-1935). Engineer and industrialist, often called the "Henry Ford of France." The son of a Parisian diamond merchant, the family name derived from the occupation of his great-grandfather, a Dutch

Citroen. Modernized mail distribution.
France B320 (1958)

fruit seller. When required by Napoleonic law to choose a patronym, he took the name "Limoenman" (lemon-man), which eventually was transformed to the French "citron." During World War I, Citroen was instrumental in maintaining and steadily increasing French ammunition production. After the war, he concentrated on his favorite project – the production of a popular, low-priced car. His idea succeeded, and Citroen rapidly expanded his industrial organization not only in France but also internationally. He organized the traffic lights in Paris and, in return, secured the use of the Eiffel Tower for advertising. Citroen sponsored Trans-African and Trans-Asian automobile crossings, developing specially built automobiles for these rigorous ordeals. In 1934, Citroen introduced front-wheel drive for his automobiles, but financial complications soon forced him out of business and the firm was taken over by Michelin.

Dassault, Marcel (1892-1986). French engineer and aircraft designer. Born Marcel Bloch in Paris, "Dassault" was his French resistance name during World War II, and he adopted it as his last name after the war. His company designed and produced the Mystere and Mirage aircraft, which were used extensively by the Israel Air Force. Dassault himself never flew, except when he was repatriated in 1945 from the Buchenwald concentration camp, where he had been interned by the Germans. In 1947, Dassault converted to Catholicism, but actively aided Israel during the 1950's and 1960's.

Top: Mystere 20 jet. *France C41 (1965)*.
Bottom: Dassault with various aircraft.
France 2087 (1988)

Durkheim, Emile (1858–1917). Pioneering French sociologist. From a long line of rabbinical ancestors and having initially prepared himself for the rabbinate, Durkeim was a towering figure in the history of sociology and one of the most prolific writers in the discipline. Durkheim believed that scientific methods should be applied to the study of society and used an empirical methodology in his own studies, especially in regard to his analyses of suicide rates. Durkheim showed that all the aspects of human society work together much like the parts of a machine (sociological functionalism), and his concept that societal organization plays the major role in the lives of humans has become the paradigm of most sociological study today. Durkheim believed that the common values shared by a society ("collective conscience"), such as morality and religion, are the cohesive bonds that hold the social order together. A breakdown of these values leads to a loss of social stability and to individual feelings of anxiety and dissatisfaction that can lead to suicide.

Emile Durkheim.
Israel 1362a (1999)

Freud, Sigmund (1856–1939). Austrian psychiatrist and founder of psychoanalysis. Born in Freiberg, Moravia, Freud graduated from the University of Vienna Medical School. One of his earliest research projects resulted in the discovery of the anesthetic properties of cocaine. Even as a general practitioner, Freud was interested in disturbances of the nervous system. In collaboration with Joseph Breuer, he conducted studies on the use of hypnosis to assess the origins of hysteria. Even before these were published, Freud replaced the use of hypnosis with his method of "free association", which became a basic technique of psychoanalysis. In 1900, Freud published *The Interpretation of Dreams*, arguing that the dream serves as a disguised fulfillment of a repressed wish. From this time on, Freud devoted himself completely to investigating the unconscious layers of the human mind. He demonstrated how the numerous unconscious slips and mistakes that people make in everyday life are not physiological or accidental, but rather have a meaning that can be interpreted. Freud developed a theory of personality based on three major facets – the id, ego, and superego – and stressed such dynamic processes as repression, regression, and sublimation. Freud was the first to demonstrate the importance of early childhood experiences and sexuality on the development of the personality. The ideas presented in his multiple books were hotly rejected and disputed, and Freud remained unrecognized in his native Austria until late in life; his first acclaim came from Germany and the English-speaking countries. After the Nazi invasion of Austria in 1938, Freud settled in England.

Although estranged from Judaism and unable to share Zionist ideals, Freud nevertheless rejected baptism and remained a steadfast member of the Jewish community and a loyal member of the B'nai B'rith lodge in Vienna.

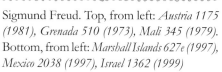

Sigmund Freud. Top, from left: *Austria 1175 (1981), Grenada 510 (1973), Mali 345 (1979).* Bottom, from left: *Marshall Islands 627e (1997), Mexico 2038 (1997), Israel 1362 (1999)*

Gurevich, Mikhail Iosifovich (1893-1976). Soviet airplane designer and builder. Together with A. I. Mikoyan, in 1940 Gurevich planned and built the high-speed fighter plane known as the MiG-I (the name being an abbreviation of Mikoyan and Gurevich). An updated version (MiG-3) was widely employed during World War II; after the war, the same duo designed the first Soviet supersonic jet fighters.

Haffkine, Waldemar Mordecai (1860-1930). Russian bacteriologist who developed the first useful vaccine against cholera and also serum therapy against plague. Born and educated in Odessa, Haffkine was a member of a Jewish self-defense organization and was forced to leave Russia for France after a political trial related to his activities. Haffkine developed the cholera vaccine at the Pasteur Institute, inoculating himself first. He tested this vaccine and later his plague treatment in Bombay, where he founded the Plague Research Laboratory that in 1925 was renamed the Haffkine Institute in his honor. An observant Jew most of his life, he created the Haffkine Foundation to foster religious, scientific, and vocational education in yeshivot in Eastern Europe.

Top: MiG and Ilyushin planes.
Egypt 408 (1957). Bottom: MiG jet and first MiG fighter plane.
Russia 3671 (1969)

Waldemar Haffkine.
Israel 1196 (1994)

Joffe, Abraham Feodorovich (1880–1960). Russian physicist. Born in Ukraine, after the Bolshevik revolution he co-founded what became the Physical-Technical Institute of the Soviet Academy of Sciences. Joffe's main scientific work dealt with the mechanical properties of crystals, the electrical properties of dielectric crystals, and semiconductors.

Katzir, Aharon (1914–1972). Israeli polymer chemist. Born Aharon Katchalsky in Lodz, Poland, Katzir was brought to Palestine in 1925. He became head of the Polymer Research Department of the Weizmann Institute of Science at Rehovot in 1948 and professor of physical chemistry at the Hebrew University four years later. Winner of the Israel Prize in Exact Science (1961), Katzir was president of the Israel Academy of Arts and Sciences from 1962 to 1968. Katzir was among those killed in the murderous 1972 terrorist attack on passengers and visitors at Lydda Airport by members of the Japanese Red Star Organization, which was acting on the instructions of the terrorist Popular Front for the Liberation of Palestine. His brother was Ephraim Katzir, the fourth president of the State of Israel.

Abraham Joffe.
Russia 4870 (1980)

Aharon Katzir.
Israel 1166 (1993)

Marcus, Siegfried (1831–1898). German inventor. After working for the Berlin engineering firm of Siemens und Halske, Marcus settled in Vienna and set up his own laboratory. In addition to a petrol-driven automobile, Marcus patented an electric lamp, telegraphic relays, a microphone, a loudspeaker, and electric fuses for submarine mines.

Marcus car.
Austria 906 (1971)

Meitner, Lise (1878-1968). Austrian-Swedish physicist who was one of the small group responsible for the discovery of atomic fission. Born in Vienna, in 1917 she

moved to Berlin to join the distinguished chemist Otto Hahn, with whom she collaborated in discovering the chemical element protactinium. After 20 years as head of the physics department in the Kaiser Wilhelm Institute for chemistry, Meitner left Germany after the Nazi takeover of her homeland and settled in Stockholm, working on the staff of the Nobel Institute. In 1939, Meitner published the first paper concerning nuclear fission (splitting the uranium atom into roughly equal parts, accompanied by a tremendous release of energy), predicting the existence of the chain reaction that contributed to the development of the atomic bomb. The chemical element with atomic number 109 was named meitnerium (Mt) in her honor.

Lise Meitner.
Austria 1093 (1978)

Olivetti, Camillo (1868-1943). Patriarch of a family of Italian industrialists. In 1909, Olivetti introduced the production of typewriters in Italy and invented the version bearing his name. Olivetti strove to make his firm one of the most advanced in Europe, both technically and socially, caring especially for the welfare and education of the workers.

Olivetti computer technology.
Italy 1688 (1986)

Politzer, Adam (1835–1920). Founder of modern otology. Born in Hungary, Politzer was professor of otology at the University of Vienna for almost 40 years and wrote the authoritative text in the field. Politzer devised many new methods for diagnosing and treating ear diseases, including a method of opening a blocked eustachian tube that bears his name.

Adam Politzer.
Austria 1326 (1985)

Racah, Giulio (Yoel; 1909–1965). Israel physicist. Born in Florence, Racah studied under Enrico Fermi and Wolfgang Pauli and at age 28 was appointed professor at the University of Pisa. An ardent Zionist, he allowed his farm outside Pisa to be used by the Zionist Organization as an agricultural training center. Settling in Jerusalem in 1939, Racah headed the department of theoretical physics at the Hebrew University. During the Israel War of Independence, Racah served as deputy commander of the Haganah on Mount Scopus, and he led research on munitions that could be produced from the raw materials available in the besieged city. He developed the "Racah method" of spectroscopy, recognized as one of the most effective ways of studying all types of nuclear structure, and was awarded the Israel Prize for natural sciences in 1958.

Giulio Racah.
Israel 1165 (1993)

Resnik, Judith Arlene (1949-1986). American astronaut and electrical engineer. In 1984, she became the second American woman (after astronaut Sally Ride) and the first "clearly" Jewish person (there is a question about one Soviet cosmonaut) to fly in space. On her second space flight, on January 28, 1986, Resnik died with six other crew members of the space shuttle Challenger, which exploded almost immediately after launch.

Crew of the U.S. shuttle Challenger, which exploded shortly after launch.
Central African Republic 823 (1986)

Rumpler, Eduard (1872–1940). German pioneer aircraft manufacturer. Born in Vienna, he built the Rumplertaube, an observation plane capable of flying at what was then the great height of 25,000 feet. Rumpler's planes made the first long-distance land flights in Germany and were used by the Germans in World War I. After the war, he conceived plans for 150-seater transatlantic airplanes, but a German aircraft industry was prohibited under the terms of the Versailles Treaty. Consequently, Rumpler turned his attention to automobiles, and in 1926 he brought out the first car with front-wheel-drive.

German Rumplertaube over Oslo Fjord.
Norway 405 (1993)

Sabin. Campaign against polio.
Brazil 2467 (1994)

Sabin, Albert Bruce (1906-1993). American virologist who developed an oral, live-virus poliomyelitis vaccine. Born in Bialystok, Poland, Sabin immigrated with his parents to the United States in 1921. He spent many years in search of protective vaccines against the strains of poliovirus that had been severely crippling or taking the lives of many children. In 1959 Sabin developed an oral vaccine for polio, which was put into mass use around the world two years later. Sabin's vaccine used a live but weakened strain of the poliovirus to create the antibody reaction that created immunity to the disease, in contrast to the inactivated, injected virus developed earlier by American Jonas Salk. Although not popularly given as much credit as Salk, Sabin's "live" form of the polio vaccine has made routine worldwide immunization possible and has almost eliminated this paralyzing disease in many areas. The Sabin vaccine does not require refrigeration and can be taken on a sugar cube, thus avoiding the need for countless needles or sterilization facilities. Inexplicably, neither Sabin nor Salk was ever awarded the Nobel Prize, even though their work saved millions of lives.

Salk, Jonas Edward (1914-1995). American physician and epidemiologist who developed the first successful polio vaccine. After working in the 1940s on an anti-influenza vaccine and developing immunological methods for distinguishing different types of the polio virus, Salk succeeded in developing an injectable polio vaccine prepared by inactivating ("killing") the virus with formalin under precisely controlled conditions. After massive field trials confirmed its efficacy, the Salk vaccine became the first effective weapon against the scourge of polio (1955). In 1963, he founded and became the director of the Salk Institute for Biological Studies at La Jolla, California.

Jonas Salk.
Transkei 261 (1991)

Dr. Salk at work.
Niger (1998)

From left: Polio victim holding crutches. *France 933 (1959)*;
Allegory of those who helped fight polio. *U.S.A. 1087 (1957)*

Schwarz, David (1845-1897). Designer of the first rigid airship (dirigible), which later became known as the "Zeppelin." Born in Zagreb, Schwarz taught himself the principles of engineering and mechanics and decided that a rigid airship could

David Schwarz with Zeppelin.
Hungary C57 (1948)

be built by using aluminum. After unsuccessfully shopping his designs for years in several countries, Schwarz literally died of shock after finally receiving a telegram informing him of the German government's willingness to finance the flight tests. In November 1897, Schwarz's dirigible took off from Tempelhof Field in Berlin but crashed and was destroyed after being flown for four hours.

Count von Zeppelin, who witnessed the flight, bought all Schwarz's plans and designs from his widow. He had the airship rebuilt with his own modifications and it became known as the "Zeppelin."

Szilard, Leo (1898-1964). Hungarian-born American nuclear physicist, who was noted for his work in the development of controlled nuclear fission. In 1934 Szilard (as did French physicist Joliot-Curie) predicted the possibility of a nuclear chain reaction arising from nuclear fission. Fearful of the results of such a reaction, Szilard tried to keep his own discoveries secret and attempted to persuade other atomic physicists to impose a voluntary censorship on the results of their research. However, when in 1939 uranium fission was announced in Europe and the chain reaction he had foreseen became a practical matter, Szilard was alarmed at the possibility that Nazi

Leo Szilard.
Hungary 3592 (1998)

Germany might make an atom bomb. He persuaded Einstein to write to President Roosevelt the famous letter that led to the creation of the Manhattan Project and the preparation of the first nuclear bomb. In 1942, Szilard and Fermi conducted the first controlled nuclear reaction at the University of Chicago. Although Szilard made important contributions to the development of the first atomic bomb, he pleaded with American authorities against using the weapon. After the war, Szilard called for international control of atomic energy and was active in efforts to restrict its use to peaceful purposes.

Volynov, Boris Valentinovich (1934-   ). Soviet cosmonaut who commanded the Soyuz 5 spacecraft. This mission accomplished the first docking and transfer of personnel in space.

Top, from left: Soyuz 4 and 5 over globe with map of Russia. *Romania C172 (1969)*; flights of Soyuz 4 and 5. Volynov is second from left. *Russia 3571 (1969)*

Wiener, Norbert (1894–1964). American mathematician and the inventor of the science of cybernetics. A child prodigy, Wiener entered college at age 11 and obtained his Ph.D. from Harvard at 18. His book *Cybernetics* (1948), a word he coined from a Greek term meaning the study of control, was a scientific bestseller and transformed him into a public figure as the pioneer of computer development.

Norbert Wiener. *Israel 1133d (1999)*

Politics

Victor Adler.
Austria 1094 (1978)

Adler, Victor (1852–1918). Leader of the Austrian Social-Democratic party and a prominent figure in the international labor movement. Born in Prague and a physician by profession, Adler devoted his life to the cause of the working class. His greatest political victory was facilitating the granting of universal suffrage by the Imperial Government in 1905.

Bauer, Otto (1881–1938). Austrian socialist leader and first foreign minister of the Austrian Republic (1918–19). Son of a Jewish industrialist, Bauer favored the granting of cultural autonomy to every national group in the Austro-Hungarian Empire. He praised the Jewish role in history, but argued that the Jews could not be regarded as a nationality, especially in Western Europe. Bauer advocated assimilation and was sharply criticized by Zionists and others for this stance. In May 1938, Bauer fled to Paris and died there a few weeks later—on the day the *London News Chronicle* published his appeal to world conscience to save the 300,000 Jews of Austria.

Otto Bauer.
Austria 1186 (1981)

Amnesty International, founded by Peter Benenson. *Denmark 790 (1986)*

Benenson, Peter (1921-). Founder of Amnesty International. Grandson of the Russian-Jewish banker Grigori Benenson and son of Flora Solomon, who raised him alone after the death of her husband, a British Army colonel, Benenson studied at Eton and Oxford, where he organized a campaign to assist refugees in the Spanish Civil War. Turning his attention to the plight of Jews who had fled from Hitler's Germany, Benenson succeeding in getting his school friends and their families to raise £4,000 to save the lives of two young German Jews by bringing them to Britain. A convert to Catholicism, Benenson was a practicing lawyer who was appalled by the conditions he found in courtrooms and prisons in countries he visited throughout the world. In 1961, Benenson founded Amnesty International, which became a worldwide symbol of hope and freedom and was awarded the 1997 Nobel Peace Prize.

Blum, Leon (1872-1950). First Jew and the first socialist leader to become premier of France (1936-1937, 1938, 1946). Always conscious of his Jewish origin, Blum was brought into active politics as a result of the Dreyfus Affair. After the French collapse in 1940, Blum was indicted by the German-dominated Vichy government on charges of being responsible for the country's military defeat. When at trial he brilliantly defended himself by showing that it was the appeasers who were the real traitors of France, the Vichy government was so embarrassed that the hearings were suspended. Blum was sent to a concentration camp in Italy and freed by U.S. forces in May, 1945. Blum played a major role in influencing the French government's pro-Jewish vote on the 1947 UN decision to partition Palestine. A kibbut in northern Galilee, Kfar Blum, is named in his honor.

Leon Blum.
France 1847 (1982)

Disraeli seen with Queen Victoria, the Albert Memorial, and the first ballot box.
UK 1190 (1987)

Disraeli, Benjamin (1804-1881). English novelist and prime minister (1868, 1874-1880), who for more than three decades exerted a profound influence on British politics and left an enduring stamp on the Conservative (Tory) Party. Born in London to a long line of Spanish Jewish ancestors who fled the Inquisition, Benjamin was twelve when his father quarreled with his Sephardic community and had his children baptized, apparently because of the political and social discrimination practiced against Jews in England at that time. Although he received a Christian upbringing, Disraeli never lost his pride in his Jewish ancestry. In one of his most famous novels, *Tancred* (1847), Disraeli spoke out energetically in favor of restoring national independence to the Jews, criticizing Jewish assimilationists "ashamed of their race and not fanatically devoted to their religion." Disraeli had great respect for Jews, terming them "the aristocracy of nature, the purest race, the chosen people."

David Dubinsky.
Maldives 1161 (1986)

Dubinsky, David (1892-1982). American labor leader. Born in Brest-Litovsk, Belorussia, Dubinsky was the head of the International Ladies Garment Workers' Union (ILGWU) from 1932 to 1966. As a self-styled "Jewish worker," Dubinsky was concerned with the special problems facing the Jewish community as a consequence of events in Germany and World War II. He was a member of the executive council of the Jewish Labor Committee, founded in 1933, which engaged in relief efforts on behalf of refugees, and became a staunch supporter of Israel, particularly the *Histadrut* (General Federation of Labor). A hospital in Beersheba, financed by his union, carries his name.

Leo Frankel.
Hungary 938 (1951)

Frankel, Leo (1844–1896). Hungarian socialist. Born in Buda and a goldsmith by trade, Frankel moved to Paris where he helped organize the uprising in the Paris Commune. After it was overthrown, Frankel fled to London and became a member of the council of the Socialist International before moving to Austria. Imprisoned for two years for his revolutionary activities, Frankel returned to Paris as Friedrich Engels' assistant in the Socialist International. Frankel was in constant correspondence with Karl Marx, whom he much admired, but also became interested in Zionism as a result of meeting Theodor Herzl.

Gompers, Samuel (1850-1924). American labor leader and long-time head of the American Federation of Labor (AFL). Born in London, the Gompers family immigrated to America in 1863, settling on the Lower East Side of New York City. When the AFL was founded in 1886, Gompers was elected president of the organization, and he was re-elected annually to that position until his death almost 40 years later. Gompers stressed cooperation between management and labor, rather than strike actions, as a means of obtaining workers' demands. Gompers played a prominent role in winning strong support from American trade unions for President Woodrow Wilson's war policies in 1917 and served as head of the War Committee on Labor that protected the interests of organized workers during the conflict.

Samuel Gompers.
U.S.A. 988 (1950)

Sir Joshua Hassan.
Gibraltar 745 (1997)

Hassan, Sir Joshua (1915–). Gibraltar lawyer and politician. Born in the British colony to a Sephardic family of North African origin, Hassan served two terms as chief minister, a post equivalent to that of prime minister. He championed the right of the colony to remain under British rule and not to be transferred to Spain. A devoted and observant Jew, Hassan served as president of the management board of the Jewish community. He was also active in Zionist affairs and president of the Jewish National Fund Commission for many years. Even while holding the highest political offices in the colony, Hassan continued to go from house to house collecting the contents of JNF blue boxes. He became a queen's counsel in 1954 and was knighted in 1963.

Hymans, Paul (1865–1941). Statesman and historian who was four times foreign minister of Belgium. Elected to the chamber of deputies in 1900, Hymans united the Belgian liberals against reli-

Paul Hymans.
Belgium 622 (1965)

gious intolerance and introduced a policy of political and social reforms. Hymans served as Belgian ambassador to London during World War I, and as foreign minister headed the Belgian delegation at the Versailles peace negotiations. Subsequently, Hymans was minister of justice and served three more terms as foreign minister before becoming president of the Assembly of the League of Nations.

Jacobs, Aletta (1854–1929). Dutch physician, feminist, and pacifist. The first woman to study at a Dutch university and to practice as a doctor, Jacobs was a champion of women's emancipation and suffrage. As a pacifist, Jacobs sponsored the International Peace Congress at The Hague in 1915, which led to the foundation of the Women's International League for Peace and Freedom.

Aletta Jacobs.
Netherlands 591 (1979)

Javits, Jacob Koppel (1904-1986). United States Senator from New York (1957-1981). Though a Republican, his moderate views appealed to liberal and Jewish voters, whose sympathies in New York were more often with the Democrats but who regarded his voting record as one of the best in Congress. Javits consistently supported greater public aid to education, health, urban housing, the arts, and small business, and backed civil rights and fair-labor legislation, pension protection, foreign aid, tariff liberalization, and curtailment of nuclear testing. Active in numerous Jewish organizations, Javits was a particularly warm friend of Israel on the powerful Foreign Relations Committee. He repeatedly argued on the Senate floor that purely American interests should dictate that the United States support Israel as unequivocally as the USSR supported the Arab states. In appreciation of Javits' years of service, the New York Convention Center was named for him.

Javits Convention Center in New York.
St. Vincent Grenadines 1728 (1992)

Kaganovich, Lazar Moiseyevich (1893–1991). Soviet politician. Born in Kiev province, Kaganovich joined the Communist Party in 1911 and rose rapidly in its hierarchy. In 1930 Kaganovich became a member of the Politburo, the nine-man committee controlling the party, and for many years he was the only Jew to occupy a top position in the Soviet leadership. Kaganovich organized the industrialization of the Moscow region and in 1935 was responsible for the construction of the Moscow subway, which was named after him.

Moscow subway stations.
Russia 1153-1158 (1947)

Kelsen, Hans (1881–1973). Jurist and drafter of the constitution of the Austrian Republic (1920). Born in Prague, Kelsen was one of the most famous legal theoreticians of the 20th century. He served on the supreme court of Austria from 1920 to 1929. Although baptized, in 1933 Kelsen was compelled to resign his post as professor of law at Cologne University because of his Jewish ancestry. Kelsen emigrated to the United States in 1944 and became professor of political science at the University of California at Berkeley.

Hans Kelsen.
Austria 1191 (1981)

Doctors without Borders.
France 2686 (1998)

Kouchner, Bernard (1939-). French humanitarian and physician. In 1971, Kouchner found "Physicians without Borders," an organization that sends doctors and nurses to disaster areas throughout the world, and it was awarded the 1999 Nobel Peace Prize. Kouchner has been health minister of France and headed the United Nations relief effort in Kosovo, championing the concept of "the right of intervention" of the medical community in humanitarian matters.

Kreisky, Bruno (1911-1990). First Jew to become Chancellor of Austria. Born in Vienna, Kreisky was the son of a rich textile manufacturer and joined the Socialist Workers Youth Association. After the Fascist seizure of power in 1934, Kreisky was active in the clandestine Socialist Party and was arrested in 1935. He spent nearly two years in prison and emigrated to Sweden at the time of the Nazi Anschluss in 1938. Returning to Austria at the end of World War II, Kreisky joined the diplomatic service, rose in the ranks of the Socialist Party, and became Austrian Chancellor in 1970. Despite his Jewish heritage, Kreisky consistently adopted a pro-Arab and anti-Israel attitude.

Bruno Kreisky.
Austria 1527 (1991)

Bela Kun.
Hungary 2970 (1986)

Kun, Bela (1886–1939). Communist dictator of Hungary. Arrested and imprisoned for incitement to violence while attempting to replace the moderate government in Hungary with an extreme revolutionary regime, Kun was released a month later when the government fell and was made a member of a new cabinet of Socialists and Bolsheviks. Soon the moderate elements were removed from the government, Hungary was proclaimed a Soviet republic, and Kun became commissar for foreign affairs and dictator. However, the communist government was short-lived and Kun was forced to flee to Vienna and then to Moscow. Appointed political commissar of the Red Army of the South and an executive of the Communist International, Kun was caught up in the Stalinist purges and executed.

La Guardia, Fiorello Henry (1882-1947). Three-term mayor of New York City. Born to a Jewish mother and an Italian father, La Guardia was raised as a Protestant. Working as an interpreter at the Ellis Island immigrant reception center while attending law school, La Guardia, who spoke Yiddish and other languages, became intimately acquainted with the needs and feelings of the immigrants upon whose support his political career would be built. In 1916, La Guardia was elected to Congress on the Republican and Progressive tickets, representing a Manhattan district composed primarily of Jews and Italians. He sponsored a resolution calling on the U.S. to protest anti-Semitic outbreaks in Poland and Eastern Europe at the Paris Peace Conference. First elected mayor of

Fiorello La Guardia.
Tanzania 1502 (1996)

New York in 1933, La Guardia became celebrated as the "Little Flower" (he stood only 5'2") for the vigor, earthiness, and flamboyance of his manner. He frequently appealed directly to the people of New York on political issues, and for several years conducted a popular weekly radio program over the municipally owned station. La Guardia fought Tammany Hall and its corruption-tainted politics, greatly enhancing the honesty and scope of municipal services and improving the city by a vast new network of parks, bridges, schools, and highways. His "urban New Deal" policies drew massive Jewish support away from the Democratic Party. Never hesitating to create international incidents in this connection, La Guardia's 1937 speech depicting Hitler as a fanatic who deserved a place in the "World's Fair Chamber of Horrors" brought official complaints from the German embassy in Washington and official State Department apologies. One of New York's major airports is named in his honor.

Luxemburg, Rosa (1871-1919). German economist and revolutionary. Born into a family of merchants in Poland, in 1889 Luxemburg fled her native land for Switzerland to avoid imprisonment for her revolutionary activities. Almost a decade later, Luxemburg migrated to Germany and became a leading figure in the revolutionary left wing of the German Socialist movement. She opposed World War I as an imperialist enterprise and spent a long period in prison as a consequence. During the unsuccessful uprising against the government in 1919, Luxemburg was arrested and murdered by German troops. Jewish in appearance and fond of Yiddish stories, she was indifferent to the frequent anti-Semitic attacks on her and had no interest in a specifically Jewish labor movement.

Rosa Luxemburg.
GDR 419 (1959)

Mandel, Georges (Jeroboam Rothchild; 1885–1944). French statesman. As a cabinet minister, Mandel urged France's speedy rearmament to meet the threat of German National Socialism and opposed Germany's remilitarization of the Rhineland. While minister of the interior from May 1940 to the fall of France, Mandel ordered the arrest of numerous suspected Nazi sympathizers. After the retreat of French troops, he opposed the policy of capitulation and collaboration. Mandel was later arrested by the Vichy militia and assassinated in 1944.

Georges Mandel.
France 1104 (1964)

Manin, Daniele (1804–1857). Italian patriot. Descended from the Jewish Medina family on his father's side, in 1848 Manin became president of the revived Republic of Venice. After leading the heroic but unsuccessful resistance of Venice in the long siege by the Austrians, Manin went into exile in Paris, where he died.

Marx, Karl Heinrich (1818-1883). German political philosopher and revolutionist who, with Friedrich Engels, was the founder of scientific socialism (modern communism) and one of the most influential thinkers of all times. His system, Marxism, became a 20th century creed for hundreds of millions of socialists, often hardening into a dogma - particularly in the communist movement and in the Soviet Bloc, the People's Republic of China, and other communist countries.

Marx's father Heinrich, whose original name was Herschel ha-Levi, was the son of a rabbi and the descendant of talmudic scholars for many generations. His brother was chief rabbi of Trier, where the family lived. A successful lawyer, Heinrich converted to Protestantism when an edict was issued prohibiting Jews from being advocates. Marx was baptized at age six, a practice common among German Jews with ambitions for their children.

Daniele Manin proclaiming the Republic of Venice. *Italy 499 (1948)*

Karl Marx with Lenin on the 60th anniversary of the founding of the USSR. *Cuba 2564 (1982)*

Exiled from Germany for political activity and moving to Paris in 1845, Marx, in collaboration with Engels, wrote *The Communist Manifesto* (1848), calling upon workers to rise in violent revolution against their capitalist oppressors. Marx and Engels saw the history of society as reflecting the ongoing struggles between the exploiting and the exploited social classes (i.e., between the rulers and the oppressed), concluding that the capitalist class inevitably would be overthrown by a working-class revolution and replaced by a classless society. As the document ended: "The proletarians have nothing to lose but their chains. They have a world to win. Working men of all countries, unite!"

After being expelled from several countries, Marx moved to London, where he partly supported himself by commenting on current world affairs as the London correspondent of the New York Tribune. For years he was an almost daily visitor to the British Museum Library, studying the great economists and governmental reports on industrial and labor relations as material for his magnum opus *Das Kapital* (Capital).

Karl Marx's attitude to Jews and Judaism evolved into what was later described as "self-hatred." Although he favored political emancipation of the Jews, Marx viewed Judaism as synonymous with the hated bourgeois capitalism. Nevertheless, Marx's Jewish origin became a catalyst of anti-Jewish emotion, especially in the fascist and Nazi regimes of the 1930s and 1940s. Spicing their anti-socialism with outright violent anti-Semitism, they used the term "Marxism" as denoting a sinister, worldwide "Jewish" plot against their national interests. In the Soviet Union, where Marxism-Leninism became the obligatory ideology, Marx's Jewish origin was generally mentioned in research works and encyclopedias until the 1940s; however, from the later 1940s, when Stalin's policy became anti-Jewish, it became studiously concealed.

Mendes-France, Pierre (1907-1982). Prolific author on politics and finance who was premier of France (1954-1955). From an old Bordeaux Sephardic family, Mendes-France advocated resistance to the Nazis even before World War II. After the fall of France, he organized opposition to the Vichy government and was imprisoned. Mendes-France escaped to England in 1941 and joined the Free French under General De Gaulle, who later made him finance commissioner of Algeria. As premier, Mendes-France offered France a "new deal," promising to end the Indochina war (the precursor of the Vietnam War), tackle the problems of European defense, and enact wide-reaching economic reforms. However, he resigned in 1955 when he was defeated over his North Africa policy to grant independence to Morocco and Tunisia. A practicing Jew, Mendes-France was a consistent supporter of Zionism and an outspoken champion of the cause of Israel. An ascetic in his private life, Mendes-France once aroused controversy when he urged Frenchmen to abandon their wine drinking for milk, his favorite beverage.

Pierre Mendes-France.
France 1906 (1983)

Julius Popper.
Romania 3393 (1986)

Popper, Julius (1857–1893). Romanian explorer. The son of the principal of the first Jewish school in Bucharest, Popper studied engineering in Paris. While on a world tour, Popper heard about gold deposits on Tierra del Fuego, at the southern tip of Argentina. His exploration of the island proved the stories to be true, and Popper accordingly designed a machine for extracting the gold. Establishing himself as ruler over the island, Popper gave it a code of laws and defended it against other adventurers.

Rakosi, Matyas (1892–1971). Hungarian Communist dictator. Following the October Revolution of 1917, Rakosi joined the Red Army and the Communist Party and was made deputy commissioner of trade in Bela Kun's Hungarian soviet republic. When this regime collapsed in 1919, Rakosi fled to the Soviet Union, secretly returning to Hungary five years later to organize the illegal Communist Party, Arrested and sentenced to death, his sentence was commuted to life imprisonment following the intervention of leading intellectuals abroad. Rakosi was released in 1940 and settled in the Soviet Union,

Matyas Rakosi, greeting workers.
Hungary 987 (1952)

where he became the leading figure and propagandist among the Hungarian exiles in Moscow. In 1944, Rakosi returned to Hungary and reorganized the Hungarian Communist Party. After several years as deputy leader of a coalition government, Rakosi gradually removed the other parties from political life and assumed dictatorial powers. Rakosi took no interest in Jewish affairs and tried to hide his Jewish origins. Indeed, his policy of trials against Zionists, the confiscation of private enterprises, and the transfer of populations from the large cities caused great suffering to many Jews.

Ethel and Julius Rosenberg.
Cuba C313 (1978)

Rosenbergs (**Julius**; 1918-1953, and **Ethel**; 1920-1953). United States citizens who in 1951 were convicted and sentenced to death for allegedly passing information concerning American atomic bomb secrets to Russia during World War II. Despite a worldwide outcry questioning their guilt and the fairness of their trial, as well as international pleas for clemency, the Rosenbergs were executed in 1953, the first civilians convicted as spies who were put to death in the United States. The case remains highly controversial and has been the subject of many books and articles.

Rowe, Leo Stanton (1871–1946). American political scientist. Appointed to a commission to revise the laws of Puerto Rico in 1900, Rowe became interested in Latin American affairs, to which he devoted almost his whole life's work. A prolific author, Rowe headed the Latin American section of the State Department for two years. Devoted to the Pan American cause, Rowe served as Director General of the Pan American Union from 1920 to his death. He showed special interest in the education of Latin American youth, whom he assisted during his lifetime and to whom he bequeathed a legacy.

Leo Rowe.
Nicaragua C253 (1940)

Salomon, Haym (1740-1785). American financier and Revolutionary War patriot. Born in Poland of Portuguese-Jewish descent, Salomon arrived in America around 1772 and established himself in New York City as a merchant and broker. He associated himself with the cause of independence and was twice imprisoned by the British. In 1778, Salomon escaped to Philadelphia, where he became an agent of American patriot Robert Morris, the financier of the Revolution. Salomon helped to negotiate subsidies from France and Holland for the conduct of the war and made substantial personal loans to the U.S. government, which were never repaid. He also lent money without charge to James Madison and other impecunious members of the Continental Congress. After the war, Salomon was a major contributor to the building of Congregation Mikveh Israel in Philadelphia. Salomon argued against a requirement that officeholders in Pennsylvania take a New Testament oath and worked for political rights of Jews.

Haym Solomon.
U.S.A. 1561 (1975)

Sverdlov, Yakov Mikhailovich (1885–1919). Russian revolutionary and Communist leader. Twice imprisoned and exiled to Siberia in 1910, Sverdlov returned to Petrograd in 1917 and became a member of the Central Committee of the Communist Party. After the October Revolution, he was elected chairman of the All-Russian Central Executive Committee and thus the first titular head of state. Sverdlov was considered one of the outstanding figures of the Bolshevik Revolution, and Lenin paid a warm tribute to him as a brilliant organizer. In 1924, the city of Yekaterinburg was renamed Sverdlovsk in his memory.

From left: 250th anniversary of the city of Sverdlovsk; portrait of Yakov Sverdlov. *Russia 4131-4132 (1965)*

The Jewish World in Stamps

Tandler, Julius (1869–1936). Anatomist and social reformer. Born in Moravia and head of the Anatomical Institute in Vienna, Tandler was a social democrat who became under-secretary of state in the Ministry of Social Administration and reorganized hospital legislation. As a city councilor in Vienna, Tandler made significant contributions to modern social medicine by creating a new system of welfare, based on a theory of societal responsibility, that became known the world over. Tandler set up advisory boards to deal with problems of young couples, pregnant women, mothers, war invalids, babies, and the elderly. Having earned an international reputation, he was a participant on the Health Committee of the League of Nations and later went to both China and Russia to help organize their hospital systems.

Julius Tandler.
Austria 1358 (1986)

Veil, Simone (1927-). French politician who became president of the European Parliament in 1979. Born Simone Jacob in Nice, she was deported by the Nazis to Auschwitz (where all the members of her family perished) and Bergen-Belsen. After earning degrees in law and political science, Veil represented France at the International Society of Criminology in 1959 and has devoted herself to the reform of the laws concerning adoption, handicapped adults, and parental authority. Veil has served as minister of health and of social security in the French government.

Above: European Parliament emblem. *Belgium 1025 (1979)*. From left: European Parliament.
France 1650 (1979), Italy 1368-1369 (1979)

Vogel, Sir Julius (1835–1899). Prime minister of New Zealand. Born in London, Vogel was attracted to Australia by the gold rush. When unable to make a fortune in the mines, Vogel emigrated to New Zealand, where he became a journalist and edited the colony's first daily newspaper. In 1873, Vogel became prime minister and set about reducing the autonomy of the New Zealand provinces and strengthening the hand of the central government. This policy lost him considerable popularity, and Vogel resigned two years later while on a visit to London to be knighted.

Sir Julius Vogel.
New Zealand 678 (1979)

Warski, Adolf (1868–1937). Polish Communist leader. Born in Cracow into an assimilated family that favored Polish independence, Warski was a founder of the Polish Labor Union and organized the Social Democratic Party of Poland and Lithuania. After World War I, Warski helped establish the Polish Communist Party and was a member of its central committee and political bureau. Elected as a Communist member of the Sejm (parliament), Warski earned a reputation for his courageous speeches and sharp criticism of the authorities. When the Communist Party was made illegal in 1930, Warski emigrated to the Soviet Union. However, during the subsequent purges Warski was executed for alleged treason and counter-revolutionary activities.

Adolf Warski.
Poland 2308 (1968)

Shmuel Yosef Agnon.
Antigua 1945a (1995)

S. Y. Agnon.
Israel 776 (1981)

Agnon, Shmuel Yosef (1888-1970). Central figure in modern Hebrew fiction. Born in Galicia and originally surnamed Czaczkes, Agnon was steeped in rabbinic and Hasidic traditions as well as general European culture. In 1907, Agnon left home and made his way to Palestine. Agnon's stories, written in classical Hebrew, are rich in Jewish folk legends and mysticism. They deal with major contemporary spiritual concerns: the disintegration of traditional ways of life; loss of faith; and the subsequent loss of identity. Agnon's many tales about pious Jews, which depict the conflict between traditional Jewish life and the modern world, are an artistic attempt to recapture the fading traditions of the European shtetl. In 1966, Agnon shared the Nobel Prize in Literature with German-Swedish poet Nelly Sachs.

Asser, Tobias Michael Carel (1838–1913). Dutch statesman and jurist specializing in international law who won the Nobel Peace Prize in 1911. Asser participated in the Hague Peace Conferences of 1899 and 1907 and was appointed a member of the Hague Permanent Court of Arbitration in 1900, where he frequently arbitrated on international issues, such as the dispute between Russia and the United States over fishing rights in the Bering Straits.

Tobias Asser.
Netherlands 800 (1991)

Adolf von Baeyer.
Sweden 689 (1965)

Baeyer, Adolf von (1835-1917). German organic chemist who received the 1905 Nobel Prize in Chemistry. Baeyer derived barbituric acid, the parent compound from which the sedative drugs known as barbiturates were developed. His most important work was defining the chemical formula for indigo, the deep blue dye produced from a tropical shrub using a time-consuming and expensive extraction process. Baeyer's success in developing synthetic indigo, which eventually displaced the natural product, was the foundation of the German dyestuffs industry. In 1885, King Ludwig of Bavaria made Baeyer a member of the nobility, allowing him to add the honorific "von" to his name.

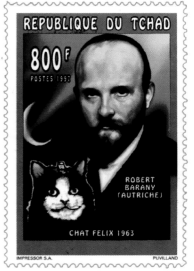

Robert Barany.
Chad 719 (1997)

Barany, Robert (1876-1936). Austrian otologist who developed the caloric test, in which cold and hot water are used to assess the vestibular apparatus responsible for regulating balance and coordination. Barany was the first to describe a practical operative procedure for patients with otosclerosis ("hardening of the ear"), and airplane pilots are still tested in a device called a "Barany chair" to see how well they cope with rapid circular motion. Barany was awarded the 1914 Nobel Prize in Physiology or Medicine, and news of the award reached him while confined in a Russian prisoner-of-war camp after being captured while serving as a medical officer in the Austrian army. Following the personal intervention of Prince Carl of Sweden on behalf of the Red Cross, Barany was released in 1916 and was presented with the Nobel Prize by the

King of Sweden in Stockholm. Returning to Vienna the same year, Barany was not made a full professor because he was a Jew, and left to become professor at the Otological Institute in Uppsala, Sweden.

From left: Barany. *Sweden 1105 (974), Austria 1031 (1976)*

Henri Bergson.
France 934 (1959)

Begin, Menachem. Winner of the 1978 Nobel Peace Prize (see page 159).

Bergson, Henri Louis (1859-1941). Influential French philosopher who won the 1927 Nobel Prize in Literature. Politically active, especially in foreign affairs, Bergson was president of the League of Nations' Committee for Intellectual Cooperation. In his later years, Bergson was attracted to Catholicism, but he remained a Jew in order to maintain his identification with the persecuted. After the French surrender to the Nazis in 1940, Bergson returned all his decorations and awards. Rejecting the offer of the Vichy French authorities to exclude him from edicts against the Jews, Bergson rose from his deathbed to register as a Jew.

Bloch, Felix (1905-1983). Swiss-born American physicist and co-winner (with Edward Purcell) of the 1952 Nobel Prize in Physics for developing nuclear magnetic resonance (NMR), a new method for the precise measurements of the strength of the magnetic field of the atomic nucleus. This work led to the development of spectroscopy as well as the powerful medical imaging tool of magnetic resonance imaging. In 1934, after the Nazis came to power in Germany, Bloch emigrated to the United States and worked at Stanford, later participating in the Manhattan Project at Los Alamos.

Felix Bloch.
Guyana 3008f (1995)

Baruch Blumberg.
Maldives 2113e (1995)

Blumberg, Baruch Samuel (1925-). American biomedical researcher who studied at the Flatbush Yeshiva before earning his M.D. and Ph.D. degrees. Blumberg received the 1976 Nobel Prize in Physiology or Medicine for discovering the antigen marking the presence of the hepatitis B virus. This led to the development of a test to screen blood and prevent this virus from being transmitted through transfusions. Blumberg also worked to develop a hepatitis B vaccine, which became available in 1982, and demonstrated the role of the virus in causing liver cancer.

Bohr, Niels Henrik David (1885–1962). Danish physicist who made basic contributions to nuclear physics and the understanding of atomic structure and won the Nobel Prize in Physics in 1922. Like most Danish Jews, Bohr and his family escaped the Nazis by fleeing to Sweden in a fishing boat. After being taken to England in the bomb rack of an unarmed Mosquito plane, Bohr eventually reached the United States, where

Niels Bohr with Albert Einstein.
Malagasy 1132a (1993)

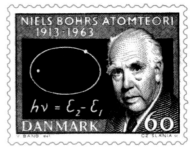

Niels Bohr with his atom theory.
Denmark 409 (1963)

Niels Bohr.
Maldives 2116a (1995)

he worked at Los Alamos in the project to develop the first atomic bomb. However, after the war Bohr saw the bomb as a threat to mankind and began working to develop peaceful uses for atomic energy. He organized the first Atoms for Peace Conference in Geneva in 1955, and two years later received the first Atoms-for-Peace Award. In 1997, Bohr was honored by having the chemical element with atomic number 107 given the official name bohrium (Bh).

Born, Max (1882-1970). German physicist who shared the 1954 Nobel Prize in Physics for fundamental contributions to the mathematical basis of quantum mechanics and modern theoretic physics. Coming from a prosperous, highly assimilated German Jewish family, Born disassociated himself from the Jewish community but refused, on principle, to convert to Christianity to advance his career or to please the aristocratic members of his non-Jewish wife's family. In 1933, he was dismissed from his academic post and settled in Great Britain, eventually returning to Germany after World War II both for financial reasons (he was eligible for a full salary and pension at the German university where he had taught) and with the hope that he could advance the cause of democratic values in his homeland.

Max Born.
Malagasy 1132b (1993)

Brodsky, Joseph (1940-1996). Russian poet and translator who received the 1987 Nobel Prize in Literature. Although widely regarded as one of the most promising Soviet poets, none of Brodsky's original verse was allowed to appear in the U.S.S.R. as late as 1970. In 1964, Brodsky was convicted as a "social parasite" in a trial that had pronounced anti-Semitic overtones, with Jewish witnesses for the defense ridiculed for their "strange-sounding" names. Released after serving 18 months of a five-year sentence in a labor camp in the far north, Brodsky left his homeland for the United States, where he became the poet-in-residence at the University of Michigan. In 1991, Brodsky was named the fifth U.S. poet laureate.

Joseph Brodsky.
Nicaragua 2135k (1995)

Canetti, Elias (1905-1994). Bulgarian-born playwright and novelist who received the 1981 Nobel Prize in Literature. Raised in a Ladino-speaking Sephardic milieu, Canetti earned a Ph.D. in chemistry but never worked in that field. His fame was established by a 1935 novel *Die Blendung*, which relates the story of the collision between the imprisoning, self-immolating intelligence of a professor and the brute sadism of an apartment porter. It was hailed as a masterpiece by critics, but seen as an attack on fascism and consequently banned in Germany. With the rise of Nazism in Germany and then in Austria, where he had been living, Canetti fled via Paris to London, where he became a citizen and resided for the rest of his life, though he continued to write in German.

Elias Canetti.
Maldives 2116d (1995)

Cassin, Rene (1887-1976). French jurist and statesman who was awarded the 1968 Nobel Peace Prize for championing the cause of human rights. A member of the French delegation to the League of Nations from 1921-1938, Cassin served in the cabinet of the Free French government in exile during World War II. His BBC broadcasts from London helped restore the courage of his fellow countrymen, and his gifts as a jurist aided de Gaulle in the work of liberation and reorganization of France from the chaos of defeat. Cassin was the principal author of the Universal Declaration of Human Rights, which was adopted by the United Nations General Assembly in 1948.

Rene Cassin.
Malagasy 943 (1989)

In 1943, General de Gaulle entrusted to Cassin the direction of the Alliance Israelite Universelle, when its central committee ceased to function in Vichy France. As its president, Cassin developed educational and cultural activities in France and its colonies, the Arab countries, and Israel. Cassin also became honorary president of the World Sephardi Federation.

From left: Universal Declaration of Human Rights. *United Nations 543 (1988), 191 (1968)*; Cassin with Eleanor Roosevelt. *France 2689 (1998)*

Ehrlich, Paul (1854-1915). German chemist and bacteriologist who shared the 1908 Nobel Prize in Physiology or Medicine with Elie Metchnikoff. He developed a technique for staining tuberculosis bacilli , discovered the diazo reaction in urine for the recognition of aromatic compounds (used to diagnose typhoid fever), and established the basic concepts of modern applied immunology. Recognizing the particular specific affinity of dyes, active organic compounds, and toxins to certain cells, Ehrlich searched for chemical compounds that would specifically attack the microorganisms causing disease without damaging healthy body cells. After years of investigation, he discovered "606", the so-called "magic bullet" known as Salvarsan (organic arsenic), to treat syphilis. This ushered in the modern era of systematic chemotherapy.

Einstein, Albert (1879-1955). Winner of the 1921 Nobel Prize in Physics (see pages 114-116).

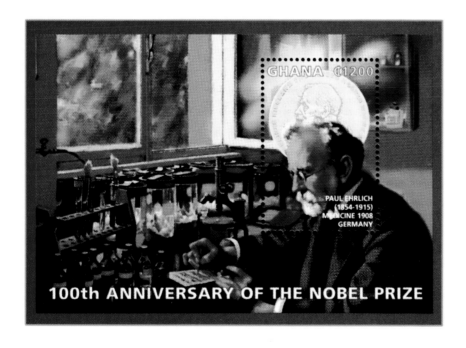

From top: Paul Ehrlich. *Gambia 909 (1989), Germany (1995)*. Left: 100th anniversary of the Nobel Prize. *Ghana 1827 (1999)*

Franck, James (1882-1964). German-American physicist who shared with Gustav Hertz the 1925 Nobel Prize in Physics for experimentally verifying the quantum theory by discovering the laws governing the effects produced by bombarding atoms with electrons. Unlike some of his co-religionist colleagues, Franck was a fairly committed Jew. As the winner of the Iron Cross, First Class, for his service in World War I, Franck was exempted from the dismissal suffered by most Jewish academics in 1933. However, he publicly resigned his chair, rather than be treated as an alien in his own country, and moved to the United States.

James Franck.
Grenada 2490a (1995)

Alfred Fried.
Austria 1484 (1989)

Fried, Alfred Hermann (1864–1921). Austrian pacifist who received the 1911 Nobel Peace Prize. Fried authored more than 70 books and pamphlets and nearly 2,000 newspaper articles devoted to the advancement of peace.

Golding, William (1911-1993). British writer who won the Nobel Prize in Literature in 1983. Golding is best known for his first novel, *Lord of the Flies*, published in 1954. The book describes the horrific exploits of a band of young children who make a striking transition from civilized to barbaric, illustrating that human beings are inherently tied to society, without which we would likely return to savagery.

Gordimer, Nadine (1923-). South African novelist who examined the tensions between whites and non-whites forced to live under apartheid, the system of strict racial segregation formerly in effect in her native country. Although many of her books were banned at home, Gordimer received the 1991 Nobel Prize in Literature for her courageous attacks on the inequalities of South African society

William Golding.
Grenada 2489g (1995)

From top: Nadine Gordimer. *Sweden 1271 (1978), Antigua 1945h (1998)*

Haber, Fritz (1868-1934). German physical chemist who received the 1918 Nobel Prize in Chemistry for his work in developing an economical method of synthesizing ammonia by directly combining hydrogen and nitrogen. In addition to its use in the production of fertilizers, ammonia is used in the manufacture of explosives. Haber's work was invaluable to the Germany military effort in World War I, and he was honored by being made head of the prestigious Kaiser-Wilhelm Institute. Although he had left Judaism to advance his career, Haber was ousted from his academic post in 1933 by Hitler's express order; he soon died, deeply embittered at his treatment.

Fritz Haber.
Sweden 1271 (1978)

Hertz, Gustav (1887-1975). German physicist who shared the 1925 Nobel Prize in Physics with James Franck for experimentally verifying the quantum theory by discovering the laws governing the effects produced by bombarding atoms with electrons. Son of a Jewish father, Hertz converted to Christianity.

Hevesy, George Charles de (1885–1966). Hungarian winner of the 1943 Nobel Prize in Chemistry for his pioneering work on the use of radioactive isotopes for chemical and biologi-

Gustav Hertz.
Grenada 2490b (1995)

cal research. When his academic position in Germany became intolerable in 1934, de Hevesy moved to Copenhagen to work with Niels Bohr; when Denmark came under Nazi occupation, de Hevesy followed Bohr by escaping on a fishing boat to Sweden.

Heyse, Paul (1830-1914). German novelist, poet, and dramatist who won the 1910 Nobel Prize in Literature. His father was a non-Jewish professor, and his mother an assimilated Jew. A conservative opponent of the naturalistic and impressionistic movements in Germany, Heyse was known for the realism and structural perfection of his writings.

George Hevesy's work.
Sweden 1479 (1983)

From left: Paul Heyse. *Sweden 878 (1970), Grenada 2490g (1995)*

Katz, Sir Bernard (1911-). German-born British biophysicist who shared the 1970 Nobel Prize in Physiology or Medicine for discovering the activation, inactivation, and storage mechanisms of neurotransmitters. He and his co-workers demonstrated that the release of acetylcholine in precise amounts from vesicles (sacs) located at the end of each neuron stimulates nerve and muscle cells.

Kissinger, Henry Alfred (1923-). German-born American political scientist and presidential counselor. Moving to the United States as a teenager, Kissinger became an expert in defense policy and international relations and taught for more than a decade at Harvard University. As National Secu-

Sir Bernard Katz.
Grenada 2489e (1995)

rity Adviser, Kissinger paved the way for President Nixon's historic visit to China in 1972. Kissinger also played a leading role in the peace negotiations with North Vietnam and shared the 1973 Nobel Peace Prize with Le Duc Tho. In that same year, Kissinger was appointed Secretary of State, the first Jew and the first person not of American birth to assume this position. After the conclusion of the Vietnam War, Kissinger played a leading role in trying to solve the problems of the Middle East. In 1975, he negotiated a disengagement agreement between Israel and Egypt, flying back and forth between the two countries as a third party mediator in a technique dubbed "shuttle diplomacy."

Henry Kissinger.
Guyana 3016 (1995)

Landau, Lev Davidovich (1908-68). Soviet theoretical physicist who received the 1962 Nobel Prize in Physics for his pioneering work in low-temperature physics (cryogenics). He developed mathematical theories explaining how super-fluid helium behaves at temperatures near absolute zero. Although awarded the Stalin Prize three times for his work in theoretical physics, Landau was imprisoned (1937-39) during Stalin's purge, allegedly as a German spy. He was released when Professor Peter Kapitza, head of his Institute and a fellow Jew, declared that he would stop all his own scientific work unless Landau were freed.

Lev Landau (right).
Malagasy 1132g (1993)

Landsteiner, Karl (1868–1943). Austrian-American immunologist and pathologist, who received the 1930 Nobel Prize in Physiology or Medicine. Landsteiner discovered the basic human blood groups (O, A, B, AB) and the Rhesus blood factor, which became the basis for matching donor and recipient in blood transfusions.

From left: Blood donor recognition. *Morocco 643 (1987), Argentina B18 (1958), France 931 (1959), Denmark 531 (1974)*

Rita Levi-Montalcini.
Sierra Leone 1844g ((1995)

Levi-Montalcini, Rita (1911–). Italian-born developmental biologist with dual American citizenship, who received the 1986 Nobel Prize for Physiology or Medicine. Barred by the Fascist government from practicing medicine and working in the university in 1939, Levi-Montalcini continued her cell research by conducting experiments in an improvised laboratory in her bedroom with embryos from eggs that she had begged for to feed "needy children." Since she was a member of the "Jewish race," the results of the experiments could not be published in Italy, but they did appear in Belgium and established her scientific reputation. Having fled to Belgium, after the German invasion she returned to Italy and hid in Florence under the name "Lovisato," claiming to be a southern Italian with a northern accent. Levi-Montalcini shared her Nobel Prize with Stanley Cohen, with whom she isolated the nerve growth factor (NGF), a protein that stimulates the growth of sensory and sympathetic nerves in animals and in cultures.

Lippman, Gabriel (1845-1921). French physicist who received the 1908 Nobel Prize in Physics for his invention of the first process for making color photographs that did not fade quickly after development.

Lippman with Eucken.
Sweden 804 (1968)

Otto Loewi.
Austria 942

Loewi, Otto (1873-1961). German-American physiologist and pharmacologist who shared the 1936 Nobel Prize in Physiology or Medicine for his discoveries concerning the biochemical transmission of impulses in the involuntary nervous system. He studied the stimulation and retardation of the frequency and strength of the heartbeats of frogs when a major nerve trunk was electrically stimulated, showing that the effects were related to the release of various chemicals, particularly acetylcholine. After the Germans took over Austria in 1938, Loewi was imprisoned for two months and deprived of all his possessions before being allowed to leave to England and then to the United States.

The Jewish World in Stamps

Metchnikoff, Elie (1845-1916). Russian biologist who shared the 1908 Nobel Prize for Physiology or Medicine with Paul Ehrlich. Metchnikoff identified the process of phagocytosis, in which white blood cells engulf and then destroy bacterial invaders. He also advocated the consumption of lactic acid-producing bacteria for the prevention and remedy of intestinal putrefaction.

Elie Metchnikoff. From left:
France B398 (1966), Russia 6000 (1991)

Meyerhof, Otto Fritz (1884-1951). German biochemist who shared the 1922 Nobel Prize in Physiology or Medicine for his demonstration of the interactions of oxygen and lactic acid in muscle tissue. In 1938, Meyerhof left Germany for France to avoid Nazi oppression; when France fell in 1940, Meyerhof escaped with his wife to Spain and later to Portugal before finally reaching the United States.

Otto Meyerhof.
Grenada 2490f (1995)

Michelson, Albert Abraham (1852-1931). German-born American physicist who received the 1907 Nobel Prize in Physics, the first American citizen of any faith to win this distinction in a scientific discipline. Using an instrument of his own design, he determined the velocity of light with a high degree of accuracy. Michelson (and Morley) established the revolutionary theory of the constant speed of light under all conditions, which has become the underlying principle of modern physics, astronomy, and cosmology.

Albert Michelson with
Buchner. *Sweden 769 (1993)*

Mottelson, Benjamin Roy (1926-). American-born Danish physicist whose research on the inner structure of the nucleus of the atom resulted in his winning the 1975 Nobel Prize in Physics with two colleagues, one of whom was Aage Bohr (the son of Niels Bohr).

Benjamin Mottelson.
Maldives 2116b (1995)

Nathans, Daniel (1928-). American molecular biologist who was awarded the 1978 Nobel Prize in Physiology or Medicine for his contribution to the discovery and use of restriction enzymes, proteins that cut chains of DNA. This ability to modify the DNA molecule has paved the way for the preparation of recombinant DNA and the production of medically useful substances. The use of restriction enzymes also supports advances in gene therapy and the Human Genome Project, which has mapped all the genes in the human body.

Daniel Nathans.
Maldives 2113f (1995)

Pasternak, Boris Leonidovich (1890-1960). Russian poet and novelist, one of the major literary figures in the Soviet Union. Pasternak's poetry was attacked by Communist critics because it did not follow the preferred patterns of socialist realism, and he was forced to earn his living from superb translations of the works of Shakespeare, Goethe, and other English and German writers. His most famous work, the novel *Doctor Zhivago*, was rejected by Soviet publishers because of its critical approach to Communism, but won international acclaim when it first appeared in the west after being smuggled out of the USSR. Pasternak was awarded the 1958 Nobel Prize in Literature, but was forced to decline the award when he was attacked as a traitor and threatened with exile from his country. In 1989, Pasternak's son accepted the Nobel Prize on his father's behalf.

Boris Pasternak.
Russia 5939 (1990)

Wolfgang Pauli.
Grenada 2487d (1995)

Pauli, Wolfgang (1900-58). Austrian physicist who was awarded the 1945 Nobel Prize in physics for his discovery of "the exclusion principle." The son of a Jewish father, Pauli was baptized as a child but left the Catholic Church as a young man in the 1920s and was drawn to various forms of mysticism and Jungian psychology. A child prodigy, Pauli is ranked among the greatest figures in the development of quantum mechanics. Though a Swiss citizen, Pauli moved to the United States in 1939 to continue working with the best European atomic scientists who had relocated to America.

Rabin, Yitzhak (1922-1995). Winner of the 1994 Nobel Peace Prize (see page 156).

Sachs, Nelly Leonie (1891-1970). German poet who shared the 1966 Nobel Prize in Literature. Like many assimilated German Jews, Sachs discovered her Jewish heritage after the Nazi takeover. Escaping to Sweden in 1940, she began the poetic output for which she is known. Her works have a profoundly Jewish theme, stressing the motif of flight and pursuit, the symbol of the hunter and his quarry, the cycle of suffering, persecution, exile, and death that characterizes the life of the Jewish people. Nevertheless, her poetry is ecstatic, mystical, visionary, and solidly within the German romantic tradition. Sharing the Nobel Prize with S.Y. Agnon, Sachs observed: "Agnon represents the State of Israel. I represent the tragedy of the Jewish people."

Nelly Sachs. From left:
Germany 1695 (1991),
Sweden (2000)

Jack Steinbeger. *Antigua 1945d (1995)*

Steinberger, Jack (1921-). American physicist and co-winner (with Melvin Schwartz and Leon M. Lederman) of the 1988 Nobel Prize in Physics for his work in providing a better understanding of elementary atomic particles and forces. They developed a method for capturing neutrinos, extremely elusive subatomic particles, and using them to discover yet other basic atomic particles.

Stern, Otto (1888-1969). German physicist who was awarded the 1943 Nobel Prize in Physics for developing a method of studying the magnetic moments of atoms, atomic nuclei, and protons by directing beams of atoms or molecules through magnetic fields. His work confirmed Planck's quantum theory and the dual nature of matter. In 1933, at the first sign of Nazi interference in his work in Hamburg, Stern left Germany for the United States.

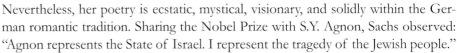

Otto Stern.
Antigua 1945f (1995)

Igor Tamm. *St. Vincent 2220k (1995)*

Tamm, Igor (1895-1971). Russian physicist who won the 1958 Nobel Prize in Physics. Tamm developed the quantum theory of acoustical vibrations and the scattering of light in solid bodies, as well as the theory of interactions of light with electrons.

Selman Waksman.
Gambia 910 (1989)

Waksman, Selman Abraham (1888-1973). Ukrainian-born American biochemist who was one of the world's foremost authorities on soil microbiology. After the discovery of penicillin, he played a major role in initiating a calculated, systematic search for antibiotics among microbes. The fruit of this research was his discovery of the antibiotic streptomycin, the first specific agent effective in the treatment of tuberculosis, for which he won the 1952 Nobel Prize in Physiology or Medicine. Waksman's work also led to the discovery of neomycin and several other antibiotics, a word that he coined. An observant Jew, Waksman founded an organization for Jewish students at his alma mater, Rutgers University.

Wallach, Otto (1947-1931). German organic chemist who was awarded the 1910 Nobel Prize in Chemistry for his pioneering work in the field of alicyclic compounds. His discoveries related to essential oils found in plants had a substantial impact on the manufacture of perfumes and flavors.

Otto Wallach (left).
Malagasy 1132k (1993)

Warburg, Otto Heinrich (1883-1970). German biochemist and physiologist who received the 1931 Nobel Prize in Physiology or Medicine for research on the oxidation process in living cells, particularly in cancerous tissue. Director of the Kaiser Wilhelm Institute for Cell Physiology, Warburg was one of the very few scientists of Jewish descent who remained undisturbed in his position during the Nazi period.

Otto Warburg.
Germany 1400 (1983)

Wiesel, Elie (1928-). Novelist and journalist who received the 1986 Nobel Peace Prize for his work in promoting human rights. Born in Sighet, Rumania, Wiesel was raised in an intensely Orthodox and hasidic environment. In 1944, the entire community was deported by the Nazis, and the adolescent Wiesel witnessed and experienced all the horrors of the Birkenau, Auschwitz, Buna, and Buchenwald concentration camps. The sole survivor of his entire family, Wiesel lived in Paris for some years after World War II, and later moved to New York. Though only *Night*, the first of Wiesel's novels (all written in French) actually relates his experience in the camps, virtually all his books are concerned with what he perceived as the religious, awesome, and haunting mystery of the Holocaust. In *The Jews of Silence*, Wiesel gives a remarkable eyewitness account of the plight of Soviet Jews. Wiesel has served as chairman of the U.S. President's Commission on the Holocaust and received the Congressional Medal of Honor.

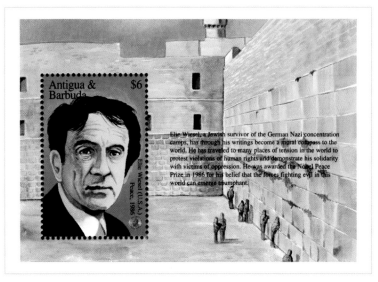

Elie Wiesel and the Wester Wall in Jerusalem.
Antigua 1947 (1995)

Richard Wilstaetter.
Sweden 1150 (1975)

Willstaetter, Richard (1872–1942). German organic chemist and winner of the 1915 Nobel Prize in Chemistry for his work regarding the properties of chlorophyll. Willstaetter was awarded the civilian Iron Cross for his research on gas masks for the German army in World War I. In 1924, he resigned his position at the University of Munich to protest the institution's failure to appoint qualified Jewish scientists. In 1939 the Gestapo ransacked his house and ordered him to leave Germany.

Yalow, Rosalyn Sussman (1921-). American medical physicist who shared the 1977 Nobel Prize in Physiology or Medicine for her work in developing the radioimmunoassay technique, which uses radioactively labeled material to quantify extremely small amounts of biological substances in body fluids.

Rosalyn Yalow.
Sierra Leone 1844e
(1995)

Zionism and the State of Israel

The Zionist Movement

Ever since the destruction of Jerusalem by the Romans in 70 C.E. and the exile of the Jewish people from their ancient homeland, Jews have clung passionately to the hope for a return to Zion. Despite extreme poverty and physical dangers that threatened their very survival, Jews turned in prayer toward Zion three times each day. The medieval poet Judah Halevi wrote glorious poems extolling his love for Zion and longing for its restoration. Over the centuries of exile, a few pious pilgrims made the arduous journey to the Holy Land, but the vast majority of Jews remained in the Diaspora with little realistic hope of ever seeing the land of their ancestors.

With the rise of nationalism in Europe during the 19th century, Jews slowly became convinced that the time was ripe for them to develop an independent state in their own land. Among those urging resettlement of the Holy Land was Judah Alkalai, who agitated among the Hasidim for a return to Zion within the framework of traditional religious thought. However, most Jews were caught up in the excitement of the Enlightenment, which stressed that obtaining a modern education and assimilating into European culture by adopting the language and manners of their non-Jewish compatriots was the best solution to the age-old problems of discrimination and anti-Semitism.

In Russia, Leo Pinsker (Judah Leib, 1821-1891) lost his faith in the struggle for Jewish emancipation in the face of tsarist persecution and pogroms. As a doctor, Pinsker diagnosed anti-Semitism as an "incurable disease," caused by fear of the alien, stateless Jew. In his 1882 essay *Auto-Emancipation*, he prescribed the establishment of a congress of Jewish leaders to achieve "a home, a land, a territory." Pinsker's call was heeded by the Hovevei Zion ("Lovers of Zion"), a movement of scattered societies that had sprung up two decades earlier with the aim of restoring Jewish national life by settling in Palestine. The members of what has been termed the First Aliyah (migration to the Holy Land) were the vanguard of the pioneering efforts at establishing Jewish settlements in the Holy Land after almost two millennia of exile.

The spark that irreversibly ignited the fire of Zionism was the infamous Dreyfus case in France and its effect on Theodor Herzl, a successful Viennese journalist and Paris correspondent of the famous *Neue Freie Presse*. Although ignorant of the early Zionist movement or its literature, when Herzl viewed virulent anti-Semitism raging in the most progressive country in Europe, he concluded that the only solution for escaping this recurrent terror was for the Jewish people to have their own state. In 1896, Herzl

Right, from top:
Rabbi Judah Alkalai, early Hasidic Zionist.
Israel 1029 (1989)
Leo Pinsker, early Zionist thinker. *Israel 880 (1984)*
Theodor Herzl, founder of Political Zionism, at the Rhine in Basel, site of first Zionist Congress.
Israel 183 (1960)
Centennial of First Zionist Congress. *Israel 1287(1997)*
Left: The casino in Basel, site of the First Zionist Congress. *Israel 1288 (1997)*

became the founder of political Zionism with the publication of his book *Judenstaat* (The Jewish State). The next year he issued a call for the first Zionist Congress, which met in Basel, Switzerland, on August 27, 1897, and announced its goal to "create for the Jewish people a home in Palestine secured by public law." Subsequent congresses developed the World Zionist Organization as the official governing body of the movement and established the Keren Kayemet (Jewish National Fund) to purchase land in Palestine. The Zionist goals were given dramatic voice by Max Nordau, a physician and writer who was a master orator and Herzl's closest supporter. Herzl engaged in endless negotiations with Turkish authorities and various European governments for a charter to Palestine. Britain did offer the territory of Uganda in East Africa for an autonomous Jewish settlement, but this was rejected by those who saw Palestine as the only valid choice for Jewish national aspirations. Although Herzl's efforts were not successful by his untimely death in 1904, they paved the way for the political achievements of the next two decades.

Max Nordau.
Israel 780 (1978)

Chaim Weizmann.
Israel 696 (1978)

The death of Herzl was a devastating blow to the Zionist movement and led to the development of bitter disagreements between its two major factions. The "political" Zionists wanted to concentrate all efforts on securing a charter to establish a Jewish state in Palestine, convinced that the practical work of mass settlement would come once the legal guarantee for the colonists had been achieved. In contrast, the "practical" Zionists of the Lovers of Zion maintained that settlement in Palestine must continue, since the presence of a large number of Jews in the land would give greater weight to the political efforts of the Zionist movement. A middle position was espoused by Chaim Weizmann, a rising young leader of the movement, who argued that a combination of both ideals would be most beneficial to the Zionist cause. A third approach was "cultural" Zionism, championed by Ahad Ha-Am, who stated that it was not sufficient to establish a Jewish state merely as a refuge for the persecuted. Instead, Palestine should be restored as a cultural and spiritual center, imbued with the ideals of the Hebrew prophets, which would serve the entire Jewish people, both in the national homeland and throughout the Diaspora.

Vladimir Jabotinsky.
Israel 706 (1978)

Aaron Aaronsohn.
Israel 742 (1979)

With the onset of World War I, the Zionist movement was faced with the splitting of its forces between Germany and Austria on one side and Britain, France, and Russia on the other. The World Zionist Organization prudently adopted a policy of neutrality, moving its central office to neutral Copenhagen. As allies of Germany, the Turks were especially suspicious of the Jews of Palestine who had come from Russia. Threatened with imprisonment by the Turks as enemy aliens, many Jews fled to Egypt, where their presence complemented the Zionist political activity among the Allies. After encountering substantial resistance, Joseph Trumpeldor and Vladimir Jabotinsky finally convinced the authorities to organize a Jewish Legion, which fought with British forces to liberate Palestine from the Turks. Other Jews joined "Nili" (acronym of the Hebrew verse

Sarah Aaronsohn. *Israel 1076 (1991)*

Netzach Yisrael Lo Yeshaker ("the Eternal One of Israel will not lie;" I Sam. 15:29), a secret pro-British spying organization that operated under Turkish rule in Syria and Palestine in an effort to realize a Jewish homeland. Major figures in this movement included agriculturalist Aaron Aaronsohn and his sister Sarah, who was arrested and executed. Meanwhile, Chaim Weizmann and other leaders of British Jewry were engaged in intensive negotia-

Lord Arthur J. Balfour.
Israel 354 (1967)

tions with the British government to obtain the charter to Palestine that Herzl had vainly sought. On November 2, 1917, the Balfour Declaration was issued in a letter from the Foreign Secretary to Lord Lionel Walter Rothschild, president of the British Zionist Federation. It stated that, "His Majesty's Government view with favor the establishment in Palestine of a national home for the Jewish people." These sentiments were accepted by the Versailles Peace Conference and readopted by the League of Nations when it affirmed the British Mandate for Palestine.

Nevertheless, the Zionist cause faced many serious obstacles. The rivalry between Britain and France for control in the Middle East, combined with budding Arab nationalism and the rival ambitions of Arab lead-

The Jewish Brigade flag.
Israel 723 (1979)

ers, led to increasing violence and Arab attacks on Jewish agricultural settlements. To appease the Arabs, Britain removed two thirds of Palestine under its mandate to create the separate Arab territory of Transjordan. A series of White Papers was issued to curtail Jewish immigration into Palestine, despite the increasing persecution of German Jews under the Nazi regime. By 1939, the Balfour Declaration with its promise of a Jewish National Home had been abandoned. With the onset of World War II and the imminent danger to the millions of Jews in Europe, the World Zionist Organization protested strenuously against the British policy prohibiting any substantial immigration to Palestine. At the same time, Weizmann pressed for permission to establish a fighting force of Palestine Jews to serve in the British army. After refusing this request for several years, the British finally agreed to the formation of a Jewish Brigade, an independent national Jewish military formation made up mainly of Jews from Palestine, which swept into Austria and Germany with the victorious Allied armies. The brigade had its own emblem, a gold Star of David on a background of blue-white-blue stripes and bearing the inscription *Chayil* (the Hebrew word for soldier and the initials of its Hebrew name, Jewish Brigade Group).

Jewish Brigade Group with its emblems.
Israel 1223 (1995)

After the catastrophic destruction of European Jewry, the Zionists pressed for the pitiful survivors of the concentration camps to be admitted freely into Palestine to be cared for by their own people. However, the British steadfastly refused, fearful of alienating the surrounding Arab states and leading to the outbreak of Arab violence in Palestine. Despite blockades by the British fleet, the "illegal immigration" begun before the war by Palestine Jewry resumed and increased. The world witnessed the shocking sight of British warships forcing Jews to return to displaced persons camps in Germany or to be interned in Cyprus in detention camps surrounded by barbed wire. In Palestine, Jewish military resistance to British rule grew steadily as underground extremist groups carried out sabotage operations and armed attacks on British military and government installations (army camps, airfields, police stations, railway trains) as well as on individual members of the British police and army. Eventually, the British grew weary of the challenge of Palestine, and in February 1947, Foreign Minister Bevin announced to the House of Commons his intention to refer the problem to the United Nations.

Jewish paratroopers in World War II.
Israel 92 (1955)

In April, the United Nations met in special session to try to reach a solution to the situation in Palestine. The Jewish side was presented by the leaders of the Jewish Agency: Abba Hillel Silver, head of the American section; Moshe Shertok (Sharett), director of its political department; and David Ben-Gurion, its chairman. The Committee of Inquiry set up to assess the various rami-

Celebrating the 1947 UN Resolution on a Jewish state. *Israel 1318 (1997)*

fications of the problem recommended the partition of Palestine into separate Jewish and Arab states, with Jerusalem to be governed by an international authority. On November 29, 1947, the majority of states in the United Nations voted to approve this compromise solution. Five months later, the British withdrew from Palestine. On May 14, 1948, the State of Israel was proclaimed in Tel Aviv, with Ben-Gurion reading its Declaration of Independence. Ten minutes after the proclamation, President Harry Truman extended de facto American recognition to the new State.

Abba Hillel Silver. *Israel 778 (1981)*

Clockwise:
Ben-Gurion reads the Declaration of Independence. *Israel 1332 (1998).*
David Ben-Gurion. *Israel 705 (1978).*
Israel's Declaration of Independence. *Israel 521 (1973).*
U. S. President Harry S. Truman. *Israel 561 (1975)*

The Jewish World in Stamps

War of Independence (1948)

The five surrounding Arab nations (Egypt, Iraq, Transjordan, Syria, and Lebanon), supported by volunteer detachments from Saudi Arabia, Libya, and Yemen, immediately launched a coordinated attack on Israel from the land, sea, and air. Urged on by their leaders, who assured them that they could return after all the Jews had been driven out, most of the Arab population fled the country. Although enormously overwhelmed in numbers and military power, the Jews were able to defeat the Arab armies. An armistice ending the conflict was signed in 1949. However, the Old City of Jerusalem fell under Jordanian control, and Jews were denied access to the Western Wall for almost two decades.

During the war, about 5,000 foreign volunteers (Machal), mainly Jews, enlisted in the Israel Defense Forces (IDF). Rather than fighting in separate formations, the Machal volunteers were absorbed into IDF units according to the need for reinforcements. Their contribution was not in numbers but in quality and experience, most necessary in a new army whose fighting tradition was that of an underground movement, as well as in the development of the air force and medical corps. Representatives also actively recruited Diaspora Jews to come to Israel as new immigrants and serve in the War of Independence (Gachal).

Soon after its establishment, the State of Israel adopted the Zionist flag as the official national flag – "a white rectangle with two blue stripes along its entire length and a Star of David in the center made up of six stripes forming two equilateral triangles." Israel also selected *Hatikvah* (The Hope) as its national anthem. The words, from a poem by Naphtali Herz Imber, were set to music by Samuel Cohen to the melody of an old Moldavian-Romanian folk song that had previously been used by the Czech composer Bedrich Smetana in "The Moldau." The simple text of *Hatikvah* is a stirring statement of the age-old Zionist dream: "As long as deep in the heart, the soul of a Jew yearns, so long as the eye looks eastward toward Zion, our hope is not lost – the two thousand year hope, to be a free people in our land, the land of Zion and Jerusalem."

Top, left to right: Battle for Safed; Battle for Jerusalem; Battle for Eilat .
Israel 1325-1327 (1998).
Middle: *Hatikvah* (national anthem);
Overseas volunteers in 1948.
Israel 697 (1978).
Bottom right: Recruitment in the Diaspora in 1948.
Israel 1322 (1997)

Flag of Israel.
Israel 15 (1949)

Six-Day War (1967)

For almost 20 years, the vague conditions of the armistice agreements (especially the provisions for demilitarized zones), the refusal of the Arabs to enter into negotiations for peace, and the absence of progress towards the solution of basic problems had inevitably led to the aggravation of relations between Israel and her neighbors.

In May 1967, Egypt closed the Straits of Tiran (the outlet for Israeli ships and cargo from Eilat to the Red Sea) and massed troops in the Sinai Peninsula for an all-out invasion. In a brilliantly conceived preemptive attack, Israel crushed the Egyptian army and air force. Although warned not to join the conflict, Jordan attacked Israel. Its forces were driven out from all the land west of the Jordan River, and Jerusalem was united under Israeli control. Finally, Israel turned its attention to the Syrian front, occupying strategic fortifications on the Golan Heights that had shelled Israeli border settlements for two decades.

Yigal Allon.
Israel 859 (1984)

Israel now controlled the entire West Bank of the Jordan, the biblical land of Judea and Samaria. A liberal military administration under Moshe Dayan rapidly restored essential services for the population of the areas and encouraged the development of trade, particularly in the field of agricultural supplies, with the rest of the Arab world. Yigal Allon (1918-1980), a member of the inner war cabinet that mapped out strategy for the Six-Day War, proposed a plan that outlined new borders to combine "maximum security for the State of Israel with a minimum of Arab population." However, despite their overwhelming defeat and repeated Israeli offers of return of territory in exchange for peace, the surrounding Arab states refused to enter into negotiations with Israel or even recognize its existence. The Palestine Liberation Organization mounted indiscriminate terrorist attacks against Israel, as well as against civilian aircraft and Israeli institutions abroad.

Yom Kippur War (1973)

In September 1973, Israel Intelligence observed a military buildup on both the Egyptian and Syrian fronts, but these were dismissed as routine training exercises that had been taking place at frequent intervals along the borders. This appraisal tallied with the assessment of Israel Intelligence that the Arab armies were not yet ready for a major all-out war, and that their leadership was not capable of launching it. Nevertheless, on Yom Kippur (October 6), Egypt and Syria launched a concerted attack that caught Israel off guard. Until Israel was able to mobilize its reserves, the Arab armies made substantial inroads and the very existence of the Jewish State was in doubt. Ironically, one of the miscalculations made by the Arabs was to launch the war on this Jewish holy day when all the manpower of the country was available either at home or in synagogue, thus saving Israel many valuable hours of mobilization. Once the reserves became available, Israeli forces eventually succeeded in recapturing all the territories taken by the invading armies and surged to within 20 miles of Damascus before the Syrians agreed to a cease-fire.

From top: Straits of Tiran. *Israel 345 (1967)*. The IDF. *Israel 346 (1967)*. The Western Wall. *Israel 347 (1967)*. Mirage fighter over Masada. *Israel 344 (1967)*. Mystere fighter over Dead Sea. *Israel 343 (1967)*

Peace Treaty with Egypt.
Israel 724 (1979)

Peace Treaties

In 1977, President Anwar Sadat of Egypt paid a surprise visit to Jerusalem, where he addressed the Knesset and held talks with Menachem Begin, becoming the first Arab chief of state to meet officially with an Israeli prime minister. Two years later, Sadat and Begin met at Camp David, under the auspices of President Jimmy Carter, to draw up the framework of a peace treaty between Egypt and Israel (see page 157). On March 26, 1979, the two countries signed a formal peace agreement in Washington, with Israel relinquishing control of the entire Sinai peninsula it had captured during the Six-Day War in return for the promise of normal relations with the most powerful Arab state. For their efforts, Sadat, Begin, and Carter shared the 1978 Nobel Peace Prize. Tragically, Sadat was later assassinated by Muslim extremists in Egypt.)

By the late 1980s, persistent unrest led to the intifada (Arabic for "liberation"), a violent struggle against continuing Israeli possession of the territories seized in the 1967 war. After the 1991 Gulf War against Iraq and its tyrannical dictator Saddam Hussein, in which Scud missiles were launched against Israel, the United States and its allies renewed their efforts to conclude a comprehensive peace treaty between Israel and its Arab neighbors. When a Labor coalition gained power in 1992, Foreign Minister Shimon Peres convinced Prime Minister Yitzhak Rabin to sign the 1993 Oslo Agreement, in which the Gaza Strip and Jericho were handed over to Arab rule under Yasser Arafat as a "good faith gesture" to begin a series of staged agreements that would eventually result in a peaceful resolution of the issues relating to the "occupied territory." One year later, Israel signed a peace treaty with King Hussein of Jordan. However, in 1995 Rabin was assassinated at a peace rally in Tel Aviv, and Likud leader Benjamin Netanyahu became Prime Minister, promising "peace with security." His successor, Labor leader Ehud Barak, reinvigorated the stalled Oslo process and eventually offered virtually all of the West Bank and East Jerusalem in exchange for peace. However, this was summarily rejected by Yasser Arafat, who demanded the "right of return" of the millions of descendants of the Arabs who had fled during the 1948 War of Independence (which would have been a demographic disaster soon resulting in Jews becoming a minority in the Jewish State). Arafat then instigated a bloody second intifada, which toppled the Barak government and led to Ariel Sharon becoming Prime Minister. As Arab terrorism continually increased and suicide bombers repeatedly wreaked devastation on the civilian population within Israel, the Oslo Peace Process effectively collapsed.

Peace Treaty with Jordan.
Israel 1209, 1216 (1994)

Celebrating the 50th Anniversary of the State of Israel

In 1998, the State of Israel celebrated the 50th anniversary of its creation. Despite multiple wars and the continued absence of peaceful relationships with most of its Arab neighbors, Israel's achievements have been spectacular. Millions of immigrants from all over the world have been successfully absorbed in the Jewish state, which is still the only free democratic nation in the entire Middle East.

Israel's 50th Anniversary.
Israel 1320 (1997)

Israel's 50th Anniversary.
Argentina 2103 (1998)

50th anniversary of the creation of the State of Israel. *Venezuela 1599a-j (1998).*

Clockwise:

a. Menorah (tab: "You shall love your neighbor as yourself;" Lev. 19:18)

b. Moses with tablets of Ten Commandments (tab: "You shall not seek revenge nor maintain anger [toward your kin];" Lev. 19:18)

c. Theodor Herzl (tab: "If I should forget you, O Jerusalem, let my right hand forget its cunning;" Psalms 137:5-6)

d. King David with lyre (tab: "The prophets were messengers of peace and justice")

e. Blowing of the shofar (tab: "The rich man is one who is happy with what he has;" Pirke Avot 4:1)

f. Shrine of the Book Museum (tab: "Man does not live by bread alone;" Deut. 8:3)

g. Knesset (tab: "All Jews are responsible, one for the other;" Shavuot 39b)

h. David Ben-Gurion (tab: "How good it is and how pleasant for brothers to dwell together;" Psalms 133:1)

i. Praying at the Wailing Wall (tab: "He who works his land has bread to eat;" Proverbs 12:11)

j. Torah (tab: "Do not do to others what you would not like them to do to you;" Deut. 8:3)

Israel's 50th Anniversary.
Left: *Dominican Republic 1275 (1998)* . Right: *Uruguay 1715 (1998)*

Major Figures and Events Prior to the Establishment of the State of Israel

Herzl, Theodor (Binyamin Ze'ev) (1860–1904). Father of political Zionism and founder of the World Zionist Organization. Born in Budapest to an affluent intellectual Jewish family, Herzl graduated in law from the University of Vienna and then turned to writing. In 1891, Herzl became the Paris correspondent of the Vienna *Neue Freie Presse*, the leading liberal newspaper of the time. Although having previously faced the anti-Semitism of fellow students and professors, Herzl had advocated assimilation as the best solution. However, this conception was shattered by the infamous Dreyfus case. As a newspaper correspondent, Herzl attended the trial and realized that it was not Dreyfus the army captain, but Dreyfus the Jew, who was on trial. With the shouts of "Death to the Jews" ringing in his ears, Herzl became convinced that the only solution to anti-Semitism was the mass exodus of the Jews from their present places of residence and their resettlement in a territory of their own.

Herzl.
Israel 695 (1978)

Herzl published his seminal work, *Der Judenstaat* (The Jewish State) in 1896; in 1897 he issued a call for a Zionist Congress, which met in Basel, Switzerland, later that year. It elected Herzl president of the World Zionist Organization, which over the next few years under his leadership established the Jewish Colonial Trust (the Zionist banking arm) and the Jewish National Fund (its land purchasing agency). Herzl worked feverishly to obtain a charter from Turkey for the creation of a Jewish state in Palestine and conducted negotiations throughout Europe to enlist diplomatic support for the Zionist goal. When Herzl saw firsthand the terrible suffering of the Russian Jews, who were subjected to periodic pogroms, he decided to accept the British offer of Uganda in East Africa as a temporary asylum for Russian Jewry. However, this proposal roused vehement opposition by those who regarded it as a betrayal of the Land of Israel as Zionism's ultimate goal, and the Uganda project was rejected.

Herzl with the seven-star design of his original flag for the new state.
Israel 86 (1954)

In his will, Herzl asked to be buried beside his father's grave in Vienna until the Jewish people would transfer his remains to the Land of Israel. Consequently, soon after the State of Israel was established, Herzl's remains were reburied on Mount Herzl in Jerusalem and a Herzl museum (including his original Vienna study) was built nearby. The anniversary of his death, the 20th of Tammuz, was declared a national memorial day in Israel.

Centennial of Zionism
Uruguay 1673 (1997)

Left: Breaking Dreyfus' sword. Tab shows French novelist Emile Zola and his article accusing the French authorities of false charges against Dreyfus. *Israel 1221 (1994)*

The 23rd Zionist Congress
Israel 51 (1951)

Ze'ev Jabotinsky.
Israel 706 (1978)

Jabotinsky, Vladimir (Ze'ev) (1880-1940). Founder of the Revisionist Zionist movement. Although born in Odessa into an assimilated Jewish family, Jabotinsky became immersed in Zionist activities. With Joseph Trumpeldor, Jabotinsky conceived the idea of a Jewish Legion and eventually convinced the British to permit the formation of a Jewish battalion. In 1920, Jabotinsky organized the Haganah in Jerusalem, openly leading it in confrontation with incited Arab masses during the Passover riots of that year. He was immediately arrested by the British authorities and sentenced by a military court to 15 years hard labor. After intense public protest, Jabotinsky was freed and left Acre prison acclaimed a hero by all sections of the *yishuv*. Jabotinsky moved to London and became a member of the World Zionist Executive, but soon resigned this post because of sharp differences with Chaim Weizmann, whom he considered too conciliatory toward Britain. In 1925, Jabotinsky organized the Revisionist Zionist party, which advocated the speedy creation of a Jewish state on both sides of the Jordan River.

After Hitler's rise to power in 1933, Jabotinsky espoused the total boycott of Nazi Germany by the Jewish people and opposed the Jewish Agency's agreement with the Berlin regime. He attempted to convince European governments that they could solve the "problem" of their Jewish minorities through emigration, and he proposed a scheme for an internationally sponsored ten-year plan for the "evacuation" of 1,500,000 East European Jews to Palestine. However, this policy was violently opposed by most sections of the Jewish public, who feared that it might be interpreted as proof of the anti-Semitic contention that Jews are essentially aliens in their countries of residence. Intent on breaking the prohibitive British regulations on immigration to Palestine, Jabotinsky forcefully supported "illegal" immigration, which became a major activity of his movement. Although he had fought the British for many years, with the onset of World War II Jabotinsky demanded the creation of a Jewish army to fight alongside England against the Nazis, but he died before the Jewish Brigade (see page 145) was formed.

Ahad Ha-Am (Asher Ginsberg) (1856-1927). Foremost thinker of Zionism, Ginsberg wrote under the modest pen name of "Ahad Ha-Am," meaning "one of the people." He taught cultural, or "spiritual" Zionism. As political Zionism emerged under the leadership of Herzl, Ahad Ha-Am argued in such essays as *Lo Zeh Ha-Derech* (This Is Not the Way) that Israel must first become a spiritual and cultural center before it could develop into a viable Jewish state. His forceful, moral personality greatly influenced Zionism and many, including Israel's national poet, Bialik, considered him their teacher. Unable to enter university in his native Ukraine, he studied in German and Austrian universities in the spirit of late 19th century humanism, but was mostly self-taught. Before World War I, Ahad Ha-Am settled in England, where he played an important role in the events leading to the Balfour Declaration. At age 66 he settled in Tel Aviv where he continued to exert his influence on the Zionist movement. (See also page 192).

Ahad Ha-Am.
Israel 1290 (1996)

Meir Bar-Ilan.
Israel 855 (1983)

Bar-Ilan, Meir (1880–1949). Leader of the Mizrachi (religious Zionist) movement. Born in Volozhin, Russia, as Meyer Berlin, he went to Berlin in 1910 where he was general secretary of the Mizrachi movement. After serving as the president of the United States Mizrachi from 1915-1926, Bar-Ilan settled in Jerusalem as president of the World Mizrachi center. After the establishment of the State of Israel, he was an initiator of the National Religious Front, the group of religious parties that presented a united platform in the first Knesset elections. A central figure in the Zionist religious movement, Bar-Ilan founded and edited a religious Zionist weekly (*Ha-Ivri;* "The Hebrew"), served as editor in chief of the Mizrachi daily (*Ha-Tzofeh*), and in 1947 initiated and organized the publishing of the Talmudic Encyclopedia. Bar-Ilan University near Tel Aviv, founded by the American Mizrachi movement, is named in his honor.

Great Philanthropists Who Helped Rebuild the Land of Israel

Montefiore, Sir Moses (1784-1885). English philanthropist and the most famous British Jew of the 19th century. Born in Leghorn, Italy, while his parents were on a visit from London, Montefiore became one of the 12 "Jew brokers" in the City of London. He married into the Rothschild family and retired in 1824 with a large fortune. Thereafter, Montefiore devoted himself to bettering the condition of Jews throughout the world and was active in trying to remove the civil restrictions of Jews in England. He made seven visits to the Land of Israel and bought land for the establishment of several agricultural colonies. Montefiore also attempted to bring industry to the country, introducing a printing press and a textile factory, and endowed hospitals, synagogues, and the first girls' school in Jerusalem. The Yemin Moshe quarter outside the Old City of Jerusalem was due to his endeavors and named after him.

Sir Moses Montefiore.
Israel 777 (1981)

Baron Edmond de Rothschild.
Israel 90 (1954)

Rothschild, Baron Edmond de (1845-1934). One of the chief builders of modern Israel. Son of one of Europe's most famous and powerful families of financiers, he was a devout Jew, avid art collector, and a philanthropist. When approached by the first Zionist pioneers in the early 1880's to save them from financial ruin, he readily responded. Gradually, Rothschild took all the new settlements under his sponsorship, thus in effect saving the Zionist enterprise. While his officials often clashed with the settlers, they did provide support and expertise in establishing Jewish agriculture and laying the foundation for the future state. For years, Rothschild was the main address for any financial needs in the newly emerging communities. His vineyards in Rishon Le-Zion and Zichron Ya'akov became world famous. After the establishment of the state, Rothschild and his wife were reinterred in Zichron Ya'akov. (See also page 160).

Wolfson, Sir Isaac (1897-1991). British financier and philanthropist. Born in Glascow, Scotland, Wolfson used the profits from his extensive business ventures in Israel to further his philanthropic interests in the land. The Edith and Isaac Wolfson Trust provided funds for building the Supreme Rabbinical Center in Jerusalem (Hechal Shlomo, named for his father), 50 synagogues throughout the country, and the Kiryat Wolfson housing projects (with schools and synagogues) for new immigrants in Jerusalem and Acre. Wolfson also contributed to the Hebrew University, the Technion, and the Weizmann Institute of Science. In 1962, Wolfson was made a baronet in recognition of his philanthropic activities.

Sir Isaac Wolfson.
Israel 888 (1984)

Members of the First Government of Israel

Ben-Gurion, David (1886-1973). First prime minister (1948-1953; 1955-1963) and defense minister of the State of Israel. Born David Gruen in Poland, he blended a fervent love for Zion with socialist ideals. At age 17, he was one of the founders of the Po'alei Zion (Socialist Zionist) movement; three years later in 1906, he moved to Palestine and took the name "Ben-Gurion" (Hebrew for "son of the young lion"). Working as a common laborer and experiencing the hardships of a young pioneer, Ben-Gurion was a founder of the Jewish self-defense movement to repel the recurrent Arab attacks threatening the settlements. Expelled from Palestine by the Turks during World War I, Ben-Gurion went to the United States, where he helped found the He-Halutz organization (preparing young Jews for settlement in Palestine) and the American Jewish Congress, and aided in organizing the Jewish Legion. Returning to Palestine in 1921, Ben-Gurion became secretary-general of the Histadrut, the General Federation of Labor. In 1933, he was elected to the Executive of the World Zionist Organization, becoming its chairman in 1940.

David Ben-Gurion.
Israel 547 (1974)

When the leaders of the Zionist movement were challenged by the combination of the onset of World War II and the infamous 1939 White Paper that severely restricted the immigration of the imperiled European Jews into Palestine, Ben-Gurion defined the position of the *yishuv* (Jews of Palestine): "We must assist the British in the war as if there were no White Paper, and we must resist the White Paper as if there were no war."

In the spring of 1948, despite great pressure from the American government and the doubts of many of his colleagues, Ben-Gurion insisted upon the establishment of the Jewish state immediately upon the termination of the British Mandate. On May 14, Ben-Gurion proclaimed the rebirth of the independent Jewish nation, becoming the first prime minister and minister of defense in the provisional government. Since no single party obtained an overall majority in the election for the first Knesset in 1949, Ben-Gurion formed a ruling coalition (setting the pattern for future governments) and soon declared Jerusalem the capital of Israel.

Ben-Gurion Airport.
Israel 943 (1986)

Perez Bernstein.
Israel 802 (1982)

Ben-Gurion exerted a profound influence on the character of Israel, making the ingathering of the exiles a supreme principle in the ideology of the state; introducing free education in an effort to mold the diversified elements of Israel into one nation and using the army as an educational medium; and placing the advancement of science and research as a central factor in the development of the country and its people. The University of the Negev in Beer Sheva, the International Airport, and the Government Buildings' Complex in Jerusalem are among the many Israeli institutions named after Ben-Gurion.

Bernstein, Perez (Fritz; 1890–1971). First minister of commerce and industry (1948–49; 1952-1955). Born in Germany, he moved to Rotterdam and became president of the Dutch Zionist Federation. In 1936 Bernstein settled in Palestine, where he edited the General Zionist newspaper *Ha-Boker* and became leader of the movement.

Yitzhak Gruenbaum.
Israel 754 (1980)

Gruenbaum, Yitzhak (1879–1970). First minister of the interior. Born in Warsaw, Gruenbaum was leader of the radical faction in General Zionism and a major spokesman of Polish Jewry between the two world wars. He moved to Palestine in 1933 when elected a member of the Jewish Agency Executive, serving as head of the Aliyah and Labor Departments.

Maimon, Judah Leib (1876-1962). First minister of religion. Born Judah Leib Fishman in Bessarabia, Maimon moved to Palestine in 1913 and took an active role in the rebuilding of the land and the development of the Mizrachi (Religious Zionist) movement. Head of the Rav Kook publishing house and editor of the scholarly monthly *Sinai*, Maimon published many important volumes on Jewish holidays, Zionism, law, and monographs about famous Jewish personalities.

Judah Leib Maimon.
Israel 1011 (1989)

The Jewish World in Stamps

Meir, Golda. First Israeli ambassador to Russia. (see below)

Rosen, Pinchas (1887–1978). First minister of justice (1948-1961). Born Felix Rosenblueth in Berlin, Rosen studied law and was a cofounder of the Blau-Weiss (Blue and White) youth movement before settling in Palestine in 1931. He was instrumental in organizing the judicial and legal system of Israel. Chairman of the Board of the Israel Philharmonic Orchestra until 1961, in 1973 Rosen was awarded the Israel Prize for Law.

Pinchas Rosen.
Israel 974 (1987)

Sharett, Moshe. First foreign minister. (see below)

Shazar, Schneur Zalman. First minister of education and culture. (see below)

Smoira, Moshe (1888-1961). First president of the Supreme Court of Israel (1948-54). Born into a Russian-Hasidic family in Prussia, Smoira settled in Palestine in 1922. An expert on labor problems, he participated in the drafting of the Workmen's Compensation Ordinance and in determining the legal status of the kibbutzim, and was president of the Jewish Bar Association.

Moshe Smoira.
Israel 1023 (1989)

Sprinzak, Joseph (1885-1959). First speaker of the Knesset. Born in Moscow and emigrating to Palestine in 1908, Sprinzak was a co-founder of the Histadrut and eventually became its General Secretary in the 1940s. As Knesset Speaker, Sprinzak greatly influenced the nation's democratic character and molded the written and unwritten rules of its parliamentary life, enjoying general confidence and respect from all sectors of the public.

Joseph Sprinzak.
Israel 946 (1986)

David Ben-Gurion.
Israel 950 (1986)

Prime Ministers of Israel

Ben-Gurion, David. First prime minister (1948-1953; 1955-1963). (see above)

Sharett, Moshe (1894-1965). Second prime minister (1954-1955). Born Moshe Shertok in the Ukraine, he moved to Palestine with his family in 1906 and was a member of the first class of the prestigious Herzliyah Gymnasium (high school). After studies in England, Shertok returned home to become deputy editor of the labor daily *Davar*. Appointed secretary of the political department of the Jewish Agency. Shertok was responsible for day-to-day contacts with the British Mandatory authorities, the preparation of the Jewish case for presentation to the various British commissions of inquiry, and a wide range of activities in the field of information and public relations. In 1947, Shertok conducted an intensive diplomatic effort to achieve the two-thirds majority in the historic United Nations partition vote. With the establishment of the State of Israel, he became its first foreign minister (changing his name to Sharett). In January 1954, upon David Ben-Gurion's temporary retirement, Sharett succeeded him as prime minister while retaining the foreign affairs portfolio. When Ben-Gurion resumed his post as the head of the government in November 1955, Sharett continued to serve as foreign minister, but growing differences between the two men led to his resignation in 1956.

Moshe Sharett.
Israel 368 (1968)

Eshkol, Levi (1895-1969). Third prime minister of Israel (1963-1969). Born Levi Shkolnik into a prosperous Hasidic family in the Ukraine, Eshkol settled in Palestine in 1914. Early recognizing the importance of securing an adequate water supply for agricultural development, Eshkol was a founder and first director of the Mekorot Water Company, and he spearheaded the construction of the National Water Carrier after the establishment of the State. From 1948-1963, Eshkol headed the Land Settlement Department of the Jewish Agency, initiating and supervising the founding of 371 new villages, almost all moshavim for new immigrants with no previous experience in agriculture. A member of the Knesset since 1949, Eshkol was minister of agriculture (1951-1952) and minister of finance (1952-1963) before becoming prime minister and minister

Levi Eshkol.
Israel 408 (1970)

of defense in 1963. During his tenure, relations with the United States were markedly improved, and he made the first official visit to the White House by an Israeli prime minister. Eshkol was successful in obtaining aircraft and other military equipment from the United States (for the first time), which was particularly important after the Six-Day War, when the air force's conventional source of supply in France was blocked. Ramat Eshkol, a community in northeast Jerusalem, was named in his memory.

Meir, Golda (1898-1978). Fourth prime minister of Israel (1969-1974). Born Golda Mabovitch in Kiev, she and her family emigrated to the United States in 1906 and settled in Milwaukee. In 1921 Golda settled in Palestine with her husband, Morris Myerson. She was appointed as head of the Political Department of the Histadrut, when the British arrested the leaders of the *yishuv* in June 1946 in an attempt to crush the Haganah and Jewish resistance, Meyerson became the principal Jewish representative in the difficult negotiations with the Mandatory power. During the critical period between the 1947 partition vote and the proclamation of the State of Israel, Meyerson visited the United States, enlisting the aid of American Jewry by successfully presenting the case for the embattled *yishuv*. Four days before the proclamation of independence, she made a dangerous and dramatic journey across the Jordan in order to meet secretly with King Abdullah, hoping to persuade him not to join the attack on the newborn Jewish State.

Golda Meir.
Israel 770 (1981)

One of only two women signers of the Independence Proclamation, Meyerson was appointed Israel's first ambassador to Moscow. Her presence elicited a massive turnout of Jews at the Moscow Great Synagogue on the High Holy Days, the first dramatic expression of long-suppressed Jewish identity in the Soviet Union. When she became foreign minister in 1956 (a post she held until 1966), Meyerson changed her surname to Meir, in keeping with the established practice that foreign service officials Hebraicize their names. Following the death of Levi Eshkol, Golda Meir became prime minister and served in that post until 1974, when she resigned amid controversy over Israel's lack of preparedness in the Yom Kippur War of 1973.

Rabin, Yitzhak (1922-1995). Fifth prime minister (1974-77, 1992-1995) and the first native-born Israeli to hold that office. Born in Jerusalem, Rabin was a founding member of the Palmach, the secret commando unit of the Haganah. During the War of Independence, Rabin was appointed commander of the Harel Brigade, which broke the Arab siege of Jerusalem and succeeded in securing the road to Tel Aviv. When the Palmach was absorbed into the new Israel Defense Forces (IDF), Rabin rose rapidly through the ranks, eventually serving as the seventh chief of staff (1964-1967). During his term of duty, Rabin led the Israeli army to its massive victory in the Six-Day War and became a national hero.

Yitzhak Rabin.

After serving as ambassador to the United States, in 1973 Rabin was elected to the Knesset and appointed minister of labor. One year later, he became prime minister when Golda Meir resigned following publication of the Agranat Report that criticized her (among others) for Israel's lack of preparedness during the Yom Kippur war. During his three-year term, Rabin succeeded in rehabilitating the army and reviving Israel's morale and sense of security. However, Rabin was less successful in managing the Israeli economy; inflation increased and strikes became rampant. The revelation that his wife had maintained an illegal bank account in the U.S. after he had completed his service as ambassador led to Rabin's resignation and precipitated new elections, in which power switched to the Likud and Menachem Begin.

One year after being re-elected prime minister in 1992, Rabin signed the Oslo Agreement for which he shared the 1994 Nobel Peace Prize. During a peace rally the following year, Rabin was assassinated by a right-wing Israeli opposed to the return of land to the Arabs.

Begin, Menachem (1913-1992). Sixth prime minister (1977-1983). Born in Brest-Litovsk, Russia, and a graduate in law at Warsaw University, Begin was a devoted follower of Jabotinsky and the head of the Polish branch of Betar, the Revisionist Zionist youth movement. Arrested by the Soviet secret police for his Zionist activities and sentenced to eight years hard labor in the Arctic region, Begin was released a year later because he was a Polish citizen, and made his way to Palestine in 1942. A gifted orator, writer, and organizer, Begin became commander of the Irgun, a guerrilla group that declared "armed warfare" against the Mandatory government and fought a determined underground struggle against the British, who offered a reward for his apprehension.

Menachem Begin.
Israel 1153 (1993)

With the establishment of Israel, Begin founded the Herut (Freedom) party, a right wing, strongly nationalistic organization that he led in the Knesset for three decades. In 1973, Begin became leader of the opposition Likud bloc; four years later, Begin became prime minister after the Likud gained a stunning political victory and emerged as the largest party in the Knesset. He immediately devoted himself to the task of establishing peace with the Arab states. This effort culminated with the dramatic visit of President Anwar Sadat to Jerusalem and his address to the Knesset in November 1977, the inception of peace negotiations, and the historic signing of the Camp David Agreements on Sept. 17, 1978. Begin shared with Sadat (and American President Jimmy Carter) the 1978 Nobel Peace Prize, and the Israeli and Egyptian leaders signed a formal peace treaty in Washington the next year. In 1982, Begin authorized an invasion of southern Lebanon in an attempt to destroy terrorist bases shelling northern Israeli communities. In failing health, despondent over his

Begin and Sadat during Camp David Accords with President Carter in foreground. *Dominica 1207d (1989)*

wife's death, and beset by controversy over the continued Israeli presence in southern Lebanon, Begin resigned in 1983 and spent the rest of his life in virtual seclusion. His writings include *White Nights* (1957), reminiscences of his imprisonment in Russia, and *The Revolt* (1964), which describes the struggles of the Irgun.

Presidents of Israel

Weizmann, Chaim (1874-1952). First president (1949-1952). Born in Russia, Weizmann moved to Germany because of the strict quotas placed on the entry of Jews to Russian universities. In 1904, Weizmann moved to England and was deeply impressed by the order, courtesy, and tranquility of the English temperament. He became convinced that the decisive turning point in Jewish history would come through intersection with British interests. Gaining the ear of Lord Balfour, Weizmann convinced the foreign secretary to issue the famous 1917 declaration that endorsed the establishment of a Jewish national home in Palestine.

A distinguished scientist, Weizmann published a pamphlet calling for the establishment of a Hebrew university that would be Zionism's spiritual center and scientific bulwark. In 1918, he laid the cornerstone for the Hebrew University on Mt. Scopus in Jerusalem. Two years later, he was elected president of first the

Chaim Weizmann.
Israel 70 (1952)

World Zionist Organization and then the enlarged Jewish Agency. Weizmann moved from England to Palestine in 1934, serving as director of the Daniel Sieff Research Institute at Rehovot. After World War II, Weizmann made a moving appeal to the General Assembly that convinced the United Nations to retain the Negev in its plans for a Jewish State. Capturing Truman's trust and imagination, Weizmann succeeded in convincing the president to overrule powerful interests within his administration by voting for the 1947 partition proposal and immediately recognizing the new Jewish State on May 14, 1948.

After being named President of Israel, Weizmann expressed fierce resentment and surprise at the rigid limitations of his office, which was virtually confined to ceremonial events. In 1949, he was named director of the newly founded Weizmann Institute of Science (which incorporated the Sieff Institute), a growing complex of laboratories and libraries that eventually raised Israel to the highest international levels of scientific research.

Ben-Zvi, Itzhak (1884-1963). Second president (1952-1963). Born in Ukraine, the eldest son of Zevi Shimshelevich (Shimshi), Ben-Zvi immigrated to Palestine in 1907. With his future wife, Rachel Yanait (see page 169), he was among the founders of Hashomer (1909), the earliest Jewish defense force in modern Palestine, and *Achdut* (Unity), the first Hebrew socialist periodical in the Land of Israel. With the outbreak of World War I, Ben-Zvi (together with David Ben-Gurion) was imprisoned and deported; they eventually arrived in New York and founded the American He-Halutz (Pioneer) movement, which was dedicated to attracting Jewish settlers to Palestine. After the war, Ben-Zvi returned to Palestine, where he participated in the establishment of the Histadrut. From 1931-1945, Ben-Tzi was head of the *Va'ad Le'umi* (National Council), the executive arm and official representative of the Palestinian Jewish community. A member of the provisional government of the newly formed

Itzhak Ben-Zvi.
Israel 255 (1964)

State of Israel, Ben-Zvi succeeded Chaim Weizmann as president in 1952 and served in that office until his death.

In addition to his political and communal activities, Ben-Zvi published numerous scholarly works on ancient and remote Jewish communities. Ben-Zvi founded the Institute for the Study of Oriental Jewish Communities in the Middle East (1948), which later was named after him.

Shazar, Schneur Zalman (1889-1974). Third president (1963-1973). Shazar (an acronym for Shneur Zalman Rubashov) was born into a Habad community near Minsk. In 1912, he left Russia for advanced study in Germany, becoming one of the founders of the Labor Zionist movement and He-Halutz in that country. Settling in Palestine in 1924, Shazar became a member of the Histadrut secretariat and later editor-in-chief and head of the Histadrut publishing firm, Am Oved. As a member of the Jewish Agency delegation to the United Nations General Assembly, Shazar established contact with the Lubavich Rebbe, who agreed to the establishment of Kfar Chabad in Israel (especially important to Shazar since he had been named for the founder of that Hasidic dynasty). First minister of education and culture, in 1963 Shazar was elected the third president of the State of Israel, succeeding the recently deceased Itzhak Ben-Zvi. Like his predecessor, Shazar did not confine himself to state duties but made his residence a center for Israeli scholars, writers, and artists, as well as for the intellectual elite of the entire Jewish world.

Zalman Shazar.
Israel 571 (1975)

Herzog, Chaim (1918-1997). Sixth president (1983-1993). Born in Belfast, Northern Ireland, his family immigrated to Palestine in 1935 when his father succeeded Rav Kook as Chief Rabbi of Palestine. During World War II, Herzog was a tank commander and later directed British intelligence in Germany, where he identified a captive soldier as Nazi chief Heinrich Himmler. After the war, Herzog served in the underground Haganah and became chief of military intelligence in the Israel Defense Forces (1948-1950; 1954-1962). During the Six-Day War (1967), Herzog was Israel's best-known political and military commentator (in both Hebrew and English), and he subsequently became the first military governor of the West Bank. As Israel's ambassador to the United Nations (1975-1979), Herzog denounced the General Assembly's resolution defining Zionism as racism and dramatically tore up the document containing the resolution at the conclusion of his speech. Elected a Labor Party member of the Knesset in 1981, Herzog was highly respected by both major political parties and elected as the sixth president of Israel in 1983.

Chaim Herzog.
Israel 1329 (1998)

Chief Rabbis of Palestine

Kook, Abraham Isaac (1865–1935). First Ashkenazic Chief Rabbi of Palestine. Born in Latvia, Kook came to the Land of Israel in 1904, serving as chief rabbi of Jaffa and then Jerusalem before being appointed the first Ashkenazic Chief Rabbi of Palestine. Rav Kook was among the few religious leaders of his time who believed that the return to the Land of Israel marked the beginning of Divine redemption, the return of the Jewish people to Zion. Terming the existing Zionist movement incomplete, since it had only addressed the revival of the secular and material needs of the Jewish people, Kook called for an emphasis on the spiritual aspects of the national revival. In 1924, Kook founded what became known as the Yeshivah Merkaz ha-Rav in his honor, which embodied his unique religious philosophy and a positive attitude to Zionism. Though a strong advocate of a synthesis of religious and secular studies, in a 1925 address to the opening ceremony of the Hebrew University he warned that an exclusive preoccupation with scientific research would alienate man from ultimate religious values.

Ouziel, Ben-Zion Meir Hai (1880–1953). Sephardic Chief Rabbi of Palestine. Born in Jerusalem, where his father was the head of the Bet Din of the Sephardi community, Ouziel worked vigorously to raise the status of the oriental congregations while serving as rabbi in Jaffa from 1911. In spirit and ideas he was close to Rav Kook, the Ashkenazic chief rabbi, and their affinity helped to bring about more harmonious relations than previously existed between the two communities.

Herzog, Isaac Halevi (1888–1959). Ashkenazic Chief Rabbi of Israel. Born in Poland and an ardent Zionist, Herzog served as Chief Rabbi of Ireland from 1921-1936, when he accepted the invitation to become the successor of Rav Kook as Chief Rabbi of Palestine. Widely respected by the vast majority of the Jews in Palestine, including the non-religious elements (particularly in the kibbutzim), Herzog enacted decrees in matters of personal status that reconciled the necessities of modern living with the demands of *halachah*. A major participant in the various conferences and commissions organized to find a solution to the Arab-Jewish conflict, Herzog eloquently set forth the Jewish spiritual claims to the Holy Land and stressed the need of a refuge for the survivors of the Holocaust.

Rabbi A. I. Kook.
Israel 699 (1978)

Rabbi B. Z. Ouziel.
Israel 700 (1978)

Rabbi I. H. Herzog.
Israel 892 (1984)

Aliyah

Pre-State Aliyah

Aliyah is the term used to describe the coming of Jews to the Land of Israel. Literally meaning "ascent," this Hebrew word also is used to describe the act of going up to read a portion from the Torah. Although generally translated as "immigration", aliyah represents the fundamental ideal of Zionism – the act of

Rishon Le-Zion centennial.
Israel 826 (1982)

personally participating in the rebuilding of the Jewish homeland, thus raising the Jew to a higher plane of self-fulfillment as a member of the renascent nation. In the early years of the modern period, many *olim* (those making aliyah) were inspired by idealistic motives; the later waves of mass aliyah were primarily driven by persecution and distress.

The First Aliyah (1882–1903) consisted of individuals and small groups, mostly from Eastern Europe, who fled pogroms, tsarist repression, and grinding poverty to establish settle-

BILU's 70th anniversary;
Well in Petah Tikvah. *Israel 72 (1952), 27 (1949)*

ments in Palestine. The first intrepid group to band together and emigrate to the Holy Land called themselves BILU, from the Hebrew initials of the biblical verse "O House of Jacob, come let us go!" Determined to work the land as a cooperative body, they were unable to overcome either the swamp-filled valleys, stony hillsides, and burning desert sands,

or the hostility of the Turkish rulers and the implacable hatred of their Arab neighbors.

The first permanent Jewish settlements in Palestine (Rishon le-Zion, Petah Tikvah, Rosh Pinna, Zichron Ya'akov) faced severe financial crises that threatened their very existence, and

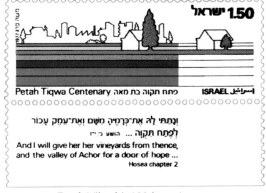

Petah Tikvah's 100th anniversary.
Israel 637 (1977)

Zichron Ya'akov's 100th anniversary.
Israel 827 (1982)

they probably would have been abandoned if financial resources had not been provided by Baron Edmond de Rothschild (1845-1934). A member of the family that became a byword for opulence and munificence, Rothschild chose to remain anonymous in this venture and was known only by his cover name, *Ha-Nadiv ha-Yadu'a* ("the Well-Known Benefactor"). As the major address for all problems of the Jews in Palestine, Rothschild was called the "Father of the Yishuv." In addition to supporting agricultural settlements, Rothschild played a major role in the development of the wine industry in Palestine and was a co-sponsor of the Palestine Electric Corporation. The early settlements of Yesud ha-Ma'alah and Nes Ziona benefited from the largesse of Michael Halperin (Mikhl; 1860-1919). When the Hovevei Zion rejected Halperin's proposal to use a large inheritance from his wealthy father to establish an industrial enterprise

Michael Halperin.
Israel 857 (1984)

Rosh Pinna's 80 anniversary.
Israel 291 (1962)

Left and middle: Yesud Ha'Ma'ala, right: Nes Ziona. *Israel 166 (1959), 849 (1983) 850 (1983)*

Pioneeer work. Left to right: clearing the land; building the harbor; plowing. *Israel 616, 617, 619 (1976)*

Road building.
Israel 618 (1976)

Clearing thistles with
hoe. *Israel 245 (1963)*

Planting trees.
Israel 620 (1976)

in the Land of Israel, Halperin instead directed his funds toward the purchase of land for these pioneering settlements.

The Second Aliyah (1904–14), which laid the foundation for the labor movement, consisted of about 40,000 pioneers, primarily from Eastern Europe, who generally worked as hired laborers in settlements or the cities. Imbued with socialist ideals and severely disappointed by the failure of the 1905 revolution (as well as shocked by the 1903 Kishinev pogroms), they decided to create their own revolutionary movement on the basis of national revival. More self-reliant than their predecessors, the members of the Second Aliyah were determined to develop a workers' commonwealth in the Land of Israel. They established the first Jewish labor parties (Po'alei Zion) and self-help institutions, associations for self-defense (Hashomer; or "Watchman"), the first collective settlements (*kvuzot*), and laid the foundations for a new Hebrew press and literature.

The Third Aliyah (1919–23), which started immediately after World War I, contained more than 35,000 young pioneers (*halutzim*) belonging to the He-Halutz, Hashomer ha-Za'ir ("Young Guard"), Betar (Revisionist Zionist) and Mizrachi (Religious Zionist) movements. These groups set up a network of training centers in the Diaspora, in which members studied the ideals of the movement, learned Hebrew and its literature, and gained experience in manual labor and farming. This ensured that the young men and women arrived in Palestine not as complete novices, but equipped with a consistent social philosophy, some experience of living in communes, and at least some rudimentary skills. The immigrants of the Third Aliyah became the most prominent leaders of the *yishuv* (Jewish community of Palestine) and the new State of Israel. Together with the veterans of the Second Aliyah, they paved the way for a future state by establishing the Histadrut (comprehensive countrywide labor organization); playing a leading role in the creation of the Haganah defense organization; providing workers for the construction of housing and roads and the beginnings of industry; strengthening the foundations of Jewish agriculture; and expanding the map of Jewish settlement by founding many kibbutzim and moshavim.

Third Aliyah.
Israel 1214 (1994)

The Fourth Aliyah (1924–28) totaled some 67,000 olim, more than half escaping the economic crisis and anti-Jewish policies in Poland. Many of these newcomers were of the middle class and had some capital of their own, which they invested in small workshops and factories and the construction of housing in the towns and main cities, considerably increasing the urban population.

The Fifth Aliyah (1929–39) of more than 250,000 Jews, many of whom were fleeing Germany and Austria following Hitler's rise to power, transformed the character of the *yishuv*. They constituted the first large-scale influx from Western and Central Europe, who transferred large amounts of capital and contributed valuable skills and business experience. A relatively high proportion of them practiced medicine or one of the other professions, and they pro-

Fourth Aliyah.
Israel 1215 (1994)

vided a majority of the musicians who formed the new Philharmonic Orchestra (as well as a considerable part of its audiences). The flood tide of immigration was halted in 1936 with the onset of the Arab revolt and almost eliminated by the infamous White Paper of 1939, which prevented thousands of Jews from escaping the impending catastrophe in Europe.

In 1933, a new type of immigration, called Youth Aliyah, was started as a branch of the Zionist movement founded for the purpose of rescuing Jewish children and young people from hardship, persecution, or deprivation and giving them care and education in Palestine. The work was largely financed by Hadassah and organized by its leader, Henrietta Szold. Youth Aliyah started its activities in Germany on the eve of the Nazis' rise to power and saved many children who had to leave their families or were orphaned by the Holocaust. Later its work was extended to other countries when the need arose; after the establishment of the State of Israel, Youth Aliyah looked after many young people entrusted to its care by new immigrant parents already in the country, either in youth communities in kibbutzim or in its own centers and children's villages. By the end of 1970, Youth Aliyah had cared for about 140,000 young people, 90% of whom received residential care.

Top: "Illegal" ship.
Bottom: Fifth Aliyah.
Israel 267 (1994), 856 (1983)

"Illegal" immigration, known as "Aliyah Bet," was the concerted effort of the *yishuv* to circumvent British restrictions severely limiting the number of Jew permitted to immigrate from Europe to Palestine to escape the terrors of Nazi Germany. The underground Mossad was set up by the Haganah to charter ships to take refugees by sea to safety in Palestine. The Mandatory government did every-

Clandestine immigration.
Israel 1305 (1997)

Youth Aliyah. Immigration by ship and plane; agricultural training, gardening, vocational training, and scientific education.
Israel 94-99 (1955)

thing in its power to stop the stream of "illegal" immigrants, exerting pressure on other governments to prevent them leaving and dispatching patrol boats to track the ships from the moment of their departure until their arrival off the Palestinian coast. Nevertheless, Aliyah Bet succeeded in bringing more than 15,000 Jews to Palestine before the outbreak of World War II. After the war, the Mossad resumed large-scale operations at sea and succeeded in bringing to Palestine more than 80,000 refugee survivors of European Jewry who had reached the shores of Italy, France, Romania, Yugoslavia, and Greece. Haganah members and local settlers received passengers on boats that arrived clandestinely at night in desolate places along the coast, carrying on their shoulders those who were unable to wade to the shore (the elderly, the sick, women, and children). Once on land, the refugees were immediately brought in buses and trucks to kibbutzim; having changed their clothes, they could not be recognized as "illegal" immigrants by the searching British police.

Intercepted boats were impounded and the passengers transferred to detention camps such as in Cyprus, where more than 50,000 were kept in prison-like conditions and 2,000 children were born. The struggle for the right of free immigration reached its peak in summer 1947, when 4,515 refugees on board the *Exodus 1947* reached the shores of Palestine. After a fight with the British on board (three killed, 28 injured), the passengers were removed from the *Exodus* to three transports that took them to France. However, the French government refused to take them off the British deportation boat against their will, and the refugees themselves chose to endure the intense discomfort of their stifling cramped quarters in the summer heat rather than disembark. Finally taken to Hamburg, the refugees were forcibly removed and transferred to a British internment camp in Germany. This incident, which aroused world opinion against Britain's policy of closing the gates of Palestine to survivors of the Holocaust, played a major role in gaining widespread sympathy for the Zionist cause.

Aliyah After the Birth of Israel

As defined in the Declaration of Independence, "The State of Israel shall be open to Jewish immigration and the ingathering of the exiles." All previous restrictions were abolished, and the official policy was to strive for the prophetic dream – the return to their homeland of all Jews who were willing and able to come and the transfer of complete Jewish communities within a short space of time. This national purpose was given legislative expression in the Law of Return

Welcoming immigrants; farm family.
Israel 362-363 (1968)

Left: Exodus of Russian Jews; middle: Airlift of Yemen's Jews; right: Teaching Hebrew to new immigrants. *Israel 487 (1972), 407 (1970), 1065 (1990)*

(1950), which guaranteed every Jew the automatic right to become an *oleh* (i.e., to settle permanently in Israel), unless deemed a danger to public health or security, and to become a citizen immediately on arrival. At an early stage, it was decided that immigration and absorption should be the joint tasks of the State of Israel and Diaspora Jewry. The World Zionist Organization, represented by the Jewish Agency, was therefore charged with encouraging and organizing immigration and assisting in the absorption of the immigrants in close cooperation and coordination with the Israeli government.

In response to emergency circumstances and pressing needs, the Jewish Agency on several occasions had to improvise the movement of tens of thousands of people within a very short time and in adverse conditions. Organized as special operations, these migrations were planned and executed by special emissaries. The most dramatic were Operation Magic Carpet, for the Yemenite Jews, and Operation Ezra and Nehemiah, which brought to Israel virtually all of Iraqi Jewry.

Top: Airlifting Chernobyl's children *Israel 1323 (1997)*. Bottom: North African immigration. *Israel 508 (1973)*

A substantial increase in immigration from Western Europe and the Americas came in the wake of the Six-Day War of 1967. This conflict also intensified Jewish consciousness and devotion to Israel among Soviet Jews, both as a reaction against official support for Arab hostility to Israel and because of renewed pride in Israel's achievements. For the first time, large numbers of Jews were allowed to leave the Soviet Union; by 1983, about 170,000 had settled in Israel. In the mid-1980s, however, the flow of Russian immigrants was drastically reduced, and almost 400,000 Jews wishing to emigrate entered a period of harassment and unemployment, acquiring the status of "Refuseniks." American Jewish groups organized mass rallies and protest meetings

Top: Immigration of Iraqi Jews. Bottom: Yemenite Jews flown to Israel and settled. *Israel 424 (1970), 178-9 (1960)*

The Jewish World in Stamps

Ethnic costumes of Jews from Asia and Africa. Left to right: Ethiopia, Kurdistan, Salonica (Greece). *Israel 1297-1299 (1997)*

that succeeded in allowing some Russian Jews to be released, but a mass exodus only occurred under the policy of *glasnost* declared by Soviet leader Mikhail Gorbachev in 1989. Over the past decade, about one million Russians have arrived in Israel, and they now constitute 20% of the Jewish population of the country. Another mass migration of a desperate people

was the airlifting of more than 22,000 Ethiopian Jews in Operations Moses (1984) and Solomon (1991). After the nuclear accident in Chernobyl, at-risk Jewish children were flown to Israel under the auspices of Chabad.

From a Jewish population in Palestine of only 24,000 in 1882, there are now approximately 5 million Jews in the State of Israel (out of a total population of 6.3 million). Since the early days of the First Aliyah, about 3 million individuals from all corners of the globe have made aliyah to Israel.

Ethnic costumes of Jews from Asia and Africa. Clockwise: Morocco, Bukhara, India, and Yemen. *Israel 1359-3560 (1999); 1373-74 (1999)*

Settlement

The settlement of the Land of Israel was the essence of "pragmatic" Zionism. The Zionist Executive assigned responsibility for this task to Arthur Ruppin (1876-1943), who became popularly known as the "father of Zionist settlement." Stressing the need for settlers and the settlement agency to work together as equal partners in every enterprise, he supported the creation of new forms of settlements (kvuzah, kibbutz, moshav) and defended them against all their opponents. From the outset of his work, Ruppin aspired to purchase contiguous tracts of land for agricultural settlement and to create a self-governing population.

Kibbutz. *Israel 921 (1985)*

Kibbutz

The kibbutz is a voluntary collective community, mainly agricultural, in which there is no private wealth and which is responsible for all the needs of the members and their families. A uniquely Israeli institution, the early *halutzim* (pioneers) established the kibbutz on the socialist principle of complete equality. Members of each settlement own the property in common, with every member having a vote in the governing body. All members must work; hired labor is employed only in times of crisis. Women share fully in the life and work of the community. Some kibbutzim set up special youth houses where the children lived, rather than residing in family homes with their parents.

Ruppin. *Israel 740 (1979)*

The first collective settlement, termed a *kvuzah*, was Deganiah Aleph. It was founded in 1909 by a group of pioneers, who, after working at first as employees of the Palestine Land Development Company, undertook collective responsibility for the working of the farm. By the end of 1918, 29 kvuzot had been established on Jewish National Fund land under the responsibility of the Zionist Organization. The early settlements had limited memberships based upon the idea that the community should be small enough to constitute a kind of enlarged family. However, as the number of immigrants rose after World War I, larger, self-sufficient villages were established to combine agriculture with industrial enterprises to increase employment opportunities, lessen the dependence of the settlements on the cities, and raise the standard of living. The first of this type (termed a "kibbutz") was En Harod, founded in 1921; many other kibbutzim soon followed, and gradually the distinction between the two terms almost disappeared. The kibbutzim and kvuzot combined to establish various national federations in accordance with their social character, political affiliations, or religious outlook. These federations coordinate the activities of their members in such matters as marketing, education, culture, credit, and relations with the government and other outside groups.

Kibbutz Degania. *Israel 167 (1959)*

The kibbutzim received their manpower mainly from pioneering youth movements abroad that were dedicated

Merhavia. *Israel 165 (1959)*

Valley of Jezreel. *Israel 459 (1971)*

The Jewish World in Stamps

to building the Jewish National Home and creating a basis for the socialist society of the future. They played an important part in expanding the map of Jewish settlement and safeguarding the growing community. In the late 1930s, many were set up overnight on the Tower and Stockade plan. The Jewish National Fund had acquired large tracts of land in areas distant from Jewish population centers, where de facto possession was in jeopardy unless the land was settled. However, ordinary methods could not be used because of Arab antagonism. Convoys carrying hundreds of helpers, prefabricated huts, and fortifications set out at daybreak, protected by Jewish Settlement Police. By nightfall they completed the erection of the settlement, surrounded by a double wall of planks with a filling of earth and stones, dominated by a central tower equipped with a searchlight and electric generator to enable the countryside to be scanned for signs of hostility. Over a ten-year period, 118 settlements were established in this way. The kibbutzim served as bases for the Haganah defense force and later its commando division, the Palmach. Most of the new villages established under emergency conditions during and immediately after World War II, especially in the Negev, were kibbutzim; by the establishment of the State of Israel, kibbutzim numbered 149 of the 291 Jewish villages in the country.

Tower and Stockade.
Israel 235-236 (1963)

Moshav

Also known as *moshav ovedim* (workers' settlement), the moshav is a cooperative agricultural village that differs from a kibbutz in that each member has a home and plot of land worked by himself and his family. However, all marketing of produce and purchase of supplies is done cooperatively, and some of the machinery is owned by the moshav as a whole. The idea of the moshav evolved during World War I in the quest for a form of settlement that would not only express national and social aspirations on the basis of collective principles like the kibbutz, but also provide scope for individual initiative and independent farm management. The first two moshavim were founded in 1921 – Nahalal in the northern Jezreel Valley and Kefar Yehezkel in the eastern part. When the State of Israel was established in 1948, there were 58 moshavim in the country.

Most of the new immigrants who arrived in large numbers immediately after the establishment of the State differed in many respects from the original pioneers, who had settled on the land after spending years in training and preparation. Instead, these newcomers consisted mainly of families with many children, elderly persons, and even entire communities brought over en masse. The moshav, with its family structure, was deemed to be the only medium of settling these immigrants on the land. By 1956, 250 new moshavim had been established.

Negev settlements.
Israel 1276 (1996)

Top: Gedera. Middle: Mazkeret Batya.
Bottom: Nahalal. *Israel 920 (1985), 828 (1982), 646 (1997)*

Nahal

Nahal ("fighting pioneer youth") is a special unit of the Israel Defense Forces whose soldiers are organized in *garinim* (literally, "seeds") of pioneering youth movements in Israel and Zionist youth movements in the Diaspora that educate their members toward cooperative settlement in Israel. During their term of military service, these soldiers simultaneously participate in intensive training and social and ideological preparation toward their future as members of new or existing cooperative agricultural settlements. All members of such a potential group are mobilized together and form a single army unit. After a period of combined agricultural and military training in a kibbutz or at a Nahal outpost, the men generally receive advanced training in paratroop, tank, artillery, engineering, or other units. Both men and women complete their military obligation by serving in a frontier settlement.

Upon conclusion of military service, those Nahal soldiers who wish to return to civilian life do so; others remain and continue to live in the settlement. As long as a new settlement is not self-supporting, it remains within Nahal, under military discipline and tied organically to the army. When the settlement has developed and begins to be self-supporting, it is transferred by the army to the civilian authority and becomes a civilian village.

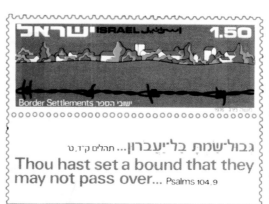
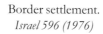

Border settlement.
Israel 596 (1976)

Nahal settlement.
Israel 646 (1977)

Southern settlements: Hevel Ha-Besor; Arava.
Israel 860-861 (1984)

Defense

The development of the self-defense force of the *yishuv* was a critical element in the history of Jewish settlement in Palestine. The Turkish regime was hostile to the first Jewish agricultural settlements that were established in the last quarter of the 19th century. The safety of the settlers depended on the good graces of the local strong man (Bedouin or village sheik), and they frequently had to cope with border friction, disputes regarding water rights, and intrusions on their crops and property. Faced with the choice of either fighting for their rights or being left to the mercy of their neighbors, individuals and groups of young people organized to protect themselves. This was the period of the first watchmen (*shomerim*), who guarded the small communities and their fields with the help of the young settlers and hired Bedouin.

Manya Shochat.
Israel 409 (1970)

Hashomer

Hashomer (literally, "the watchman") was the first organized self-defense group of the Jewish settlers in Palestine. It was founded in 1909 by pioneers of the Second Aliyah, many of whom had been active in revolutionary movements and Jewish self-defense in Russia and were critical of the use of non-Jewish guards to protect life and property in the Jewish settlements. The members of Hashomer spoke Arabic, wore a mixture of Arab and Circassian dress, and carried modern weapons. Some became expert horsemen and were romantic figures throughout the *yishuv*, creating for the first time the image of the Jewish fighter. The small body of professional watchmen carefully studied Arab methods of fighting, trying to outdo their enemy in organizational ability, discipline, and force of arms. Among the leaders of Hashomer were Israel and Manya Shochat, Alexander Zaid, and future Israeli president Itzhak ben Zvi and his wife Rachel Yanait. In late 1912, Israel Shochat sent a memorandum to the Executive of the Zionist Organization suggesting the establishment of a country-wide organization for the defense of the settlements that would incorporate every male capable of bearing arms.

Top: Tel Hai monument.
Bottom: Alexander Zaid monument.
Israel 846, 863 (1984)

Rachel Yanait (Ben-Zvi).
Israel 1096 (1991)

Jewish Legion

During World War I, under the leadership of Vladimir Jabotinsky, a Jewish Legion was established with the express purpose of helping the British army to conquer Palestine and, on the conclusion of the war, to serve as the garrison of the country ensuring the security of the Jewish settlements. After the Balfour Declaration (1917) proclaimed support of a

The Jewish Legion.
Israel 1001 (1988)

national home for the Jews in Palestine, Arab opposition to Jewish immigration and settlement became increasingly violent. When Arab riots broke out in Jerusalem during Passover 1920, the British prevented a self-defense force under Jabotinsky from entering the Old City; instead, they arrested him and his men and sentenced them to long prison terms. In response to an Arab uprising in French-ruled northern Upper Galilee that endangered settlements, the Jewish authorities were inclined to transfer the settlers to the area of Palestine under British occupation. This suggestion was indignantly rejected by Hashomer, which sent reinforcements of men and ammunition to the besieged villages and entrusted the organization of their defense to Joseph Trumpeldor. The stand against the Arabs at Tel Hai in March 1920, during which Trumpeldor and several of his comrades fell in battle, became a symbol of Jewish resistance. It also established a new principle in the *yishuv*'s defense policy — "No Jewish settlement is to be abandoned for any security consideration whatsoever." Both of these events convinced the Jewish leaders that the *yishuv* could rely on neither a foreign army nor a Jewish Legion under a foreign command, whose policy was guided by extraneous military and political considerations. Instead, the *yishuv* needed to develop an independent defense force, completely free of foreign authority which, unlike the elite Hashomer, would encompass large numbers of people and be subordinate to a public Jewish authority

Haganah

The Haganah was the underground military organization of the *yishuv* in Palestine from 1920 until the establishment of the State of Israel in 1948. For the first nine years of its existence, the Haganah was a loose organization of local defense groups in the large towns and in several of the settlements. It enjoyed sympathy but no material support from the Zionist Organization, which regarded the Haganah as merely a local version of the Jewish self-defense organizations of Eastern Europe. This attitude changed dramatically following the Arab riots of August 1929, when it became evident that the bloodiest anti-Jewish riots and the heaviest looting had occurred in those places where there was no Haganah, such as Hebron, or where the Haganah was weak, as in Safed. In contrast, the Jewish population of Jerusalem, Tel Aviv, Haifa, and several of the settlements had been saved by the stand of the Haganah forces. Following the riots, the Haganah went through a difficult organizational crisis, during which a group of local commanders seceded and established the Irgun, consisting mainly of right-wing and Revisionist elements. From 1931 to 1936, under the leadership of Eliyahu Golomb, the Haganah became a large organization encompassing nearly all the youth and adults in the settlements as well as several thousand members from each of the cities. It initiated a comprehensive training program for its members, ran officers' training courses, and established central arms depots into which a continuous stream of light arms (rifles and pistols) flowed from Europe. At the same time, the foundation was laid for the underground production of arms. During this period, the Haganah developed two basic principles that made it even closer to becoming a national army – the concept of a single defense organization, subject to a unified central command, which inevitably entailed opposition to the existence of dissident groups; and the recognition of the authority of the political leadership of the *yishuv*, the Jewish Agency and the National Committee).

From 1936–39, the *yishuv* in both the cities and the countryside was under a perpetual siege and attacked by Arab guerilla bands. With the outbreak of these riots, the Jewish Agency declared that the *yishuv*'s response to Arab acts of terror would be "restraint." In

Haganah oath and badge.
Israel 1058 (1990)

Eliyahu Golomb.
Israel 688 (1978)

Moshe Sneh.
Israel 689 (1978)

Orde Wingate.
Israel 881 (1984)

The Jewish World in Stamps

addition to the moral side of the question, the Jewish Agency believed that a policy of restraint would lead to a positive response from the British authorities, who would provide the beleaguered Jews with arms. Although the British did not officially recognize the Haganah, they established the Jewish Settlement Police and provided this auxiliary force with rifles and even light machine guns. Units were stationed in all agricultural settlements and in many urban quarters in the country, and this force served as a cover for the activities and training of Haganah members. The British administration attempted to make the establishment of the police units conditional upon the surrender of all illegal arms, but this was resolutely rejected by the Haganah command, which saw these legal units as only one aspect of its activities. Indeed, the Haganah soon became more proactive, setting up field squads that were trained specifically for war against terrorist gangs. Coordinated by Moshe Sneh, these units learned the methods of guerilla warfare and gained battle experience with the establishment of the Special Night Squads under the command of Charles Orde Wingate (1903-1944), a British captain who became a passionate supporter of the Jewish cause. Known in the *yishuv* as *Ha-Yedid* (the friend), Wingate had a profound impact, on the Palmach and the Haganah and trained such future Israeli military leaders as Yigal Allon and Moshe Dayan. The Wingate Institute for Physical Education and Sport in Netanya is named in his honor.

During and after World War II, the central point of the struggle between the British administration and the Jews of Palestine was the issue of free Jewish immigration, which was virtually prohibited by the 1939 White Paper issued by the British to appease the Arabs. The task of organizing the "illegal" entry of immigrants from all over Europe into Palestine fell to members of the Haganah. The British concentrated a force of 100,000 in the area to control the Jews. Searches for hidden arms were conducted day and night, and many Haganah leaders were arrested and sent to detention camps. In the spring of 1947, David Ben-Gurion assumed the task of preparing the Haganah for the possible showdown with the armed forces of Arabs in Palestine and those of the Arab states. Plans were laid for full-scale mobilization of the *yishuv*, the founding of an air force, and the expansion of arms manufacture and acquisition. Within weeks after the onset of the War of Independence, the Haganah was transformed into the Israel Defense Forces – the regular army of the State of Israel.

Palmach song.
Israel 1108 (1992)

Palmach

The Palmach (acronym for *plugot mahatz*, translated as "assault companies" or "shock troops") was the commando unit of the Haganah under the leadership of Yitzhak Sadeh. Organized in 1939 when Axis forces had moved dangerously close to the approaches to Palestine, its members achieved high standards in physical fitness, field training, and guerilla fighting by day and night. The Palmach carried out numerous daring missions – rescuing thousands of Jews from Nazi Europe, running the British blockades of Palestine in the "death ships" of the "illegal immigration" period, and guarding the settlements and highways as the British were preparing to leave Palestine. During the War of Independence, Palmach members bore the brunt of the Arab attack, and a large number lost their lives in action. Many of the Palmach commanders, including Yigal Allon, Moshe Dayan, and Yitzhak Rabin, became leaders of Israel.

Yitzhak Sadeh.
Israel 691 (1978)

Major Palmach battles in War of Independence: Left, Metsudat Yesha (Galilee); right, Kastel (on road to Jerusalem). *Israel 46-47 (1951)*

Irgun and Lehi

The Irgun (*Irgun Zeva'i Leumi*, IZL, or Etzel; "National Military Organization") was an underground military force that was ideologically linked to the Revisionist movement and accepted the authority of its leader, Vladimir Jabotinsky. Rejecting the "restraint" policy of the Haganah,

the Irgun carried out armed reprisals against Arabs. The Irgun took as its symbol a hand gripping a rifle over a map of all of Mandatory Palestine, including Transjordan. After the publication of the White Paper in 1939, the Irgun directed its activities against the British authorities, sabotaging government property and attacking security officers. The British retaliated with widespread arrests, and at the outbreak of World War II, when hundreds of Revisionists and members of the Irgun (including its commander David Raziel) were in prison, the Irgun declared a truce for the duration of the conflict. This led to the splitting off of a new underground group (*Lohamei Herut Israel*, Lehi; "Fighters for the Freedom of Israel", or "Stern Gang") led by Avraham (Ya'ir) Stern, which resorted to terror tactics, including assassination, in continuing the attempt to drive the British out of Palestine. When the British continued to block Jewish immigration into Palestine even once the full extent of the Holocaust in the Nazi-occupied territories became known, the Irgun under Menachem Begin declared war against the British administration, attacking and blowing up government offices and police stations and capturing weapons and ammunition. However, each Irgun exploit was countered by an act of British repression, and the arrests swelled to thousands after the Irgun blew up a wing of the King David Hotel, the administrative headquarters of the Mandatory government.

Top: Lehi. Bottom: Avraham Stern. *Israel 1099 (1991), 692 (1978)*

After the establishment of the State of Israel, the several thousand members of the Irgun cooperated with the Haganah, by then the official army of the State, in fighting off Arab invaders. However, open hostility briefly erupted between the Irgun and the Haganah in June 1948 when an Irgun ship, Altalena, clandestinely reached the shores of Israel carrying 800 military volunteers and a huge quantity of weapons and ammunition. Fearing that the Irgun meant to start a revolt to topple Israel's provisional government, the leaders of the Haganah ordered that the ship be handed over to them. When the Irgun countered by demanding 20% of the arms for the use of its military units in Jerusalem, Ben-Gurion ordered Israeli artillery to blow up the ship. Contrary to the fears of some, the Irgun did not rebel, and soon most of the Irgun members were incorporated into the Israel Defense Forces.

Top: Etzel. Bottom: David Raziel. *Israel 1100 (1991), 690 (1978)*

Israel Defense Forces

Israel Defense Forces (*Zeva Haganah le-Israel,* or *Zahal*) was established on May 26, 1948, as the army of the new State of Israel. A true citizen's army, the IDF has a relatively small number of career soldiers and is essentially based on reserve service of the civilian population, retaining much of the pre-state character of a popular militia. Because almost all the Jewish youth of the country have to pass

Monument to Dov Gruner (Irgun member executed by the British) by Chana Orloff. *Israel 865 (1984)*

The Jewish World in Stamps

Sword and Laurel (20th anniversary of the IDF).
Israel 365 (1968)

through its ranks, the IDF has proved to be one of the most important factors, together with the school system, in integrating new immigrants as well as the various cultural elements of the population of Israel. Soldiers are taught Hebrew, Jewish history, and the geography of the county, as well as trained in the trades of their choice so that they will be better prepared for productive work when they return to civilian life. Most yeshiva students, married women, and mothers are exempted from the draft. Women from strictly Orthodox homes who have religious objections to serving in the army must perform national service as teachers or nurses. Israeli Arabs are also exempt, but Druze men are drafted at their own request. Following their term of national service, men and women without children remain in the reserves, and men generally report each year for various periods of training. This arrangement enables able-bodied citizens to be mobilized for combat within hours if there is a national emergency.

Gadna (*Gedudei No'ar*, "Youth Corps") is a voluntary pre-army youth movement that trains 13- to 18-year-olds in defense and national service. Functioning in high schools and youth clubs, Gadna provides firsthand knowledge of Israel's geography and topography, physical fitness, marksmanship, scouting, field exercises, comradeship, teamwork, and mutual aid. During the Sinai Campaign of 1956 and the Six-Day War of 1967, Gadna youngsters effectively replaced reservists mobilized for active duty in their civilian jobs in the postal system, civil defense, schools, hospitals, industry, and agriculture.

Israel Defense Forces'
50th anniversary.
Israel 1333 (1998)

Gadna (Youth Corps).
Israel 818 (1982)

First Major Israel Defense Figure

Trumpeldor, Joseph (1880-1920). Zionist leader, soldier, and founder of the pioneer movement He-Halutz. Born in the northern Caucasus of Russia, Trumpeldor fought in the Russo-Japanese War of 1904, where he lost his left arm and was decorated four times for conspicuous bravery. In 1912, together with a group of his comrades, Trumpeldor moved to the Land of Israel. When World War I broke out, Trumpeldor refused to take Ottoman citizenship and was deported to Egypt. In Alexandria, he, with Jabotinsky, advocated the establishment of a legion of volunteers from among fellow deportees that would put itself at the disposal of the British to help liberate the country from the Turks. He organized the Zion Mule Corps and assisted in the development of the Jewish Legion. When the tsarist government fell in 1917, Trumpeldor returned to Russia hoping to organize an army of 10,000 Jews to lead over the Caucasus and Anatolia to Palestine. However, this plan failed when the Bolsheviks took power and Russia signed a peace treaty with Germany in January 1918. Trumpeldor then devoted himself to the establishment of the He-Halutz pioneer movement and succeeded in getting a group of them out of Russia.

Back in Palestine, Trumpeldor turned to Jewish self-defense work. At the end of World War I, the border between Syria and Palestine was unsettled, and there were three small Jewish settlements (Metulla, Ayelet Hashachar, and Tel Hai) in the disputed area. After the British and French forces had withdrawn, these communities lay exposed to bands of hostile Arabs. Realizing the importance of keeping these settlements within the boundaries of Palestine, Trumpeldor organized a small force to defend them. Reaching Tel Hai, Trumpeldor and his band succeeded in defending the settlement, but he was killed in battle. His last words were, "Never mind; it is good to die for our country." The life and death of Trumpeldor became a symbol to pioneer youth from all parts of the Diaspora, and songs, poems, and stories were written about him. His memory inspired both the pioneering socialist movements and right-wing youth groups.

Joseph Trumpeldor.
Israel 408 (1970)

Leading Israeli Defense Figure During Israel's Formative Years

Dayan, Moshe (1915-1981). Military commander and statesman. Born in Kibbutz Degania and raised in Nahalal, the first moshav, at age 14 Dayan joined the Haganah. While serving with the Allied forces that liberated Lebanon and Syria from the Vichy French in World War II, Dayan lost his left eye and adopted the black eye patch that became his distinguishing feature. During the War of Independence, Dayan was commander of the Jerusalem front. He was Chief of Staff of Israeli forces from 1953-1958 and supervised the 1956 Sinai Campaign. After leaving the army, Dayan was elected to the Knesset and served as minister of agriculture (1959-1964). With the buildup of tension between Egypt and Israel in 1967, by popular demand Dayan was appointed minister of defense just before the brilliant success of the Six-Day War, which greatly enhanced his reputation. After the war, Dayan headed a liberal military government over the new territories. Widely blamed for Israel's lack of preparedness for the 1973 Yom Kippur War, Dayan resigned his defense portfolio. Four years later, Dayan quit the Labor Party and crossed the floor of the Knesset to become foreign minister under Likud prime minister Menachem Begin. In this capacity he played a vital role in the American-mediated Egyptian-Israeli peace talks and emerged as one of the chief architects of the Camp David accords.

Moshe Dayan.
Israel 1000 (1988)

Top, left to right: Auster plane in 1948 war; Vautour fighter-bomber in the 60's; fighter-bomber formation.
Israel 342 (1967), 222-223 (1962).
Middle, from left: Kfir C2 fighter; Merkava-MK1 battle tank.
Israel 852 (1983), 854 (1983).
Bottom, from left: . Destroyer; Reshef-class missile boat.
Israel 382 (1969), 853 (1983)

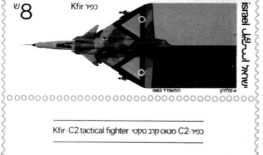 

 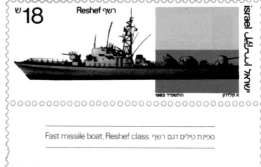

Independence Day and Memorial Day

Independence Day

Independence Day (Yom ha-Atzma'ut) is celebrated on the 5th of Iyar, the Hebrew date of the promulgation of the Declaration of Independence and the establishment of the State of Israel on May 14, 1948. When the anniversary falls on a Sabbath or a Friday, it is celebrated on the preceding Thursday. Independence Day is marked by dancing in the streets, fireworks displays, picnics in the countryside, and a variety of official ceremonies and organized open-air entertainment. Although usually translated as "Independence Day," *atzma'ut* comes a Hebrew root word meaning "bone," and thus may better reflect the positive affirmation of "Identity" day. Rather than celebrating a past event, *atzma'ut* indicates continued striving in the present and future to affirm one's own identity.

The festivities of Independence Day begin on the eve of the holiday with a ceremony on Mt. Herzl in Jerusalem, at the grave of the prophet of Jewish statehood. The speaker of the Knesset ushers in the festival by lighting a torch, from which are kindled 12 other torches to symbolize the tribes of Israel. Each year, the torchbearers are chosen to represent outstanding phases in the modern history of the nation and its struggle for statehood and survival. For years, the main official event was a military parade, but this was discontinued after the 1968 march in reunited Jerusalem to mark the 20th anniversary of the State. Israel Prizes for distinction in various fields of literary, artistic, and scientific endeavor are presented at a ceremony held at the Hebrew University in Jerusalem.

Clockwise: immigration struggle; Yad Mordecai battlefield (with thistle); Safed (with anemone); Degania battlefield (with cornflower). *Israel 33 (1950), 62-64 (1952)*

At the Hebrew Song Festival, new songs compete for popular approval (this was the venue where Naomi Shemer's "Jerusalem of Gold" was first heard in 1967, shortly before the Six-Day War), and an International Bible Contest is held for Jewish youth.

In the Diaspora, Yom ha-Atzma'ut is celebrated with a variety of parades, cultural events, fairs, and public ceremonies designed to foster solidarity with the State of Israel.

Beginning in 1950, Israel has issued stamps to commemorate Independence Day. Through 1965, these stamps were also issued to remember those who died fighting for Israel's freedom. Starting in 1966, there were separate stamps for Independence Day and Memorial Day. Israel continued to issue stamps for Independence Day each year through 1973 (25th anniversary); since that time, they have been issued only every 5 years.

Marigold at Yehiam; narcissus at Gesher. *Israel 84-85 (1954)*

Anemones and State emblem. *Israel 73 (1953)*

Israel Independence Day stamps

From left: Lit Menorah; "Eight Years of Israel;" jet marking "9;" menorah and olive branch.
Israel 93 (1955), 119 (1956), 128 (1957), 142 (1958)

Anemone, cyclamen, narcissus. *Israel 157-159 (1959);* sand lily; Oenothera. *Israel 180-181 (1960)*

Myrtle, sea onion, oleander.
Israel 204-206 (1961)

The Jewish World in Stamps

Israel Independence Day stamps
(continued)

Left: White lily, hollyhock, tulips.
Israel 238-240 (1963)

Below, left to right: terrestrial spectroscope, macromolecules of the living cell, electronic computer.
Israel 256-258 (1964)

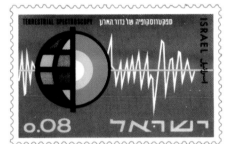
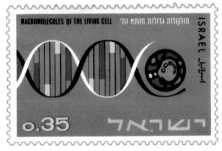

Below, left to right: Irrigation of the desert; flags on rooftops; fireworks over Tel Aviv; warships and Super Mirage jets, Haifa. *Israel 293 (1965), 308-310 (1966)*

Swamp orchid, Maria iris, lupin.
Israel 414-416 (1970)

Memorial Day

Yom ha-Zikaron (Day of Remembrance) is a memorial day for those who died fighting for the State of Israel. It is observed on the 4th of Iyar (the day before Israel Independence Day) in solemn civil, military, and religious ceremonies throughout the country. Memorial candles are lit in army camps, schools, synagogues, and public places; flags are flown at half-mast. By law, all places of entertainment are closed on the eve of Yom ha-Zikaron, and broadcasting and educational bodies are required to stress the solemnity of the day. At 11 A.M., sirens are sounded throughout Israel, signaling two minutes of silence as the entire country comes to a halt.

Soldiers' memorial,
Upper Galilee.
Israel 311 (1966)

War of Independence (road to
Jerusalem) memorial.
Israel 341 (1967)

Left to right: Rifles and helmet; Israel's flag at half
mast; memorial flame. *Israel 366 (1968), 383 (1969),
413 (1970)*

Defense Forces emblem.
Israel 446 (1971)

Flowers.
Israel 493 (1972)

Left: Memorial flame. Right:
Soldier with prayer-shawl.
Israel 524 (1973), 535 (1974)

Top: Paratroopers' memorial, Bilu-Gedera.
Right: 8th Brigade monument,
Ben-Gurion Airport.
Israel 632 (1977), 600 (1976)

Left: Eternal flame over soldier's grave. Right:
Memorial tablet for the unknown soldiers.
Israel 562-563 (1975)

Navy memorial, Ashdod.
Israel 729 (1979)

Left to right: Road of Courage monument; Bik'at ha-Yarden
memorial; Armor memorial; Steel Division memorial.
Israel 750 (1980), 782 (1981), 819 (1982), 837 (1983)

Left to right: Druse memorial, Daliyat ha-Carmel;
Golani memorial and museum; Negev Brigade
memorial. *Israel 866 (1984), 905 (1985), 937 (1986)*

Top: Ammunition Hill memorial,
Jerusalem;
bottom: Intelligence Service memorial,
Glilot. *Israel 961 (1987), 1080 (1991)*

Top left: Israel at 40; top right:
Fallen airmen memorial; left:
Artillery Corps memorial.
*Israel 988 (1988), 1013 (1989),
1055 (1990)*

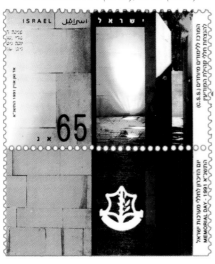

Left: Border Police
memorial; right:
Medical Corps
memorial.
*Israel 1113 (1992),
1158 (1993)*

Left to right: Monument to fallen of Communications/Electronics/Computer Corps, Yahud; Ordnance Corps, Netanya; Israel Police. *Israel 1200 (1994), 1227 (1995), 1272 (1996)*

Left to right: Monument to fallen of Logistics Corps; 50th anniversary of the War of Independence; Bedouin memorial. *Israel 1301 (1997), 1331 (1998), 1363 (1999)*

Left to right: Volunteers who fell in World War II; Nahal fallen; pre-state freedom fighters fallen and executed. *Israel 1405 (2000), 1441 (2001), 367 (1968)*

Archeology

Derived from two Greek words *archaios* (ancient) and *logos* (knowledge), archeology is the scientific study of the remains of the past. In Palestine, archeology has supplemented the written record of the Bible to provide insight into the lifestyles of the Jewish people in antiquity. In addition to information concerning the material side of life, such as the transition from food-gathering to agriculture, the beginnings of irrigation, and the types of wheat and other products grown, archeology has mapped out the development of architecture, from the earliest fortifications at Jericho, by way of the Israelite four-room house, the Canaanite palaces and temples, and the revolution effected by the introduction of Greek models in the Hellenistic period.

The principal method of archeology is excavation, the systematic removal of accumulated earth and debris covering ancient remains. Whole cities and settlements have been discovered arranged one atop the other, forming artificial mounds (*tel*, in Hebrew). The dating of various strata is sometimes based on absolute criteria, by demonstrating levels of destruction associated with known events, inscriptions, and coins. Relative dating can be accomplished by the discovery of artifacts such as pottery. Pottery is easily broken, and though its shards are valueless they are practically indestructible. As pottery styles changed and developed through the ages, these shards are the best indication of the chronology of a settlement.

The pioneering archeologist in modern Israel was Yigael (Sukenik) Yadin (1917-1984), who also was the second chief of staff of the Israel Defense Forces and a deputy prime minister. Yadin led the expeditions that unearthed the fortified city of Hazor, dating from the conquest of the Promised Land by Joshua in the 13th century B.C.E., and the ancient fortress of Masada, famed for the last stand of the Zealots in the desperate struggle against the Romans in 70 C.E. Other famous archeological sites in Israel include the Canaanite cities of Lachish, Gezer, and Megiddo, as well as the Herodian harbor and walls of Caesarea, the fortress of Herodian, the temple and walls of Samaria, the palace at Jericho, and the wall surrounding the Cave of Machpelah in Hebron.

After the Six-Day War of 1967, extensive excavations were begun in many parts of Israel, especially in the vicinity of the Western Wall and the Old City of Jerusalem. The broad city wall that surrounded Jerusalem in First Temple times (around 700 B.C.E.) has been demonstrated. Archeological investigations in Jerusalem have indicated the magnificence of this metropolis in Herodian times and its utter destruction by Titus. Large-scale excavations south and south-west of the Temple Mount revealed the superb planning of this area, its gates, stairways, paved streets, and water systems. The so-called Robinson's Arch was shown to belong to the monumental stairway leading to the Royal Stoa. Along the southern side of the Temple Mount, archeologists have discovered a large paved plaza and a broad series of stairs in front of the Double Gate, which were used by the pilgrims at major festivals. Beautiful architectural fragments with floral reliefs have also been found. Paved streets and mansions of the well-to-do were unearthed in the Jewish Quarter, which was the Upper City in Herodian times.

Archeologists have succeeded in discovering facets of life in Jerusalem during the Byzantine, Crusader, Mamluk, and Ottoman (Turkish) periods. A spectacular discovery in the Jewish Quarter of the Old City is the Cardo, the main north-south street (*cardo maximus*) that once served as the "shopping mall" of Jerusalem in Roman and Byzantine times. After almost 1500 years, the Cardo has reopened and again features fashionable shops. The excavations of the Umayyad palaces at the Southern Wall in Jerusalem have revealed a new dimension of Moslem art, including stucco sculptures of the Caliph, his warriors, dancers, and dwarfs, together with the beginnings of the typical Islamic arabesque decoration.

City wall, First Temple period, 7th century B.C.E. *Israel 611 (1976)*

Arch, Second Temple period, 1st century B.C.E. *Israel 613 (1976)*

Staircase, Second Temple period, 1st century B.C.E. *Israel 614 (1976)*

Top, left to right: Corinthian capital, Second Temple period, 1st cent. B.C.E.; Ionic capital, Second Temple period, 1st century B.C.E.; rosettes and rhomboids, frieze and columns, facade of eastern Gate of Hulda, Temple compounds; carved relief from sepulcher entrance, end of Second Temple period. Below: Byzantine capital, 6th century; Islamic relief from Umayyad caliphs, 8th cenutry; Crusader Corinthian capital from Church of the Ascension, Mount of Olives, 12th-13th century. *Israel 930-931 (1986), 1014,1020, 1015 (1988), 1016-1017 (1989)*

Byzantine building, 6th century; Umayyad palace, 8th century.
Israel 612, 615 (1976)

Ottoman relief with star of David,
16th century. *Israel 1018 (1989)*

The Jewish World in Stamps

Coins

The earliest coins found in the Land of Israel date from 550-450 B.C.E. They are Greek coins that were probably brought by merchants visiting the country. Imitations of the Athenian coinage were issued in Judea a century later, but it cannot be determined whether the Jewish high priest or the local Persian governor was the issuing authority.

The consecutive history of ancient Jewish coinage begins after the establishment of the independent Hasmonean dynasty in the 2nd century B.C.E. The bulk were bronze coins of small denomination (*perutah* or *dilepton*). In accordance with the Second Commandment, they contained no likeness of living beings, humans or animals. The emblems found on the coins (e.g., cornucopia, wreath, anchor, flower, star, helmet) were copied from those issued by the Seleucids. All Hasmonean coins bear Hebrew words, but those of Alexander Yannai and Mattathias Antigonus also have writing in Greek. With one exception, all Hasmonean coins are undated, making it difficult to arrange them chronologically (especially since different rulers went by the same names).

Some of the bronze coins of Herod the Great (37–4 B.C.E.) are dated, all with the year three (i.e., three years after the Romans appointed him as king of Judea). All are inscribed with Greek legends. Emblems on the coins of Herod and his successors include the tripod, caduceus, pomegranate, shield, helmet, palm branch, anchor, double and single cornucopia, and eagle. It may be concluded from this selection of symbols that Herod the Great did not wish to offend the religious feelings of his subjects.

By the time the Jewish War broke out (66-70 C.E.), the mint in Tyre had ceased to issue the coins required by every Jewish adult male for the payment of the annual Temple tax of a half-shekel. For this reason, as well as the desire of the Jewish authorities to demonstrate their sovereignty over their own country, it was decided to mint the shekel, the first silver coins Jews struck in antiquity. The emblems are as simple as they are beautiful – a chalice with pearl rim and three pomegranates. The legends, which are only in Hebrew and written in the old script, read *Yerushalayim ha-Kedoshah* (Jerusalem the Holy) and *Shekel Yisrael* (Shekel of Israel). They contain abbreviated dates – the letter *shin* (for *shanah*, meaning "year") followed by a letter indicating the specific year (i.e., *aleph* = one; *bet* = two, etc). Bronze coins were also struck during the war, bearing such emblems as the vine leaf, amphora, lulav, etrog, palm tree, fruit baskets, and chalice.

The last Jewish coin series in antiquity was issued during the Bar Kochba War (132-135 C.E.). Most bear the name Simeon and eventually his title, "prince of Israel." Those issued during the first two years are dated, either "Year one of the redemption of Israel" or "Year two of the freedom of Israel." During the third year and until the end of the war, the coins issued were undated and bear the war slogan, "For the freedom of Jerusalem." This series of silver and bronze coins is exceptional in that all were overstruck on coins then current in Palestine. It is thought that Bar Kochba may have obtained the gentile coins needed for overstriking by means of a public loan for the national war effort.

Top, left to right: Bronze coins of the Maccabean period (2nd century B.C.E.), reading: "Freedom of Zion;" "For the Redemption of Zion;" "Third Year." Coins of the First Revolt (66-70 C.E.), reading: "Silver Shekel, Second Year;" "First Year of the Redemption of Israel." *Israel 1-6 (1948)*. Bottom: Bar Kochba Revolt coins. *Israel 60/62/64 (1950-1954)*

Seals

Seals were employed in antiquity to identify property, as protection against theft, and to mark the clay stoppers of oil and wine jars. With the spread of writing in the early days of the Mesopotamian dynasties, seals were used as signatures on clay-tablet inscriptions. In Egypt, seals were used to sign papyrus scrolls. Seals were made of a variety of stones, which were usually semiprecious. The carving and relief were done by means of a simple drill, an auger, or a stylus.

Scaraboid seals became widespread in Israel from the ninth to fifth centuries B.C.E, primarily for signature or to mark possessions. The base of these seals was generally engraved with an inscription, which often was combined with decorative designs, mythological subjects, flora and fauna, and geometrical patterns. The name of the owner of the seal was frequently given together with that of his father (with or without the word "son"). While most of the seals were personal, a few contained the name of a "servant" (official) and his monarch (e.g., Shema, the servant of Jeroboam). The king's ring was synonymous with the king's seal, and it symbolized royal power.

Seals with inscriptions (left to right): "Belonging to Tamach son of Miknemelech;"
"Belonging to Shema, servant of Jeroboam;" "Belonging to Natanyahu Ne'avadyahu."
Israel 129-131 (1958)

Cultural Life In Israel

Ahad Ha-Am, the spokesman for "cultural Zionism," stressed the need to establish a great academic institution in Palestine and emphasized that the Hebrew language was essential in developing the new Jewish culture. He advocated "a concentration of genius and talent in the service of Jewish culture to restore the Jewish people to its rightful place in the comity of human culture... when the work of the returned wanderers will serve as the starting point for an advance into higher realms of achievement." Until the 19th century, Jewish cultural creativity in the Diaspora had been expressed mainly within a religious framework. The bulk of the literature had been on religious subjects, art had been confined to ritual spheres, and musical expression was liturgical. Only with the dawn of emancipation could there be a flourishing of the universal aspects of Jewish cultural and artistic talents. It was the strong upsurge of intellectual and cultural creativity in European Jewry that Ahad Ha-Am sought to attract and harness to the Jewish nationalistic expression within the Zionist movement. Subsequently, the intermingling of the Ashkenazic, Sephardic, and oriental traditions has provided Israel an immense opportunity to develop a vibrant and diverse culture.

Centennial of the Hebrew Language Council. *Israel 1028 (1989)*

The first generations of settlers consciously struggled with the interrelations of the different components that they felt would be required for an Israeli culture. Although it must be solidly based within Jewish traditions and the Hebrew language, it also needed to relate to a universal context. Initially, particularist tendencies were dominant and a marked continuity with the East European Jewish tradition was perpetuated in all forms of cultural expression. However, as aliyah from various countries increased and the new state of Israel became dominated by *sabras* (native-born Israelis) with their newly found self-confidence, Israeli culture has become more universalistic and outward looking, seeing itself as one expression of contemporary world culture.

Hebrew Language

The revival of Hebrew as a spoken language was an essential part of Zionist ideology. Although not spoken as an everyday tongue for some 17 centuries, Hebrew had remained a language of literature and of prayer, never forgotten and always cherished. As early as the middle of the 19th century, Hebrew was being spoken in Jerusalem, where it provided a common link between the Ashkenazic and Sephardic Jews who had no other language in common.

Eliezer Ben-Yehuda, father of modern Hebrew. *Israel 156 (1959)*

The major proponent of the revival of Hebrew as a spoken language after more than 2,000 years was Eliezer Ben-Yehuda (1858-1922), who arrived in Palestine in 1881. Ben-Yehuda launched a single-minded campaign that succeeded in making Hebrew the language of instruction in schools, with the Sephardic pronunciation becoming standard due to its having the closest resemblance to the Hebrew speech in ancient times. He coined many Hebrew words needed in modern life and began the publication of the first dictionary of the modern tongue. However, Ben-Yehuda and the Hebraists met with determined opposition from various quarters. The Orthodox elements in Jerusalem were openly hostile to this secular use of the holy language of prayer. Speakers of French, Yiddish, and Ladino feared that the development of Hebrew would lead to the neglect of their languages, as eventually was the result. The Palestine Mandate of 1922 gave Hebrew official recognition as one of the three languages of the country (alongside English and Arabic), and it was used in administrative activities as well as on coins and stamps. Hebrew became the official language of the State of Israel when it was established in 1948.

Chaim Nachman Bialik, national Hebrew poet. *Israel 155 (1959)*

The mass immigration of the ensuing years led to the development of the ulpan, which provided an intensive Hebrew course for newcomers to the country. In 1954, the Knesset established the Academy of the Hebrew Language (which succeeded the Hebrew Language Council that was co-founded by Ben-Yehuda in Jerusalem in 1889) to determine correct and grammatical Hebrew usage. Working through various committees, each specializing in a particular field, the Academy has determined the proper Hebrew words for tens of thousands of technical terms.

Literature

Until World War I, Hebrew literature was centered in Eastern Europe. After the war and the Russian Revolution, many Hebrew writers found their way to Palestine and essentially continued the European tradition. The 1920s and 1930s witnessed the emergence of Palestine as the dominant center of Hebrew literary activity, the site of a Hebrew press, Hebrew publishers, and a Hebrew-reading public. Those Hebrew writers for whom the return to Zion had been one of their basic themes (Chaim Nachman Bialik, Ahad Ha-Am, Saul Tchernichowsky), now seized the opportunity to spend their last years in Tel Aviv and exerted a great influence on younger Hebrew writers. Chaim Nachman Bialik (1873-1934), generally considered the greatest poet of modern times, combined the fervor of folk spirituality with the Hasidic ambience and mystic lore that he experienced as a child in his native Lithuania. Like the ancient prophets, Bialik rebuked his people and exposed their weaknesses in fiery and sharp-edged verses. Nevertheless, the poet inspired the Jewish masses with hope, pride, and self-respect. His poem "The City of Slaughter," written after the Kishinev pogrom in 1903, roused the younger generation to take up arms in self-defense. Today, Bialik prizes are awarded for the best in Hebrew literature. Ahad-Ha-Am ("one of the people") was the pseudonym of Asher Hirsch Ginsberg (1856-1927), an ardent advocate of cultural or "spiritual" Zionism. In his essays, Ahad Ha-Am argued that Palestine must first become a spiritual and cultural center of Judaism before it could develop into a viable Jewish state. The poetry of Saul Tchernichowsky (1875-1943) reflected the wholesome and happier phases of Eastern European traditional life and was distinguished by a vigorous sense of beauty and closeness to nature. Some of his first poems dealt with the Palestine landscape and its historical themes. In addition to his original works, Tchernichowsky also translated some classic foreign works of literature into Hebrew.

Saul Tchernichowsky.
Israel 1269k (1996)

Immigrant arriving by ship and plane, with quote from Tchernichowsky ("Our sun will also rise in the east.")
Israel 34 (1950)

J. H. Brenner.
Israel 1269f (1996)

Yehuda Burla.
Israel 1269b (1996)

Joseph Hayyim Brenner (1881–1921), who emigrated from the Ukraine in 1909, was the spokesman from the "uprooted" generation, ruthlessly exposing the anxieties, self-probing, and despair of intellectual anti-heroes overwhelmed by life in a society that had lost meaning and direction. His fiction, though bleak and fiercely honest, nourished a belief in artistic truth even when faith in all else has failed. Yehuda Burla (1886–1969) was one of the first modern Hebrew writers of Sephardic Middle Eastern background. Born in Jerusalem, he was the descendant of a family of rabbis and scholars that had settled in the Land of Israel some three centuries previously. Observing that the classical modern Hebrew authors portrayed only the life of the Ashkenazim of Eastern Europe, Burla determined to correct this imbalance and depicted the language, customs, and thinking of the previously neglected Middle Eastern Sephardic community, a way of life

The Jewish World in Stamps

that is fast disappearing as a result of immigration and acculturation to Israeli life.

The next generation of writers - such as Abraham Shlonsky, Uri Zvi Greenberg, Yocheved Bat-Miriam, Nathan Alterman, Lea Goldberg, and Rachel - found in the Land of Israel the requisite antidote to the rootlessness of the Diaspora. The Hebrew poetry of Abraham Shlonsky (1900-1973), written with mastery of language and style and excelling in rich imagery, reflected his pioneering experience. He also translated classic works from world literature into Hebrew. Uri Zvi Greenberg (1895-1981) wrote passionately and eloquently about the rebuilding of the land and the vision of Jewish sovereignty over all of historical Palestine. During World War II, Greenberg penned powerful and dramatic poems on the Nazi slaughter of the Jewish people, which were published in the volume *Streets of the River*. The bulk of the poetry of Yocheved Bat-Miriam (Zhelezniak; 1901-1980), reflected her personal experiences as a child in Belorussia and a settler in Israel or the problems faced by Jews in the period between the two world wars.

Shlonsky translates Pushkin's *Eugene Onegin*. Joint issue with Israel.
Russia 6418 (1997)

Polish-born Nathan Alterman (1910–1970) was a poetic spokesman for the national struggle against the policies of the British authorities, and his popular satirical verse reflected the political aspirations of the *yishuv*. However, Alterman also was a sophisticated modern poet, who was recognized as a leader of Israel's literary avant-garde. Lea Goldberg (1911-1970) was a poet, theater critic for *Davar*, and literary adviser to Habimah (Israel's national theater), who later served as the first chair of the Department of Comparative Literature at the Hebrew University in Jerusalem. Rachel, the pseudonym of Rachel Bluwstein (1890-1931), was among the first modern Hebrew poets to write in a simple conversational style with an uncomplicated lyrical line. Invariably short, her poems are elegaic and have a nostalgic tone, many reflecting the pessimism of a young writer on the brink of an untimely death. Stricken with tuberculosis and no longer able to till the land, Rachel's longing and loneliness poured out in such poems as the beloved *Ve-ulai* (And Perhaps). Many of her poems, including *Kinneret*, have been put to music. Other writers active during this period included Devorah Baron (1887-1956) and poet Amir Gilboa (1917-1984).

Those who emerged around the time of the War of Independence (such as S. Yizhar and Moshe

Top: Lea Goldberg. Bottom: Rachel ("Oh my Kinnert, was it only a dream?")
Israel 1078, 1077 (1991)

Abraham Shlonsky.
Israel 1269g (1996)

Uri Zvi Greenberg.
Israel 858 (1984)

From top: Yocheved Bat-Miriam; Devorah Baron; Nathan Alterman; Haim Hazaz.
Israel 1269m, c, d, g (1996)

Shamir) were all sabras or had been brought to the country at an early age. For them, Israel was an established fact, to be criticized and fought for like any other country. They were strongly influenced by other literatures, especially Western. The 1948 war was their great moment, but the euphoria was later replaced by a feeling of emptiness and of searching for new values, leading to experiments in exploring other Jewish communities in Israel or the Jewish past. Haim Hazaz (1898–1973) wrote about the broad spectrum of the Jewish experience in various times and locales, seeing the modern period as a link in the great chain of Jewish national history. A political activist, Hazaz was prominent in the Land of Israel movement calling for settlement in the territories captured during the 1967 war and for their permanent inclusion in the State of Israel.

A leading contemporary Israeli poet was Yehuda Amichai (1924–2000). His first volume of poetry (1955) and subsequent works revealed that Amichai was engaged in a distinctly modern literary enterprise, both in content and in language. Subjects previously considered prosaic became appropriate poetic images; tanks, airplanes, fuel, administrative contracts, and technological terms figure in his work, reflecting Amichai's conviction that a modern poetry must confront and reflect contemporary issues. In addition to a non-conventional choice of subjects, Amichai employed an innovative use of language, ranging from classical Hebrew to the post-modern colloquial.

The Hebrew Writers' Association was established in 1921 in Tel Aviv, with the stated objectives of "the cultivation and growth of Hebrew literature through the cooperative efforts of Hebrew writers; and the defense of the spiritual and material interests of those in the field of literature." Distinguished presidents of the organization have included Nahum Sokolow, Bialik, and Tchernichowsky.

Until modern times, little literature was written especially for children. Hebrew literature for children written in the Diaspora developed in a somewhat artificial milieu, since for most writers and readers Hebrew was neither the mother tongue nor the daily means of expression. Thus, it was only in Israel that a vibrant Hebrew children's literature finally emerged.

The first Hebrew children's magazine, *Olam Katon,* appeared in Jerusalem in 1893, but disappeared after only seven issues because of problems of language, lack of writers, a limited reading public, and small circulation.

From top: Yehuda Amichai; Yaakov Shabtai; 50th anniversay of the Hebrew Writers' Association.
Israel 1453 (2001), 1269h (1996), 536 (1974)

Hebrew Children's Books:

From left: *Why Is the Zebra Wearing Pajamas?* by Omer Hille; *Apartment to Let* by Lea Goldberg; *Across the Sea* by Chaim Nachman Bialik; *Stars in a Bucket* by Anda Amir-Pinkerfield. *Israel 894, 893, 895 (1984), 1238 (1995)*

Hurry, Run, Dwarfs by Miriam Yallan-Stekelis; *Daddy's Big Umbrella* by Levin Kipnis; *Olam Katan* (Small World), first Hebrew children's magazine. *Israel 1239, 1240 (1995), 1179 (1993)*

Libraries

Israel's main library is the Jewish National Library which also serves as the library of the Hebrew University. In addition to rare manuscripts and prayer-books and special collections on Jews in medicine and Jewish autographs and portraits, the Jewish National Library also houses the personal archives of Ahad Ha-Am, Martin Buber, Joseph Klausner, Stefan Zweig, and Shmuel Yosef Agnon.

Jewish National and University Library, from left: Parables, Brescia, 1491; Machzor, Italian Ms., 15th century; Buber, draft of Bible translation. *Israel 1121-1123 (1992)*

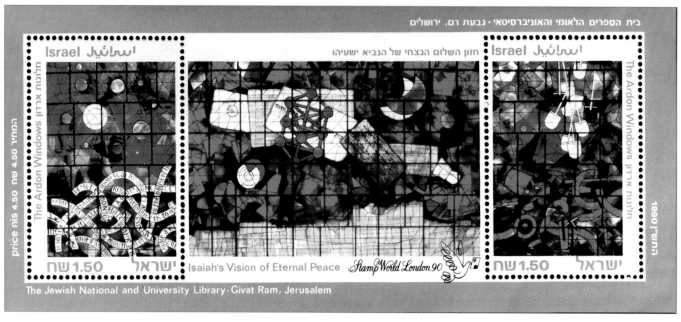

Stained-glass windows by Ardon at the Jewish National Library, Givat Ram, Jerusalem, depicting eternal peace. *Israel 1041 (1990)*

Press

The earliest Hebrew newspaper in Palestine was *Halbanon*, which initially appeared in Jerusalem in March 1863 and continued for 20 years, providing the first opportunity for Hebrew journalists in the Land of Israel. Another important Hebrew publication was *Ha-Shilo'ah*, a Hebrew-language literary, social, and scientific monthly founded in Russia in 1896. Until 1903, *Ha-Shilo'ah* was edited by Ahad Ha-Am, who endeavored to have it be a journal devoted to Zionism, Jewish scholarship, and *belles lettres* in a style accessible to the general reader. It expressed Ahad Ha-Am's bitter antagonism to Herzl and political Zionism, thus eliciting a strong reaction from the Zionist movement. His successor as editor was Joseph Gedaliah Klausner (1874-1958), who edited the monthly until it ceased publication in 1926. Unlike Ahad Ha-Am, Klausner was an adherent of political Zionism, yet *Ha-Shilo'ah* reflected all the trends within the movement. When Klausner immigrated to Palestine in 1920, *Ha-Shilo'ah* resumed publication in Jerusalem, though in its new locale

the journal did not enjoy the same importance as it had in Russia. The oldest Jewish periodical still in existence is the weekly Jewish Chronicle, which published its first edition in London in 1841.

In Israel today, the major newspapers are the Hebrew-language *Ha-Aretz*, *Yedi'ot Aharonot*, and *Ma'ariv*, and the English-language *Jerusalem Post*.

From left: *Jewish Chronicle* of London, 150th anniversary; *Ha'Lebanon* with typesetter in the 19th century. *Israel 1092 (1991), 241 (1963)*

Joseph Klausner
Israel 804(1982)

Theater

Three major theaters developed in Palestine before the establishment of the State of Israel. The Ohel (tent) theater, which began to perform publicly in 1926, was originally a volunteer group under the auspices of the Histadrut's cultural committee, whose objectives were the theatrical expression of the ideals of the Jewish workers' movement as well as the creation of an original Hebrew drama. Consequently, its repertoire was based on plays of specific Jewish and socialist interest. However, increasing financial difficulties caused it eventually to disband in 1969.

The Habimah (literally, "stage") was founded in Moscow in 1918 as the world's first professional Hebrew theater. It had achieved an international reputation before making its permanent home in Palestine in 1928. The declared objective of Habimah was to act as a cultural bridge between the Jews of Palestine and those in the Diaspora. A favorite production was Anski's *The Dybbuk*, which often featured founding member Hanna Rovina (1889-1980). Members of Habimah made pioneering attempts at writing original Hebrew plays; most were based on Jewish history, though some dealt with the new life in Palestine. Unfortunately, few were successful and it took some time before the Hebrew drama developed out of its experimental period. In 1958, on the occasion of its 40th anniversary, Habimah was officially recognized as the Israel National Theater.

The third major company, the Cameri (Chamber) Theater, was founded in 1944 by a group of actors led by Joseph Millo, who wanted to establish a theater in the European tradition. Critical of what they deemed Habimah's stylized and dated performances, which were inspired by the methods taught by Stanislavsky some 30 years previously in Russia, the Cameri sought to break away from the East European influences that had dominated the Hebrew stage, combining avant-garde productions with up-to-date methods of acting and production. The Cameri provided an outlet for talented actors who had not been absorbed by the existing theaters and put on programs that reflected the attitudes and behavior of their own generation. The first productions were foreign works, since no original Hebrew plays were available; however, the translations were into modern idiomatic Hebrew, the acting style was natural, and the standard of production was high.

From top: Habimah National Theater at 50; Hanna Rovina; Cameri Theater at 25. *Israel 412 (1970), 1102 (1991), 441 (1971)*

Cinema

Newsreels and Zionist propaganda films were made in Palestine, especially after World War I, but they in themselves did not constitute a true film industry. The pioneer in film making in Palestine was Natan Axelrod, who immigrated from the Soviet Union in 1926. In 1932, Axelrod produced the first Hebrew feature film, *Oded the Wanderer*. After inde-

75 years of Hebrew films. From left: *Judah Released* (first Hebrew film, 1918); *Oded the Wanderer* (first Hebrew feature, 1932); *This is the land* (first Hebrew talkie). *Israel 1130-1132 (1992)*

pendence, the government recognized a need to develop a film industry, especially for propaganda abroad and educational purposes in Israel. Several documentary films achieved high technical and artistic standards and even won international prizes, but the few feature films made at the time were rather primitive and failed at the box offices. Some foreign movies made in Israel, especially Otto Preminger's *Exodus*, *The Juggler*, and *Cast a Giant Shadow*, enabled local film workers to gain experience in the Hollywood type of production.

Israeli films came of age after the Six-Day War in 1967, with the most active producer and director being Menahem Golan. The subjects have primarily been taken from life in Israel (such as the various communities and the relations between them, the three wars since the establishment of the state, satires, and kibbutz life), with the stories generally written specifically for film. However, there also have been adaptations of literary works, plays, and Jewish classics. The introduction of television in 1968 further strengthened the movie industry. Studios became overloaded with work for television, which encouraged expansion and the building of new studios, as well as more intensive training of film personnel. One year later, the Ministry of Commerce and Industry established the Israel Film Center to deal with all matters concerned with the making of films in Israel and the marketing of them abroad.

A century of cinema (Marx brothers, Signoret, Sellers, Kaye, Jolson).
Israel 1253 (1995)

Instrumental music

There was little organized musical life in Palestine until the 1930s, when the immigration of Jews from Central Europe swelled potential audiences and brought many professional musicians (instrumentalists, teachers, composers) who soon applied their knowledge and talents to teaching and performing. In 1936, the Palestine Orchestra (later the Israel Philharmonic Orchestra) was established, and in the same year the Palestine Broadcasting Service was inaugurated in Jerusalem.

The Palestine Orchestra was the vision of violinist Bronislaw Huberman, who saw it as a rescue operation for musicians persecuted by the Nazis, as well as a contribution to the cultural life in Palestine. He succeeded in convincing Arturo Toscanini, the eminent Italian conductor, to conduct the first concerts in December 1936, thereby immediately establishing the international rank of the orchestra. In 1948, after the foundation of the State, the orchestra changed its name to the Israel Philharmonic Orchestra. The musicians formed a cooperative, taking over management and financial responsibility. In subsequent years, membership expanded to more than a hundred players, of whom an increasing number were born and trained in Israel. The major home of the Israel Philharmonic Orchestra is now the Mann

Israel Philharmonic Orchestra at 50. From left: Bronislaw Huberman; Arturo Toscanini.
Israel 954-955 (1986)

Klezmer festival, Safed.
Israel 1317 (1997)

Israel Philharmonic at 25.
Israel 214 (1961)

The Jewish World in Stamps

Auditorium in Tel Aviv, though it continues to also present performances throughout the country and abroad.

Although the Israel Philharmonic is the major orchestra in the country, the wealth of musical talent (especially after the influx of Russian and Eastern European immigrants in the 1990s) has filled the ranks of professional groups such as orchestras in Jerusalem, Haifa, and Beer Sheva, as well as the Israel and Kibbutz Chamber Orchestras.

Vocal Music

The Israel National Opera, founded by Edis De Philippe in 1947 and directed by her until her death in July 1978, fought valiantly for survival with insufficient budgets but rarely achieved high standards. Far superior opera productions were those presented occasionally by the Israel Philharmonic Orchestra, in concert form, semi-staged, or even in full stage production. In 1985, three years after the National Opera closed, operatic activity resumed with the founding of the New Israel Opera.

The biennial Zimriya Choir Festival, founded by A. Z. Propes in 1952, was originally conceived as an exclusively Jewish festival. However, for years it has become an ecumenical event, in which non-Jewish choirs from throughout the world (now the majority) sing together with Israeli groups in friendly collaboration.

From top: Israel National Opera (*Samson and Delilah*); Zimriya (World Assembly of Choirs). *Israel 440 (1971), 1315 (1997)*

Dance

Israeli folk dance emerged as an amalgam of Jewish and non-Jewish forms from many parts of the world. For several decades the *hora* (a circle dance from Eastern Europe that may have been based on the fervent celebrations of the Hasidim) typified the new life of the Jews in Palestine. The tightly closed circle gave equal status to all participants; simple movements such as stamping

and jumping enabled everyone to take part; and the linked arms symbolized the new ideology. The Yemenite tradition became an important part of Israel's dance culture, as did the Arab *debka*, which was originally a dance of men linked in a row that expressed strength and self-confidence. The

International Folklore Festival, Haifa. *Israel 1056-1057 (1990)*

From top: *Dancing the Hora* by Aman. *Romania 2248 (1971);* Inbal Dance Theater; Karmiel Dance Festival. *Israel 442 (1971), 1316 (1997)*

challenge to create a dance culture came largely from the settlers' need to find roots in the soil after having left urban society. They wanted to return to the original motivation of dancing, without consciously imitating fertility rites, and to find contemporary meaning in ancient festivals preserved by religious practices. This vitality of the new settlers was expressed in experiments to create songs and dances for the nature festivals.

The *Inbal* Dance Theatre (*inbal* is the "clapper" of a bell), an Israeli dance company based mainly on Yemenite traditions, was founded in 1949 by Sara Levi-Tanai (choreographer and artistic director) and Ovadia Tuvia (musical director). Its repertoire is based on various Jewish religious traditions and the Bible, and the company has combined dancing, singing, and acting into one indivisible unit.

The Batsheva and Bat-Dor dance companies, founded and financed by Baroness Batsheva de Rothschild in Tel Aviv, aim to foster the art of dance in Israel. The first company was started in 1964, using techniques based on the method of the American dancer Martha Graham, who became its artistic adviser. After establishing a dance studio with classical ballet among the basic training methods, Rothschild decided that there also was a need for a second company that would be more closely linked with the studios and provide scope for developing an indigenous style.

In 1988, the first annual dance festival was held in Karmiel in the Galilee. Attracting thousands from Israel and abroad, the Karmiel Dance Festival is primarily a folk dance event, but also includes performances by Israeli professional dance companies and foreign groups.

Bezalel Academy at 75.
Israel 597 (1976)

Fine Arts

Art in the modern Land of Israel can be dated from the first Zionist immigration to Palestine. It generally evolved in relation to the pattern of the successive waves of immigration. The first Palestinian artists, who were all immigrants, had been artistically active before their arrival and came to Israel with a vision reflecting their European origin. The artists of later generations, however, were influenced by the special circumstances of Israel.

In 1906, Boris Schatz (1867–1932) emigrated to Palestine from Bulgaria, where he had been a painter, sculptor, and head of the Royal Academy of Art in Sofia. In the year of his arrival, Schatz realized his dream of founding an academy of arts and crafts in Jerusalem, which he called the Bezalel School after the biblical architect of the Tabernacle. This was an adventurous undertaking, both because the Jewish population of the *yishuv* was small and because the Orthodox were certain to protest vigorously against a school that might violate the biblical prohibition against the making of a graven image. Nevertheless, Schatz received the full backing of the Zionist Organization for the school, which can be considered the beginning of genuine artistic activity in the land since previously the only art forms produced locally consisted of arts and crafts and pictorial representations for devotional purposes by the small Jewish communities of Jerusalem, Safed, and Tiberias. Other Eastern European pioneers of art in

The Scribe by Boris Schatz.
Israel 479 (1972)

Sarah by Abel Pann.
Israel 480 (1972)

From left: *Old Jerusalem* by Rubin. Romania 4081(1996); *An Alley in Safed* by Levanon; *Jerusalem Scen*e by Zaritsky.
Israel 684 (1978), 772 (1981)

From left: *A Street in Jerusalem* by Gliksberg; *Resurrection* by Kahana.
Israel 682 (1978), 483 (1972)

From left: *Pastorale* by Paldi; *Safed* by Shemi.
Israel 817 (1982), 481 (1972)

JACOB STEINHARDT   יעקב שטיינהרט

ISRAEL   إسرائيل   0.85

ISRAEL   إسرائيل

ANNA TICHO   אנה טיכו

ש 0.50   ישראל   1980 תשמ"א

ישראל   ש 25.00

ISRAEL   إسرائيل

כ"ה שנים לעצמאות ישראל   AGAM אגם יעקב   החשמ"ג 1983

From top: *Old Jerusalem* by Steinhardt; *Jerusalem Scene* by Ticho; *Israel at 35* by Agam. *Israel 482 (1972), 771 (1981), 838 (1983)*

Palestine included Ephraim Moses Lilien (1874-1925) and Abel Pann (1883-1963).

Almost two decades later in 1923, the younger generation of Palestine artists organized the first important exhibition in the land, which was held in the Tower of David in Jerusalem. This group, of which Reuven Rubin (1893-1974) became the best known, criticized the style and ideas of their teachers as anachronistic. Most were primarily landscape artists, such as Mordecai Levanon (1901-1968), Israel Paldi (Feldman) (1892-1979), Nahum Gutman (1898-1980), and Yossef Zaritsky (1891-1985), and they formed the nucleus out of which Israeli art developed. Some young painters, such as Menahem Shemi (1897–1951) and Haim Gliksberg (1904–1970), were heavily influenced by Jewish expressionism of the Paris School, especially the work of Chaim Soutine. The 1930s saw a wave of German artists who had fled the Nazis, such as Jacob Steinhardt (1887–1968), Aharon Kahana (Hermann) (1905-1967), and Mordecai Ardon (Bronstein) (1896–

90   ישראל   א   ISRAEL
ITZHAK DANZIGER, SERPENTINE
פארק הירקון, תל אביב   YARKON PARK, TEL AVIV

LEOPOLD KRAKAUER

3.80   ישראל   إسرائيل   ISRAEL   1978

From top: *Yarkon Park* by Danziger; *Thistles* by Krakauer. *Israel 1222 (1995), 683 (1978)*

1992). Most settled in Jerusalem, creating a "Jerusalem School" that was dominated by certain aspects of German expressionism. These artists were preceded by two Viennese painters, Anna Ticho (1894–1980) and Leopold Krakauer (1890–1954). More recent Israel artists include Igael Tumarkin (1933-), Uri Lifschitz (1936-), and Yaacov Agam (Gipstein) (1928-), who resides in Paris.

Sculpture also has flourished in Israel. Ze'ev Ben-Zvi (1904-1952), teacher of sculptor at the Bezalel School, exerted a substantial influence upon many of the major figures in this discipline. Among the most famous Israeli sculptors were Yitzhak Danziger (1916-1977), who was commissioned by the Tel Aviv Foundation to produce a sculptured environment for the Yarkon Park; David Palombo (1920-1966), whose first monumental work was the entrance gate to the Yad Vashem Memorial in Jerusalem, which embodied a rhythmic composition of welded iron bars and steel electroplatings (see page 60), and who later designed the massive iron gates at the entrance to the Knesset; and Avraham Melnikoff (1892–1960), who is known for his famous "Lion" at Tel Hai (see page 171).

The Jewish World in Stamps

Architecture

The architecture in Jewish towns and settlements in the modern Land of Israel was primarily conditioned by the urgent housing requirements of the various waves of immigration. The aesthetic aspect mostly reflected the trends prevalent in the architects' countries of origin. During the Ottoman period, there were two broad categories of buildings – Arab village buildings, constructed on the traditional pattern, without architects, using building materials found nearby and in distinctive harmony with the terrain; and town architecture, which was typically Mediterranean, based on southern Italian mixed with traditional Arab styles. In addition, there were buildings erected by the Turkish government, which employed German architects and were of a high standard. The buildings erected by the Jewish Colonization Association, in a French style, were attractive and less pretentious.

Large-scale Jewish immigration after World War I brought in its wake an acute housing shortage, and there was a rush of building unprecedented in Middle Eastern countries. The building boom provided full employment for the architects and engineers then in the country, but also allowed the entry of a number of self-taught technicians into the building field. Consequently, many of the buildings of the period were badly designed. During the same period, there also was an attempt by creative architects to achieve a modern Oriental style. However, some European architects who immigrated to Palestine made no attempt to adapt the styles of their former homes to local topography or climate.

The establishment of the State of Israel in 1948 led to a tidal wave of immigration and the immediate need for mass housing. In the early 1950s, thousands of new immigrants were living in tin huts, wooden prefabricated structures, and tents. Permanent accommodation had to be built quickly and cheaply. Thus the famous *shikkun* (quickly constructed housing project) became a feature of many parts of the country. Quantity was the sole criterion; the qualitative side was neglected with respect to the building, the materials, and the efficiency of execution, as well as the architectural and aesthetic aspects.

Israel now boasts a host of striking and noteworthy buildings by world-renowned Israeli architects, many of them public buildings and at major educational institutions throughout the country.

From top: Amal Technical Center, Tel Aviv; Library, Tel Aviv University; Rest home, Zichron Yaakov; Library, Hebrew University of Jerusalem; Yad Mordecai museum; Bat Yam City Hall. *Israel 544-546(1974), 558-560 (1975)*

Israeli Scenes

Acre seen from the sea.
Israel 471 (1971-75)

Acre (Akko). Ancient seaport town on the northern hook of Haifa Bay. A leading Phoenician port in Canaanite times, Acre was seized alternately by Egypt and Assyria. Later, Acre served successively as a Greek and Roman port, Crusader fortress, Moslem battlefield, French trading center, and Ottoman outpost. In 1947, Jewish underground fighters succeeding in freeing 250 prisoners from the British-controlled Acre fortress. The mosque complex, with subterranean Crusader vaults, is named for Ahmed Jezzar Pasha, the Ottoman Turkish governor of Acre during the late 1700s.

Afula and the Valley of Jezreel.
Israel 848 (1983)

Afula. City founded in 1925 by the American Zion Commonwealth as the future urban center of the Jewish settlements in the Jezreel Valley. However, the kibbutzim and moshavim of the valley rarely used its facilities, except for the regional hospital of Kupat Holim (the first in the country), instead developing their own services or using those of Haifa. The town was raised to the status of a municipality in 1972.

Arava. Part of the Jordan rift valley and mostly below sea level, the Arava is the area most remote from populated centers in Israel. South of the Dead Sea and bordering Jordan, the Arava has a unique desert landscape. It is on the ancient spice route and produces almost half of Israel's fresh vegetable exports and 12% of its exported flowers.

View of the Arava.
Israel 465A (1974)

Ashdod harbor.
Israel 379 (1969)

Ashdod. 4,000-year-old port but neglected for centuries, Ashdod is now the largest deep-water harbor in Israel.

Avdat. Nabatean town in the Negev desert built in the 2nd century B.C.E. as a caravan stop on the route from the Red Sea to Petra to Beer Sheva and on to the Mediterranean coast. The plain between Avdat and Sde Boker (where Ben-Gurion retired) is traversed by a ravine with a lake, the En Avdat nature reserve.

View of En Avdat.
Israel 466 (1971-75)

Beer Sheva. Capital of the Negev. The Hebrew name of this ancient town can be translated as either "well of the seven" or "well of the oath," referring to the biblical account of the covenant Abraham made with Abimelech over a well that the Patriarch had dug in the desert. The phrase "from Dan to Beer Sheva" occurs frequently throughout the Bible, indicating the northern and southern boundaries of the Israelite territory. In Roman and Byzantine times, Beer Sheva was a prosperous station on the route from the Red Sea to the Mediterranean. The pride of the modern city is the Ben-Gurion University of the Negev.

Modern Beer Sheva with view (bottom right) of local Bedouins. *Israel 1067 (1990)*

Church of the Nativity,
Bethlehem. *Jordan 662 (1970)*

Bethlehem. Town in the Judean hills south of Jerusalem in the area once occupied by the tribe of Judah. Bethlehem is the burial place of Rachel, the wife of Jacob; the setting of the Book of Ruth; and the ancestral home of the royal family of David. According to the Christian Bible, Bethlehem was the birthplace of Jesus of Nazareth, and the 4th-century Church of the Nativity is a major Christian shrine. To Israelis, Bethlehem is Bet Lechem ("house of bread"); for Arabs it is Bet Lahm ("house of meat").

Caesarea. Named by King Herod in honor of Augustus Caesar, this seaside town south of Haifa was the headquarters of Roman rule in Palestine. Extensive archeological excavations have uncovered ruins from the Roman, Byzantine, and Crusader periods, including a magnificent 5,000-seat amphitheater that is now a venue for summer concerts. Just north of the city is a great aqueduct almost 6 miles long, though most of it has been buried by the shifting sands.

Caesarea port.
Israel 338(1967)

Dead Sea. *Israel 1008 (1989), Jordan 522a (1965)*

Dead Sea. Lowest point on earth at about 1,300 feet below sea level. This inland sea, 47 miles long and 9.5 miles wide, is known in Hebrew as *Yam ha-Melach* (Salt Sea) because of the huge quantities of minerals it contains. Six times as salty as the ocean, the waters are so heavy that they hold the human body buoyant and it is virtually impossible to sink. Israelis and tourists alike flock to area spas for therapeutic black mud applications and sulfur and mineral baths. The Dead Sea Works has been established to commercially exploit the millions of tons of salt, potash, and bromides of these mineral-rich waters.

Eilat. Israel's leading winter resort, at the southern tip of the Negev. Blessed with fine beaches, coral reefs filled with exotic fish, and year-round sunshine, Eilat lies on the Gulf of Aqaba, a finger of the Red Sea where the borders of Israel, Egypt, Jordan, and Saudi Arabia meet. About 950 B.C.E., Solomon built the twin cities of Eilat and Ezion-Geber for his navy and copper industry, but they were abandoned with the discovery of a sea route around Africa to India. Eilat was developed by Israel both as a tourist mecca and as a seaport window to East African and Asian markets.

Eilat: Diving and sea view. *Israel 1007 (1989), 470A (1971-75)*

En Gedi. Oasis on the western shore of the Dead Sea. Literally meaning "fountain of the goat," En Gedi was a place of abundant fertility in ancient times, with its vineyards extolled in the Song of Songs and its palms used as a symbol of beauty. The rare herbs and spices grown at En Gedi were famous throughout the ancient world and used to produce exotic incense, lotions, and perfumes. Today, the environs of En Gedi are a national park featuring spectacular waterfalls, where the Bible records that the youthful David took refuge from King Saul.

En Gedi.
Israel 479 (1971-75)

En Gev and the Sea of Galilee.
Israel C10 (1953-57)

En Gev. Site of a kibbutz founded in 1937 on the eastern shore of the Sea of Galilee. A famous statue of a mother and child by Chana Orloff commemorates those who stood fast against the Syrian aggressors in 1948. The En Gev music festival is a popular yearly event.

Gamla. Seven miles southeast of Kazrin, the Israeli "capital" of the Golan received its name because it is situated on a hill that looks like the hump of a camel (gamal). Shortly after the revolt against Rome broke out in 66 C.E., Gamla filled with Jewish refugees fleeing Roman control. The inhabitants of Gamla initially held out against the Roman siege. However, once their defenses were breached, about 9,000 people flung themselves from the cliff, choosing death before subjugation. The archeological excavations at this "Masada of the North" have revealed one of the earliest synagogues, dating back to the Second Temple period.

Nature reserve at Gamla.
Israel 1052 (1993)

Gan Ha-Shelosha. Magnificently landscaped recreation park near Tiberias, with naturally warm freshwater pools fed by En Harod (Herod's Spring). Much loved by Israelis, who bring their families to picnic and swim, Gan HaShelosha has been engineered into a full-fledged water park with waterfalls and slides.

Top: Gan Ha-Shelosha.
Bottom: Hadera. *Israel 462(1971-75), 1079 (1991)*

Hadera. Town 10 miles north of Netanya that was founded in 1890 by immigrants from Lithuania.

Haifa. Israel's principal port and third largest city. The capital of the north overlooking a stunning bay, Haifa extends over the foot, slopes, and crest of Mount Carmel. The city is divided into three tiers – a lower industrial area fringing the harbor; the central business area (Hadar); and the upper Carmel district, a verdant residential section with panoramic vistas. Haifa's most impressive tourist attraction is the huge domed Baha'i shrine with its majestic gardens. The city has two major institutions of higher learning, the Technion and the University of Haifa.

Baha'i World Center, Haifa.
Israel 1443 (2001)

From left: View of Hebron in 1839. *Palestinian Authority 67 (1997)*;
Mosque at Cave of Machpelah in Hebron. *Jordan 28 (1951)*

Hebron. Ancient city southwest of Jerusalem and the site of the Cave of Machpelah, which Abraham bought from Ephron the Hittite as a burial ground for his wife Sarah. Isaac and Rebecca, and Jacob and Leah are also buried in this Tomb of the Patriarchs. Their remains are housed in a fortress build by Herod, which later was converted into a mosque. King David reigned for seven years in Hebron before establishing his capital in Jerusalem. In more recent times, Arabs massacred Hebron's 700 Jews in the 1929 riots. After the War of Independence, Hebron came under Jordanian rule, but was captured by Israel in the Six-Day War. Today, conflict often erupts between the large Arab majority and Jews living either in a

Haifa harbor. *Israel 380 (1969)*

small community in the heart of Hebron or in the nearby settlement of Kiryat Arba (a biblical name for Hebron).

Hula Valley. Once a desolate swampland north of the Sea of Galilee, Zionist pioneers drained the malaria-infested marshes to reclaim the land. In addition to settlements, there is now a prominent nature reserve in the Hula Valley.

Ilaniyya. Moshav in eastern Lower Galilee. Long known by its popular Arabic name Sejera (both terms mean "tree"), Ilaniyya was founded in 1899. Some of the settlers were Kurdish Jews and Russian converts to Judaism. Among the Second Aliyah immigrants who worked at Ilaniyya as hired laborers was David Ben-Gurion.

Lake Huleh.
Israel C15 (1953-57)

Ilaniyya.
Israel 1428 (2001)

Jaffa. Now an integrated component of the sprawling Tel Aviv metropolitan area, Jaffa has a long and colorful history dating back to biblical times. King Hiram of Tyre floated the cedars of Lebanon down to Jaffa for the building of Solomon's Temple. Jonah sailed from this port en route to his encounter with the "great" fish. According to Greek legend, Andromeda was chained to a rock and on the verge of being sacrificed to a sea monster when saved by Perseus on his winged white horse. Jaffa played a major role in the Crusades and in Napoleon's invasion. It was a predominantly Arab town until captured during the War of Independence; most of the Arabs fled and Jaffa was incorporated into Tel Aviv. The "Jaffa orange," developed in the coastal area of Israel, has become internationally famous.

From left: Jaffa harbor; view of Jaffa from the sea. *Israel 339 (1967), C16 (1953-57)*

Jethro's tomb.
Israel 492 (1972)

Jethro's Tomb. Near Tiberias, this holiest place for the Druze people is the tomb of the prophet Nebi Shu'eib, known in the biblical tradition as Jethro, the father-in-law of Moses.

Jordan River. River that arises from headwaters in the Lebanese mountains, flows south through the Sea of Galilee (Kinneret), and empties into the Dead Sea. The Children of Israel crossed the Jordan River from the east to reach the Promised Land. The waters of the Jordan became sacred in Christian eyes because it was the site where John the Baptist performed his ritual immersions.

View of the Jordan River by F. Geyer (circa 1850). *Israel 1370 (1999)*

Juara. *Israel 1409 (2000)*

Juara. Situated between Yokneam and Megiddo, Juara was the site of a defense installation and is near the training and operations base used by Palmach freedom fighters.

Judean Desert. Just east of Jerusalem, the Judean desert is a land of rugged splendor – hot, dry, and inhospitable, but rich in history. Jericho, the oldest inhabited city on earth, surrounds an oasis deep within this desert. Abraham and Lot camped in the Judean Desert as they journeyed to Egypt; Lot's wife cast her last unlucky glance

Judean Desert.
Israel 461 (1971-75)

back toward the burning cities of Sodom and Gomorrah. Jacob laid his head on a rock to dream of angels; Moses gazed on the place he was never to reach from the top of a high mountain in this desert — Mount Nebo (today within Jordan), and the tribes of Israel streamed through the craggy heights of this wilderness on their way into the Promised Land. The Judean Desert is also the site of the Dead Sea, Herod's mighty fortress of Masada, and Qumran, where the Dead Sea Scrolls were discovered.

Qumran Caves.
Jordan 522b (1965)

Kefar Tavor. Moshav at the foot of Mt. Tabor. Founded in 1901 about 10 miles northeast of Afulah by the Jewish Colonization Association, Kefar Tavor was a center for the activity of Ha-shomer until World War I.

Kiryat Shemona. Literally meaning "Town of the Eight," the name of this Upper Galilee community refers to Joseph Trumpeldor and his seven comrades who died at nearby Tel Hai defending their settlement from Arab attackers in 1920. Unfortunately, this development town still periodically comes under attack by *katushya* rockets fired from Lebanon.

From top: Kefar Tavor; Kiryat Shemona.
Israel 1431 (2001), 1382 (1999)

Masada, the northern palace. *Israel 274 (1965)*

Masada. Magnificent palace and fortress complex built by King Herod in the Judean wilderness on an isolated mountain plateau that rises to 1,440 feet above the western shore of the Dead Sea. In 73 C.E., three years after the fall of Jerusalem, Masada was the last stand of the Jewish Zealots in the war against Rome. The Romans launched a massive attack with siege engines, flaming torches, rock bombardments, and battering rams, but Masada remained in Jewish hands. At last, it became clear that the end was near. As the historian Josephus reports, Zealot-leader Eliezer Ben-Yair made an impassioned speech that persuaded the 900 men, women, and children who inhabited Masada to accept death bravely on their own terms, rather than surrender to the Romans. Ten men chosen by lot served as executioners; one of these then killed the other nine before falling on his own sword. This tragic yet heroic stand has inspired the confident slogan of modern Israel – "Masada shall not fall again!"

From top: Masada, view from the west; lower terrace. *Israel 272-273 (1965)*

Mediterranean Sea. Western border of Israel.

Mediterranean Sea.
Israel 1009 (1989)

Metulla. Northernmost city in Israel, situated on the Lebanese border in the foothills of Mt. Hermon. Founded in 1896 by a Rothschild grant, Metulla is a picturesque, pine-scented oasis where residents farm and cultivate bees. Just west of Metulla is the "Good Fence," the former border crossing between Israel and Lebanon that received its name in 1976 when a Lebanese child was brought into Israel to receive medical care. Nearby is the Ayun nature reserve with

Tanur waterfall at Metulla.
Israel C14 (1953-57)

the 100-foot Tanur waterfall, a name derived either from the Arab word *tanura*, the skirt worn by Arab women in this region, or the Hebrew word *tanur*, meaning "oven."

Mitzpe Revivim. One of the first settlements in the Negev (1943). Although water, food and shelter were hard to find in this desert area south of Beer Sheva, with foresight and courage the pioneers succeeded in building a fort-like compound. During the War of Independence, Israel's Negev forces relied on an underground hospital and secret airfield buried in the desert of Mitzpe Revivim.

Mount Hermon. Highest mountain in Israel with a 9,232-foot summit. The moshav of Neve Ativ has developed a ski center on the upper slopes of Mount Hermon, which has a snow season that usually begins in December or January and lasts until about mid-April.

Mitzpe Revivim.
Israel 1427 (2000)

Mount Hermon.
Israel 467 (1971-75)

Mount Meron nature reserve.
Israel 1054 (1990)

Mount Meron. Just beyond Safed, the highest city in Israel, Mount Meron is the highest peak within the Green Line (3,926 feet) and offers a panoramic view of the Sea of Galilee.

Mount Tabor. Tallest mountain in the Lower Galilee (1,800 feet), about 6 miles southeast of Nazareth. At this dramatic peak, Deborah and Barak let the Israelites to victory over the Canaanites. According to Christian tradition, Mount Tabor is the site where Jesus was transfigured as he spoke to Moses and Elijah in the presence of three of his disciples.

Mount Tabor.
Vatican City 1111 (1999)

Nazareth (19th century watercolor).
Vatican City 1108 (1999)

Nazareth. Major Arab city in Israel with a Christian majority, Nazareth nestles in a secluded glen in the hills of lower Galilee in the shadow of Mount Tabor, overlooking the great Plain of Jezreel. The home of Jesus as a child and young man, Nazareth is the site of the Church of the Annunciation, where according to tradition the angel Gabriel told Mary of the coming birth of her son. A Jewish suburb to the north is known as Upper Nazareth (Nazareth Ilit).

Upper Nazareth.
Israel 472C (1975)

Negev. Still largely uninhabited southern region that constitutes about 60% of the total area of Israel. For years the Negev was a forsaken wasteland of wind-sculpted mountains, high plateaus, canyons, and wide dry riverbeds. "Making the desert bloom" has been a Zionist dream; although the Negev is sparsely populated, settlements have been established to grow winter crops and early vegetables.

From left: Negev landscape; Nahal Baraq canyon. *Israel 538 (1972), 404 (1970)*

Netanya. Seaside town north of Tel Aviv. Founded in 1929 as a citrus center among the sand dunes of the fertile Sharon Plain, Netanya was named after American philanthropist Nathan Strauss. Perched on verdant cliffs overlooking the Mediterranean, Netanya is also the center of Israel's diamond-cutting industry, which was developed in the late 1930s by immigrants from Antwerp and South Africa.

Rehovot. Site of the Weizmann Institute of Science, a major center of fundamental and applied research set in a stunning complex of futuristic buildings, verdant lawns, and colorful gardens.

Rosh Pinna. Small town about 15 miles from Tiberias up the winding road to Safed. Founded by Jewish pioneers in 1882 as a cooperative farming settlement, its name means "cornerstone" – an apt designation since Rosh Pinna was the first new Jewish community founded in the Galilee in modern times and paved the way for resettlement of the region.

Safed (Zefat). Capital of the Upper Galilee. In the 15th century after the expulsion of the Jews from Spain, the mystical town of Safed became a great spiritual and educational center. In Safed, Joseph Caro wrote the *Shulchan Aruch* (the major code of Jewish law) and Isaac Luria developed the *Kabbalah*. Much of Safed was destroyed by an earthquake in the 18th century. After heavy fighting in the War of Independence, the Arab population fled. Today, its beautiful mountain setting has made Safed an art center and a popular resort.

From top: Netanya; Rosh Pinna; Sea of Galilee (19th century drawing); Kinneret. *Israel 469 (1971-75), 672 (1977), Vatican City 1109 (1999), Israel 469 (1971-75)*

Sea of Galilee. In Hebrew *Kinneret* (from a root meaning lyre or violin), it is a harp-shaped fresh-water lake, 13 miles long and seven and a half miles wide at its broadest point. Surrounded by the hills of Galilee and the Golan, the Kinneret is about 700 feet below sea level and is filled from the north by the Jordan River. A rich fishing ground, the Sea of Galilee is encircled by towns and villages, including Tiberias, Capernaum, Migdal, Ginossar, and En Gev.

Sha'ar Hagay. Situated 11 miles west of Jerusalem, during the War of Independence Sha'ar Hagay was the site of the bloodiest combat between Israeli and Arab armies over control of the route leading upward from Tel Aviv. Convoys were repeatedly attacked as they brought relief supplies to the beleaguered Israeli forces in Jerusalem. Today, Sha'ar Hagay offers a panoramic view of the valley where Joshua defeated the Amorites, King David smote the Philistines, and the Maccabees battled their way to Jerusalem.

From top: Rehovot; Safed (with tab); Safed; Sha'ar Hagay; Shuni. *Israel 1040 (1990), 1346 (1999), 427B (1971-75), 1442 (2001), 1400 (2000)*

Shuni. Compact semi-circular Turkish fortress nestled amid the lush lawns of Jabotinsky Park north of Caesarea. While masquerading as an agricultural commune, the fortress became the

The Jewish World in Stamps

Soreq Cave nature reserve.
Israel 406 (1970)

chief military training camp of the underground Etzel (Irgun) movement, which fought against the British Mandatory forces. The fortress is now the Etzel Museum, and the original gravestones of nine Jews hanged and buried by the British, plus that of first Etzel chief David Raziel, form a memorial in the park.

Soreq Caves. Twelve miles west of Jerusalem, these limestone caves contain incredible stalactite and stalagmite formations.

Tel Dan. East of Kiryat Shemona, Tel Dan is the site of extensive excavations including a prehistoric settlement and a pre-Israelite cult center. Settled by the tribe of Dan, this area marked the northern limit of the Promised Land (the southern limit was Beer Sheva). Cold-water springs gushing up from the ground in the Tel Dan Nature Reserve form the Dan, which is one of the three principal sources of the Jordan River.

Tel Dan.
Israel 464A (1971-75)

Tel Aviv. Commercial and cultural center of Israel. Founded in 1909 as the first all-Jewish city, Tel Aviv ("Hill of Spring") was initially developed by a group of Jewish residents from Jaffa (immediately to the south), who bought two stretches of sand dunes to build a garden suburb. Its first and long-time mayor was Meir Dizengoff (1861-1936), who donated his house on Rothschild Boulevard for the establishment of the Tel Aviv Museum. With Jerusalem under siege in 1948, Ben-Gurion proclaimed the independence of Israel in Tel Aviv. The city is home to the Israel Philharmonic Orchestra, Habimah Theater , New Israel Opera, and the campus of Tel Aviv University, which houses the Diaspora Museum.

From top: Tel Aviv at 50; Tel Aviv at 40.
Israel 160 (1959), 44 (1951)

Meir Dizengoff.
Israel 919 (1985)

Tiberias. On the western shore of the Sea of Galilee, Tiberius was built by King Herod in honor of the reigning Roman emperor, Tiberius Caesar. With its hot springs and mild climate, Tiberias became one of the most elegant winter resorts in this part of the ancient world. After the failure of Bar Kochba's revolt, Tiberias became a major Jewish center and the home of the Sanhedrin. In this city, Rabbi Judah ha-Nasi completed the Mishnah (c. 200 C.E.), the Jerusalem Talmud was compiled (c. 400 C.E.) and scholars introduced vowels and punctuation into Hebrew grammar and developed a standard "Masoretic" text of Scripture. Pilgrims have flocked to Tiberias to pray at the tombs

From left: Tomb of Rabbi Meir, Tiberias; Tiberias. *Israel C17 (1953-57), 1347 (1999)*

of Maimonides, Rabbi Yochanan ben Zakkai, and Rabbi Meir Ba'al Ha-Nes. Today, Tiberias is the economic center and metropolis of Lower Galilee.

Yavne'el (Jabneel). Moshav in eastern Lower Galilee. Founded in 1901 by Russian pioneers, after the War of Independence Yavne-el gained a number of new members from Yemenite and North African refugees who were sent to a nearby absorption camp.

Yavne'el's 100th anniversary.
Israel 1429 (2001)

Jerusalem

Capital of the Jewish people ever since King David established his throne there about 3,000 years ago, the Holy City of Jerusalem is now the capital of the modern State of Israel. From a Hebrew root meaning "peace" or "whole," Jerusalem has been the Jews' unending object of longing throughout the centuries of dispersion. As they wept for their lost land by the rivers of Babylon, the Jews cried out, "If I should forget you, O Jerusalem, let my right hand forget its cunning." Each year at the end of the Passover feast and the Yom Kippur fast, Jews throughout the world fervently hope for "Next year in Jerusalem!"

In commemoration of the 3000th anniversary of Jerusalem in 1996, many nations issued single stamps or souvenir sheets illustrating major sites in the city.

Above: Approach to Jerusalem. Below: Children's drawing of Jerusalem. *Israel 24 (1949), 737 (1979)*

Views of Jerusalem on souvenir sheets. From top: *Uganda 1415 (1996), Azerbaijan 582 (1996), Guyana 3069 (1996)*

Historical Jerusalem

Jerusalem is situated in the Judean Hills at an elevation of more than 2,000 feet above sea level. The triad of hills (Mount Zion, Mount Moriah, Mount of Olives), separated from other hills by the deep ravines of Hinnom and Kidron, made Jerusalem a natural stronghold. A center of Canaanite civilization in Abraham's time (about 1,900 B.C.E.), it was twice destroyed, once by Nebuchadnezzar of Babylon (586 B.C.E.) and again by Titus of Rome (70 C.E.). Jerusalem was turned into a Christian holy city by Emperor Constantine in about 330 C.E. and fell under the control of the Muslims in 836. After the initial success of the First Crusade in 1099,

Jerusalem changed hands several times between Crusaders and Muslims (most notably under Saladin). Under Turkish control from 1517, Jerusalem was conquered by the British under General Allenby in the final year of World War I. After the War of Independence in 1948, the ceasefire lines left Jerusalem split down the middle, from north to south, by a wall of concrete, barbed wire, and minefields. The modern western section of the city remained in Israeli hands, but the Old City (including the Jewish Quarter from which all Jews were expelled) and the modern Arab neighborhoods north of it were annexed by Jordan. In the Six-Day War, East Jerusalem was captured by Israel and the city was reunited once again.

Mount Zion, Jerusalem.
Israel 1348 (1998)

Mount Zion. This hill southwest of the Old City has borne its name since Byzantine times, because the prophetic literature and the Psalms use the term Zion for Jerusalem and it was believed to be the site of the City of David. The central building on Mount Zion is the Dormition Abbey, which is said to stand on the site where the Virgin Mary died. Nearby is the traditional site of Kind David's tomb; above it is the Coenaculum, where Jesus is said to have sat with his disciples to celebrate the Passover seder (Last Supper).

Tomb of Absalom (Absalom's Pillar). Free-standing monument dating from Herodian times that contains two burial chambers. At one time, religious Jews would throw stones at this so-called tomb in condemnation of Absalom, who rebelled against his father, King David.

Tomb of Zechariah. Hewn entirely from rock in Herodian times and with a pyramidal roof, tradition associates it with the prophet Zechariah, who called for the rebuilding of the Temple in Jerusalem after the return from Babylon.

Absalom's Pillar. From left: *Guyana 3069c (1996)*, *Israel 370 (1968)*

Above: Tomb of Zechariah
Antigua 2009 (1996).
Right, clockwise: Absalom's
Pillar, Holy Sepulcher, Western
Wall, Gate of Mercy.
Gambia 1790-1793 (1996)

Medaba map. Oldest known representation of the city of Jerusalem. The Byzantine-era Medaba map is actually a mosaic floor (25 by 5 meters), made up of two million stones, that illustrates the entire eastern Mediterranean region and has a detailed depiction of Jerusalem at its center.

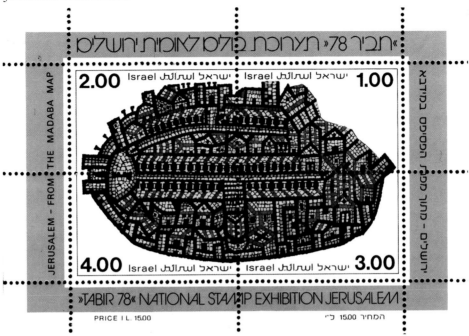

Medaba map: Overview of Jerusalem. *Israel 693 (1978)*

Medaba map: Coned view. *Argentina 1923-1924 (1996)*

Damascus Gate.
Grenada Grenadines 1840b (1996)

Old City Wall. Built in the 1500s by Sultan Suleiman the Magnificent, a 40-foot-high wall surrounds the Old City of Jerusalem. There are eight gates in the wall – Jaffa, Damascus, New, Herod, Lion, Dung, Zion, and Golden. The Jaffa Gate opens into the Christian and Armenian Quarters of the Old City from West Jerusalem; the Damascus Gate is the largest and most beautiful and leads into the Muslim Quarter from East Jerusalem. The Dung Gate, closest to

Zion Gate. *Netherlands Antilles 826 (1998)*

the Temple Mount and Jewish Quarter, was so named because it was where the inhabitants of Jerusalem threw their refuse into the valleys below. Israeli paratroopers gained access to the Old City in the 1967 war through the Lion's Gate (also called St. Stephen's Gate). According to legend, this gate was the only one still open in the eastern part of the city wall after Suleiman had been instructed in a dream to construct a wall surrounding Jerusalem or be torn to pieces by lions. Jewish tradition maintains that the Golden Gate, which has been walled up for centuries, will be the site of the entry of the Messiah into Jerusalem.

Lion Gate.
Israel 375 (1968)

St. Stephen's (Lion) Gate.
Ghana 1891 (1996)

Western Wall (Kotel). Part of the Herodian retaining wall surrounding and supporting the Temple Mount. It was formerly called the "Wailing Wall" by European observers because Jews for centuries came here to bewail the loss of their Temple. The holiest of Jewish sites, the wall is a major venue for prayers day and night. Many of the faithful place private petitions on bits of paper stuffed into the lower cracks of the massive stone blocks.

Pool of Siloam. Collection of overflow water from an open channel, constructed during the reign of Solomon or earlier, that carried water from the Gihon spring along the eastern slope of the City of David to irrigate the gardens of the Kings of Judah. It later was enhanced by the overflow of water in Hezekiah's tunnel, built in 701 B.C.E. This remarkable underground structure led from the Gihon spring into Jerusalem, providing a hidden water supply that allowed the inhabitants of the city to withstand the Assyrian siege.

Pool of Siloam.
Antigua 2010 (1996)

Pool of Bethesda. Lower section of the Bethesda Brook, one of ancient Jerusalem's most important sources of water, which was walled off when the Temple Mount platform was built during the reign of King Solomon. The pool was probably used for washing sheep before they were sacrificed in the Temple. Long known for the curative qualities of its waters, the pool is the site where Jesus is said to have healed a long-paralyzed man.

Citadel and **David's Tower.** Destroyed and rebuilt many times, the Citadel stands to the right of the Jaffa Gate and is now an excavation site and city museum. Originally a Maccabean fortress, it became successively Herod's palace, a Roman garrison, a Byzantine monastery, and a Crusader castle. The present structure dates mainly from the early 14th century.

Pool of Bethesda.
Grenada Grenadines 1840a (1996)

UPON YOUR WALLS, O JERUSALEM, I HAVE SET WATCHMEN...
ISAIAH 62.6

Tower of David.
Israel 372 (1968)

Citadel and Tower of David. *Ghana 1892 (1996)*

Gates of Jerusalem: Jaffa, New, Damascus and Herod Gates. Lion, Golden, Dung, and Zion Gates.
Israel 447-450 (1971), 488-491 (1972)

Jews praying at the Wall.
Azerbaijan 582a (1996)

Jews praying at the Wall.
Panama 854 (1996)

Top: Western Wall with paper note tucked in, praying for peace. *Israel 724 (1979)*
Left: Praying at the Wall (Children's drawing).
Israel 739 (1979)

David's Tower with coat of arms of the City of Jerusalem.
Gambia 1794 (1996)

Holy Sepulcher. *Grenada Grenadines 1841 (1996)*

Church of the Holy Sepulcher. One of the most sacred Christian sites, the church stands above the traditional place where Jesus was crucified, died, entombed, and rose again. Control of the church, which has been the subject of bitter disputes, is divided among six Christian sects (Roman Catholic, Armenian Orthodox, Greek Orthodox, Egyptian Coptic, Ethiopian, and Syrian Orthodox), each of which has its own space and celebrates its own religious rites. The first church was built by Emperor Constantine, who made Christianity the state religion of Rome after his mother, Queen Helena, made a pilgrimage to the Holy Land and located what was believed to be the tomb from which Jesus rose and the True Cross.

Holy Sepulcher. Above: *Azerbaijan 582b (1996).* Below: *Israel 1371 (1999)*

Dome of the Rock. Dazzling mosque covered with a façade of blue tiles originally installed by Sultan Suleiman the Magnificent in the 1500s. In 1994, under the auspices of Jordan's King Hussein, the great dome was completely reconstructed

Left: Dome of the Rock. *Yemen Arab Republic 307 (1972).*
Right: Dome of the Rock. *Morocco 372A (1976)*

Church of the Resurrection.
Israel 371 (1968)

Left to right: Saladin riding to Jerusalem. *Egypt 1532 (1993)*; Dome of the Rock. *Maldives 1960 (1994)*; Holy City of Jerusalem (with symbols of the three major religions). *Niger 857 (1993)*

and regilded with 80 kilograms of 24-karat gold. The Dome of the Rock is built over the Foundation Stone, which according to Islamic tradition was the site from which Mohammed ascended to view paradise on his Night Journey. It is also the traditional site of the *Akedah* (binding of Isaac) as well as the altars used for burnt offerings in the First and Second Temples.

Hurva Synagogue. Once the great synagogue of the Jewish Quarter, it was heavily damaged in the 1948 war and destroyed after the Jordanians captured the area. From a Hebrew word meaning "ruin," all that remains is a single broad, graceful arch marking the line of the building's former domed roof, a memorial to its prior grandeur.

Windmill. Built for grinding flour, the windmill is the most recognizable landmark of the first residential quarter outside the walls of the Old City, which was built by Sir Moses Montefiore to bring indigent Jews into a more healthful environment. For years an impoverished neighborhood, today Yemin Moshe is a beautifully restored area with spectacular views of the Old City wall.

Left: Dome of the Rock. *Azerbaijan 582c (1996)*.
Right: Dome of the Rock. *Panama 856 (1996)*.
Below, left: Hurva Synagogue. *Antigua 2011 (1996)*.
Below, right: Hurva Synagogue (tab shows remaining arch). *Israel 1164 (1993)*.

Windmill at Yemin Moshe.
Top: *Israel 373 (1968)*.
Right: *Azerbaijan 583 (1996)*

Church of All Nations. Built in 1924 by people from 16 different nations and also known as the Basilica of the Agony, the church is situated on the site where Jesus is traditionally said to have prayed the night before his arrest.

Church of All Nations.
Grenada Grenadines 1840c (1996)

Chapel of the Ascension. Christian shrine under Muslim control that marks the spot where according to tradition Jesus ascended to heaven.

Church of the Ascension.
Ghana 1893 (1996)

Church of Mary Magdelene. Russian Orthodox church with multiple onion-shaped spires, built in 1888 by Czar Alexander III on the lower slopes of the Mount of Olives.

Church of the Visitation. Located in Ein Kerem, the church commemorates the visit of Mary to her cousin Elizabeth, the mother of John the Baptist. This meeting is often depicted in medieval and early Renaissance paintings as a scene in which the two expectant women touch each other's stomachs.

Church of Mary Magdelene.
Ghana 1894 (1996)

Saint Andrew's Church. Built by the people of Scotland and dedicated by General Allenby in 1929, the Presbyterian church is situated on a hilltop near Abu Tor and the Jerusalem railroad station.

Church of the Visitation.
Israel 1398 (2000)

St. Andrew's Church.
Israel 1397 (2000)

Views of modern Jerusalem (40th anniversary of independence).
Israel 987 (1988)

Jerusalem proclaimed capital
of Israel (50th anniversary).
Israel 1383 (1999)

Right: Jerusalem, panoramic view. *El Salvador 1456 (1996)*.
Below: "Jerusalem 2001" Multinational Stamp Exhibition. *Israel 1440 (2001)*

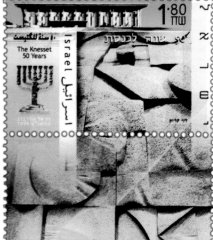

Top: Knesset building. *Israel 312 (1966).*
Middle: Menorah in front of the Knesset.
Uganda 1414a (1996).
Right: 50th anniversary of the Knesset.
Israel 1356 (1999)

Knesset. Israeli Parliament. This modern landmark houses mosaics and tapestries by Chagall. Opposite the building is a large Menorah, the symbol of the State of Israel.

Supreme Court. Opened in 1992, its contemporary architectural design incorporates traditional Middle Eastern motifs of domes, arches, and passageways.

Shrine of the Book. Site of the Dead Sea Scrolls, its distinctive onion-shaped top is contoured to resemble the jar covers in which the scrolls were discovered. Part of the Israel Museum complex, it also houses the Bar Kochba letters and some finds from Masada.

Hebrew University. One of the largest institutions of higher learning in the Middle East, it is housed in a vast fortress-like complex on Mount Scopus. Opened

Israel's Supreme Court building.
Israel 1124 (1992)

Top: Shrine of the Book (mislabeled as Knesset!). *St. Vincent 2308 (1996).*
Bottom: Page from the Dead Sea Scrolls. *Jordan 522b (1965).*
Right: Israel Museum and Shrine of the Book. *Israel 374 (1968)*

The Israel Museum
complex.
Uganda 1414c (1996)

in 1925, it lay empty under Jordanian control from 1948-1967. Since the Six-Day War, the Hebrew University campus has been restored and greatly enlarged, and it offers a sweeping view of both the New and Old City of Jerusalem.

Jerusalem Center for the Performing Arts. Modern complex opened in 1975 that includes the Jerusalem Theater, Henry Crown Auditorium, and the smaller and more intimate Rebecca Crown Hall. The theater presents original Israeli plays and Hebrew translations of foreign classics and modern works, as well as performances by visiting groups in foreign languages. The Auditoriums are the home of the Jerusalem Symphony Orchestra and Israel Chamber Ensemble.

Overview of the Hebrew University.
Dominica 1859 (1996)

YMCA. Historic landmark, opened in 1933, which is located across from the King David Hotel and was designed in an art deco Byzantine-Islamic style by Arthur Loomis Harmon, who also did the Empire State Building in New York City.

YMCA's 100th anniversary. *Israel 698 (1978)*

Yad Vashem. Literally meaning "Monument and Memorial," Yad Vashem is Israel's memorial to the Jewish communities and individuals who perished in the Holocaust. Located on a ridge called Mount of Remembrance, Yad Vashem is reached by the Avenue of the Righteous Among the Nations, which is lined with trees planted in tribute to individual gentiles who helped save Jewish lives during the Nazi era. The Hall of Remembrance is a huge stone crypt-like room in which an eternal flame sheds an eerie light over plaques on the floor listing the major concentration camps. Other memorials include a 20-foot high monument dedicated to the 1.5 million Jewish soldiers among the allied armies, partisans, and ghetto fighters; the Valley of the Destroyed Communities that commemorates the 5,000 Eastern European communities that disappeared during World War II; and the most recent memorial, to the Children of the Holocaust, in honor of the more than 1.5 million murdered youth. Yad Vashem also contains an extensive library and the Hall of Names, which contains more than 3 million pages of testimony as well as the names, photographs, and personal details of many of those who perished in the Holocaust.

Memorial at Yad Vashem. *Guyana 3070 (1996)*

The Twelve Tribes of Israel by Chagall (at the Hadassah Hospital, Jerusalem). *Israel 509-520 (1973)*

tribes of israel שבטי ישראל

DAN · דן

חלונות שאגאל – הדסה, ירושלים
chagall windows – hadassah, jerusalem

tribes of israel שבטי ישראל

GAD · גד

חלונות שאגאל – הדסה, ירושלים
chagall windows – hadassah, jerusalem

tribes of israel שבטי ישראל

ASHER · אשר

חלונות שאגאל – הדסה, ירושלים
chagall windows – hadassah, jerusalem

tribes of israel שבטי ישראל

NAPHTALI · נפתלי

חלונות שאגאל – הדסה, ירושלים
chagall windows – hadassah, jerusalem

tribes of israel שבטי ישראל

JOSEPH · יוסף

חלונות שאגאל – הדסה, ירושלים
chagall windows – hadassah, jerusalem

tribes of israel שבטי ישראל

BENJAMIN · בנימין

חלונות שאגאל – הדסה, ירושלים
chagall windows – hadassah, jerusalem

Jerusalem Post Office.
Israel 89 (1954)

The Jerusalem Theater.
Uganda 1414b (1996)

Jerusalem Convention Center.
Israel 144 (1958)

Jerusalem 3000. From left: King David playing the harp (Gaza synagogue, 6th century); map of Israel drawn by
Rabbi Pinie, 19th century; aerial view of the Knesset and Supreme Court. *Israel 1245-1247 (1995)*

The Jewish World in Stamps

Jewish Institutions and Organizations

Museums

Israel Museum. Situated in the heart of modern Jerusalem, the Israel Museum houses a collection of Jewish and world art, and the archeology of the Holy Land. It was founded to collect, preserve, study, and display the cultural and artistic treasures of the Jewish people throughout its long history as well as the art, ethnology, and archeology of the Land of Israel and its neighboring countries. The Israel Museum houses the world's largest collection of Judaica, including two whole 18th-century synagogue interiors. The ethnography division includes costumes, jewelry, and articles typical of Jewish ritual and daily life in Diaspora communities. Included in the Arts Wing is the extensive collection from the Bezalel National Arts Museum. Other highlights include the 100-piece sculpture collection of the Billy Rose Art Garden and the Shrine of the Book, repository for Israel's Dead Sea Scrolls.

Gold drinking horn (ram's head), Persia, 5th century BCE. *Israel 328 (1966)*

Clockwise: Bronze panther, Avdat (1st cent. BCE); stone menorah, Tiberias (2nd cent. BCE); Phoenician ivory sphinx (9th cent. BCE); gold earring (calf's head), Ashdod (6th-4th cent. BCE); miniature gold capital, Persia (5th cent. BCE). *Israel 323-327 (1966)*

Bezalel Museum's 50th anniversary. *Israel 127 (1957)*

Tel Aviv Museum of Art. Originally established in 1932 in the donated house of Meir Dizengoff on Rothschild Boulevard, the Tel Aviv Museum of Art expanded with the addition of the Helena Rubinstein Pavilion in 1958 and moved to a new building in 1971. It houses a rich collection of modern paintings, sculpture, and graphic art, sponsors many visiting exhibits, and is the venue for concerts and film screenings.

Youth Wing of the Israel Museum. *Israel 505 (1973)*

Paintings from the Tel Aviv Museum of Art

From left: *The Jewish Wedding* by Josef Israels; *Paris Quai* by Camille Pissarro; *Flowers in a Vase* by Fernand Leger.
Israel 432-434 (1970)

Lady in Blue by Moshe Kisling.
Israel 537 (1974)

Tel Aviv Landscape by Aryeh Lubin.
Israel 815 (1982)

Landscape by Sionah Tagger.
Israel 816 (1982)

Children's drawing.
Israel 506 (1973)

Youth workshops.
Israel 507 (1973)

Ha'Aretz ("Homeland") Museum. This complex facility in Ramat Aviv, a suburb of Tel Aviv, incorporates nine separate pavilions covering the history of writing, glass, ceramics, numismatics (coins), ethnography and folklore, science and technology (including a planetarium), antiquities of Jaffa and Tel Aviv, the history of Tel Aviv, and an archeological site with a reconstructed Canaanite period house.

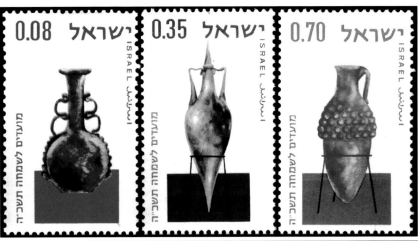

Ancient glass vases (1st-3rd century) at Ha'Aretz Museum.
Israel 264-266 (1964)

Haifa Music Museum. Houses a worldwide collection of musical instruments from all periods of history and a library of recordings of Jewish music.

Institute for Islamic Art. Named for the Swiss orientalist Leo Ary Mayer, the museum has an extensive collection of Islamic art, jewelry, vessels, textiles, and musical instruments, as well as a comprehensive library with slides and photographs of Islamic art and archeology.

Educational Institutions

Hebrew University of Jerusalem. The 1913 Zionist Congress voted to develop a "University of the Jewish People" and appointed an illustrious committee (including Chaim Weizmann, Martin Buber, Ahad Ha-Am, James de Rothschild, and Judah L. Magnes, its first president) to execute the project. Unfortunately, the first meeting never took place because World War I broke out on the day it was scheduled. Nevertheless, while war with the Turks was still being waged in 1918, the cornerstone of the university was laid on Mount Scopus (north of the Old City of Jerusalem) in the presence of General Allenby, commander of British Forces in Palestine. Although the first faculty of the university did not open until seven years later, Albert Einstein gave the initial lecture on his theory of relativity in 1923. Einstein spoke the first sentences in Hebrew, which was to be the language of instruction. In an impressive ceremony, the Hebrew University

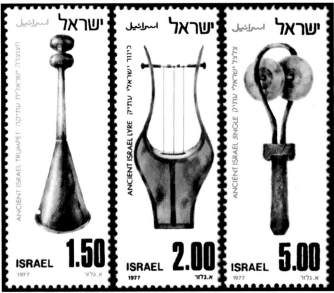

Ancient musical instruments (trumpet, lyre, cymbals), Haifa Music Museum. *Israel 628-630 (1977)*

Institute for Islamic art. From left: vase (India, 18th cent.); elephant with howdah (Iran, 13th cent.); mosque lamp (Syria, 14th cent.). *Israel 709-711 (1978)*

was officially opened by Lord Balfour on April 1, 1925.

The Nazi persecution of Jews in Germany and their exclusion from institutions of higher learning gave fresh importance to the Hebrew University, which was a haven for exiled scholars and scientists. In April 1948, the murder by an Arab mob of a convoy of doctors, nurses, and students en route to Hadassah Hospital on Mount Scopus compelled the evacuation of the site to avoid further losses. Cut off from the New City of Jerusalem by the fighting, the area of Mount Scopus was demilitarized after the Armistice. Until its liberation by Israeli forces in 1967, the Mount Scopus campus stood empty except for Israeli guards, since the Jordanians controlled the road leading to it from Jerusalem.

The work of the Hebrew University resumed in western Jerusalem, housed in improvised and unsuitable buildings scattered over the city. The rooms for lectures were bare; there were no laboratories or equipment and very few books. At the same time, the rapid building of the newly created State of Israel required intensified expansion of university departments to provide the needed civil servants, teachers, doctors and lawyers, scientists and agronomists. Faculties of medicine and law were established, and an extensive new campus was dedicated at Givat Ram in the western part of the city. A larger Hadassah University Hospital (opened in 1961), as well as a medical school and a dental school, were built at Ein Kerem on the outskirts of Jerusalem. Finally, the Hebrew University returned to its original home on Mount Scopus after the Six-Day War.

Mikveh Israel. First and for many years the only agricultural school in Israel. Situated southeast of Tel Aviv, Mikveh Israel (literally, "Hope of Israel") was founded in 1870 by the Alliance Israelite Universelle on the initiative of Charles Netter, in response to an appeal to help Jews in the Holy Land learn a productive occupation. The first BILU pioneers trained at Mikveh Israel immediately upon their arrival in the country, and the school became an important education center for

Hebrew University campus on Mount Scopus.
Israel 551 (1975)

The Hebrew University.
Israel 23 (1950)

Left: Charles Netter, founder. Right: Mikveh Israel Agricultural School.
Israel 417-418 (1970)

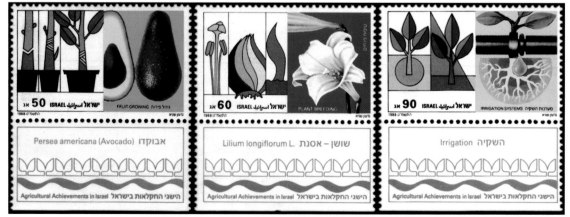

Agricultural achievements in Israel. From left: avocado (fruit growing); lilium longiflorum (horticulture); irrigation. *Israel 1004-1006 (1988)*

The Jewish World in Stamps

Youth Aliyah. Mikveh Israel has been instrumental in developing novel techniques in citrus and other farm branches, introducing avocado cultivation and the acclimatization of many livestock strains.

Technion (Israel Institute of Technology).

Major engineering university in Israel. Paul Nathan of Berlin, one of the leaders of the Relief Organization of German Jews (Hilfsverein), was the father of the plan for a technical school in Haifa, the cornerstone of which was laid in 1912. As the date approached for the opening of the school, then known by the German name Technikum, a struggle broke out in the governing board over the language of instruction. The Zionist minority insisted on Hebrew, but the majority voted for German. This decision aroused a storm of controversy, and practically all Jewish institutions and organizations passed resolutions of protest. The Hebrew Teachers' Association issued a ban against its members accepting posts or registering students in the Technikum; pupils at the Hilfsverein's other schools struck in support of having Hebrew as the sole language of instruction, and many of the teachers resigned. Consequently, the opening of the Technion was delayed and World War I broke out before the controversy could be settled. After the war, the Zionist Organization acquired the property, and in 1924 the first classes on a university level were held – in Hebrew. Since then, graduates of the Technion have supplied more than half of the technically trained manpower for scientific and industrial development programs in Israel. In 1953 the Technion began its move from the original building in midtown Haifa to a 300-acre campus on Mt. Carmel, popularly known as Technion City. The Technion established a new medical school in 1970.

  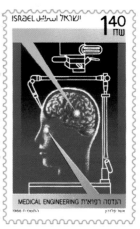

Industrialization of Israel. From left: computer technology; genetic engineering; medical engineering. *Israel 979-981 (1988)*

Technion, Israel Institute of Technology. *Israel 118 (1956)*

Technion's 50th anniversary. *Israel 528 (1973)*

Tel Aviv University.

Largest institution of higher learning in Israel. First established in 1956, the university's 220-acre campus in the suburb of Ramat Aviv comprises faculties and research institutes, student dormitories and facilities, a sports center, zoological and botanical gardens, an art gallery, and a statue garden. The Middle East peace process and ensuing regional cooperation opportunities are important research fields at the university, notably through such institutes as the Dayan Center for Middle Eastern and African Studies and the Jaffee Center for Strategic Studies. One of the main attractions on campus is the Diaspora Museum, which houses exhibits detailing the history of the Jewish people.

Volcani Institute.

Complex of research facilities that began as agricultural experimental stations at Rehovot and Bet Dagon. Established by Yizhak Elazari-Volcani (Wilkansky; 1880-1955) in conjunction with the Zionist Organization in the 1920s, the Volcani Institute today has three large research farms and sponsors several regional facilities. Its activities are organized in divisions of soil and water, garden and field crops, fruit-tree plantations, livestock, plant protection, mechanization, food technology, and afforestation.

Volcani Institute of Agricultural Research. *Israel 460 (1971)*

Weizmann Institute of Science. Center of scientific research and graduate study located on 300 acres of lawns and gardens in Rehovot. It developed from the Daniel Sieff Research Institute – founded in 1934 by Dr. Chaim Weizmann, the distinguished scientist, Zionist leader, and first president of Israel – and was renamed and formally dedicated as the Weizmann Institute of Science in 1949. Institute scientists were the first to introduce cancer research in Israel and designed and built the first computer in the country. In addition to having the initial nuclear physics department in Israel, the Weizmann Institute had the first research accelerators for the study of atomic nuclei, submicron research facility for advancing the electronics industry, and advanced solar energy research facility.

Hebrew Union College (HUC). Dedicated to the training of Reform rabbis, it is the oldest rabbinical seminary in the United States. HUC was founded in Cincinnati, Ohio in 1875 by Isaac Mayer Wise under the auspices of the Union of American Hebrew Congregations to "educate American rabbis for the American pulpit." In 1952, HUC merged with the Jewish Institute of Religion (JIR) in New York, which had been founded in 1922 by Stephen S. Wise to provide training "for the Jewish ministry, research, and community service." HUC-JIR also has a branch in Los Angeles and a Moshe Safdie-designed campus in Jerusalem.

From left: Weizmann Institute of Science (atom diagram and test tube); Koffler Accelerator at the Weizmann Institute. *Israel 400 (1969); 647 (1977)*

Jewish Theological Seminary (JTS). Educational and spiritual center of Conservative Judaism. Opened in New York in 1887, JTS became a major academic institution under the leadership of Solomon Schechter (1847-1915). To reach the rapidly growing Jewish community on the West Coast, in 1947 the seminary opened the University of Judaism in Los Angeles, which now is a separate institution. In 1984, the seminary established the Beit Midrash (Seminary of Jewish Studies) in Jerusalem, which trains rabbis and educators for Masorti synagogues and schools in Israel.

Yeshiva University. Site of the Rabbi Isaac Elchanan Theological Seminary for the training of Orthodox rabbis, which was founded in 1897 as the first advanced yeshiva in the United States. At the undergraduate college for men (Yeshiva College, opened in 1928) and the college for women (Stern College, 1954), students pursue a dual program of studies, taking courses in Jewish subjects as well as a normal load of secular subjects in order to achieve "synthesis" – a mastery of two intellectual worlds. Secular, non-sectarian divisions of Yeshiva University include the Albert Einstein College of Medicine and the Benjamin Cardozo School of Law.

Major rabbinical seminaries in the United States. From left: Hebrew Union College (Reform); Yeshiva University (Orthodox); Jewish Theological Seminary (Conservative). *Israel 939-941 (1988)*

Medical-related institutions

Hadassah. The Women's Zionist Organization of America, Hadassah is the largest women's and Jewish membership organization in the United States. In Israel, Hadassah sponsors medical training, research, and healing, along with educational programs; in the United States, members participate in fund-raising and Jewish educational activities focused on five main themes: health, life skills, Jewish growth and continuity, social action and advocacy, and partnership with Israel.

Founded in 1912, Hadassah flourished under the long-time leadership of Henrietta Szold. In 1939, the Hadassah University Hospital opened on Mount Scopus; however, the Medical Center was evacuated in May 1948 after an Arab ambush that killed 75 medical personnel. The Hebrew University-Hadassah Medical School was launched in 1949 in temporary quarters, and the new Hadassah-Hebrew University Medical Center in Ein Kerem was dedicated in 1960. Today, the Hadassah Medical Organization is renowned as a state-of-the-art diagnostic, research, and treatment center, the largest such facility in the Middle East.

Israel Medical Association. Professional organization of Israeli physicians, based in Ramat Gan.

Kupat Holim. The first health insurance institution in Israel, Kupat Holim was founded in 1911 by a small group of agricultural workers and taken over in 1920 by the Histadrut. The largest countrywide fund, which insures more than 70% of the population, Kupat Holim covers workers in town and country, manual laborers and professionals, salaried and self-employed, Israel-born, veterans, and new immigrants, all on a basis of mutual aid. Kupat Holim operates its own clinics and hospitals, laboratories, pharmacies, and convalescent homes.

Magen David Adom. Hebrew for "Red Shield of David," Magen David Adom was founded in 1930 as Israel's emergency medical first aid society (equivalent to the Red Cross). It operates first aid, ambulance, and mobile-intensive-care services; national blood banks, including a fractionation institute for plasma by-products; and provides instruction in first aid.

Sha'are Zedek ("Gates of Righteousness"). First Jewish hospital built in Jerusalem outside the walls of the Old City. From its opening in 1902 as a 20-bed facility on Jaffa Road, Sha'are Zedek has grown to a 500-bed modern complex opposite Mt. Herzl. Known as the "hospital with a heart," Sha'are Zedek has a long reputation for treating patients rather than just their illnesses and for its adherence to traditional Jewish precepts and values.

Return of Hadassah to Mount Scopus, Jerusalem.
Israel 576 (1975)

Henrietta Szold and the Hadassah Medical Center. *Israel 188 (1960)*

From left: Kupat Holim; Israel Medical Association. *Israel 973 (1987), 824 (1982)*

Sha'are Zedek Medical Center. *Israel 708 (1978)*

Magen David Adom ambulance. *Israel 104 (1955)*

Other Organizations

Association for the Rehabilitation of the Mentally Handicapped. Established in 1952 by a group of parents with mentally and developmentally handicapped children, the organization (AKIM in Hebrew) has fought for the right of people with mental disabilities to lead rewarding lives, in dignity and self-fulfillment, as integral members of the community.

B'nai B'rith. World's oldest and largest Jewish service organization. Founded in 1843 in New York City as a new fraternal order for American Jews, the organizers chose the name B'nai B'rith (Sons of the Covenant) and the Menorah as its insignia. After 1881, when the mass immigration from Eastern Europe poured into the country, B'nai B'rith sponsored Americanization classes, trade schools, and relief programs. When anti-Semitism in the United States increased prior to World War I, in 1913 B'nai B'rith founded its Anti-Defamation League (ADL) to protect the status and rights of Jews. Other organizations established under the auspices of B'nai B'rith include the Hillel Foundation, which serves the religious, cultural, and social needs of university students on campuses throughout the United States and around the world, and the B'nai B'rith Youth Organization (BBYO), which offers a broad range of activities for Jewish teenagers.

Histadrut (abbreviation of *Ha-Histadrut ha-Kelalit shel ha-Ov'dim be-Eretz Israel*; the General Federation of Labor in Israel). Founded in 1920, the Histadrut became the largest labor union in Israel as well as the most powerful non-governmental organization in the country. More than 90% of wage earners in Israel are organized within the Histadrut's trade union framework. Each member pays dues to the federation and in return receives full medical coverage through Kupat Holim (Workers' Sick Fund), old age and disability benefits, and the right to participate in all its cultural and social activities and elections.

The Histadrut also initiated and developed many economic enterprises, some in the form of autonomous cooperative societies and others owned directly and collectively by the entire membership. The earliest and best known of these ventures were the *kibbutz* (collective village) and *moshav* (cooperative settlement of private farmers). The major centrally run economic agencies have included: Solel Boneh, the biggest Histadrut enterprise, which comprises a Building and Public

B'nai B'rith, 150th anniversary.
Uruguay 1478 (1993)

...I will remember my covenant...
Leviticus 26, 42

B'nai B'rith, 150th anniversary.
Israel 1177 (1993)

B'nai Brith, Jerusalem.
Israel 990 (1988)

Association for the Rehabilitation of the Mentally Handicapped.
Israel 1459 (2002)

Histadrut labor union.
Israel 435 (1970)

From top: Egged bus cooperative; the International Labor Organization at 50.
Israel 1219 (1994), 384 (1964)

Working Youth Movement.
Israel 540 (1974)

Teachers Association.
Israel 91 (1955)

Works Company; Tnuva, which markets the products of the Histadrut agricultural settlements and is cooperatively owned by them; Bank ha-Po'alim (Workers' Bank); Shikkun, the Cooperative Housing Society; and the Egged and Dan transport cooperatives, in which the great majority of drivers and employees are shareholding members. In the educational and cultural realm, for years the Histadrut published the daily newspaper *Davar* and ran the publishing house Am Oved (Working People). In the 1990s, however, the Israeli government dramatically decreased the power and scope of the Histadrut in response to calls for it to adapt to current realities and shed its image as a wasteful and bloated bureaucratic organization that had lost touch with the Israeli worker.

Israel Bonds. Organization founded in 1951 to enable the government to raise capital for the rapid economic expansion of Israel and the absorption of the hundreds of thousands of immigrants who arrived after the proclamation of the State in 1948. Since that time, billions of dollars have been raised throughout the world for such projects as the development of Israeli agriculture and industry; exploitation of natural resources; development of existing harbors at Haifa and Eilat and construction of the deepwater port of Ashdod; housing; electric power plants; and the establishment of new tourist facilities.

Above, left and right:
Israel Bonds.
Israel 207 (1961), 45 (1951)

Jewish Agency (*Ha-Sachnut ha-Yehudit le'Eretz Israel*). International non-government body centered in Jerusalem, which is the executive and representative of the World Zionist Organization, whose aims are to assist and encourage Jews throughout the world to help in the development and settlement of Israel. The term "Jewish Agency" first appeared in Article Four of the League of Nations Mandate for Palestine (1922), which stipulated that "an appropriate Jewish agency shall be recognized as a public body for the purpose of advising and cooperating with the (Mandatory) administration of Palestine in such economic, social, and other matters as may affect the establishment of the Jewish National Home and the interests of the Jewish population in Palestine." The Jewish Agency organized the movement and absorption of immigrants, fostered settlement on the land, took part in the development of the Jewish economy, and promoted educational and social services. After the White Paper of 1939, the Jewish Agency fought restrictions on land purchase and immigration, mainly by organizing "illegal" immigration of survivors from Europe in the face of determined British opposition. In May 1948, the Jewish Agency relinquished many of its functions to the newly

Jewish Agency.
Israel 733 (1979)

created government of Israel, but continued to be responsible for the absorption of huge number of immigrants, land settlement, youth work, and other activities financed by voluntary Jewish contributions from abroad.

Jewish Institute for the Blind. In the Old City of Jerusalem in 1902, Nachum Nathanson witnessed a blind boy run into an alley into the path of a camel and suffer serious injuries. The merchant joined with Rabbi Avraham Moshe Lunz, a blind scholar, to found the Jewish Institute for the Blind. Originally opened on the Street of the Prophets in downtown Jerusalem, since 1937 the institute has been located in the Kiryat Moshe neighborhood of the city.

Jewish Institute for the Blind.
Israel 1461 (2002)

Jewish National Fund (JNF). Land purchase and development fund of the World Zionist Organization. Founded in 1901 at the Fifth Zionist Congress, its Hebrew name, *Keren Kayemet le-Israel*, comes from the talmudic dictum about good deeds, "the fruits of which a man enjoys in this world, while the capital abides (*ha-keren kayemet*) for him in the world to come." The JNF's initial principles, which were greatly influenced by the agricultural laws of the Bible, provided that the land it purchased must remain the

Jewish National Fund: Left, tractor and wheat; right, olive tree. *Israel 48-49 (1951)*

Reforestation work of JNF: pine cone and symbolic trees. *Israel 212-213 (1961)*

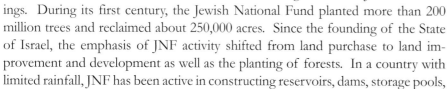

Inset shows 1902 JNF stamp. *Israel 50 (1951)*

inalienable possession of the Jewish people. It cannot be sold or mortgaged and may be leased only to individual pioneers or groups of settlers at a normal rental period of 49 years, renewable only by the original contractor. JNF made its first land purchases in the lower Galilee and continued to acquire property that would form the foundation of the future State of Israel. These purchases determined the future sites of forests, cities, kibbutzim, universities, settlements, and strategic outposts. Many of the first Jewish settlements in Palestine were founded with the aid of the JNF, which in addition to land provided farm equipment, livestock, and expert advice. By 1947, the JNF had bought and controlled more than half the total Jewish property in Palestine, and the UN Partition Plan drew Israel's borders along the lines of JNF land holdings. During its first century, the Jewish National Fund planted more than 200 million trees and reclaimed about 250,000 acres. Since the founding of the State of Israel, the emphasis of JNF activity shifted from land purchase to land improvement and development as well as the planting of forests. In a country with limited rainfall, JNF has been active in constructing reservoirs, dams, storage pools,

JNF's 100th anniversary.
Israel 1454 (2001)

and water purification plants. For years, funds for the JNF came from coins and bills placed in the Blue Box, which has remained a popular Zionist symbol.

American Jewish Joint Distribution Committee (popularly known as the JDC or the "Joint"). Founded in 1914 by a group of wealthy Jews of German background who were alarmed by the suffering of Jews in World War I, the JDC later set up health and child-care institutions to aid Jews fleeing from Polish and Ukrainian pogroms. The JDC established medical stations, loan cooperatives, and vocational training schools, and in 1939 joined the United Palestine Appeal (UPA) to form the United Jewish Appeal (UJA) to coordinate fund-raising activities in the United States. As the conditions of the Jews in Eastern Europe declined in the 1930s, the JDC was forced to return to its relief activities. These reached a peak after the war, when the JDC expended huge sums on the feeding, clothing, and rehabilitation of the 250,000 in displaced persons camps as well as the remnants of Jewish communities in Europe. After the establishment of the State of Israel in 1948, the JDC was closely involved in the airlifting of Yemenite, Iraqi, Kurdish, and Ethiopian Jews to Israel. In recent years, the JDC has focused efforts on Jews in the former Soviet Union, attempting to bring them back to their Jewish heritage by establishing a network of Russian-language Judaic libraries and training Jewish educators, religious leaders, and communal professionals.

Joint Distribution Committee.
Israel 882 (1984)

Dead Sea Works: crane and extraction plant.
Israel 296-297 (1965)

Keren Hayesod (Palestine Foundation Fund). Financial arm of the World Zionist Organization. Founded in 1920, Keren Hayesod was the major institution for financing the Zionist budget for immigration and colonization in Palestine in order to lay the foundations of the Jewish National Home.

From 1925 the fund operated in the United States as the United Palestine Appeal, which combined in 1939 with the American Jewish Joint Distribution Committee and the National Refugee Service to form the United Jewish Appeal. With its head office in Jerusalem, Keren Hayesod coordinates operations in countries outside the United States, including the State of Israel. In addition to establishing and developing more than 820 villages and towns in Israel, funds collected through the Keren Hayesod have helped finance such

First power station, Tel Aviv.
Israel 1084 (1991)

El Al Airlines: Boeing 707.
Israel 228 (1962)

Keren Hayesod.
Israel 422 (1970)

S.S. Shalom. *Israel 250 (1963)*

Zim Israel Navigation Company.
Israel 1241 (1995)

National Labor Federation.
Israel 867 (1984)

important enterprises as the General Mortgage Bank, Israel Land Development Corporation, Mekorot Water Company, Rassco (Rural and Suburban Settlement Company), Solel Boneh (the Histadrut's building and contracting company), Palestine (Israel) Electric Corporation, Palestine Potash Works (Dead Sea Works), Anglo-Palestine Bank (now Bank Leumi), Amidar Housing Corporation, Zim Navigation Company, and El Al Airlines. In the early 1990s, Keren Hayesod achieved unprecedented results from its fund-raising campaigns to support the massive exodus of Russian Jews to Israel and the dramatic rescue of Ethiopian Jews in Operation Solomon, as well as in response to the Scud attacks on Israel during the Gulf War.

National Labor Federation (*Histadrut ha-Ov'dim ha-Leumit*). Organization of Revisionist workers who criticized the Histadrut for its socialist philosophy and expanding beyond its trade union activities. Found in 1934, its symbol was the blue and white flag (rather than the red flag of the Histadrut); its anthem was *Hatikvah* not the *Internationale*; and it chose the anniversary of Herzl's death (20th of Tammuz) rather than the First of May as its annual workers' holiday. Although substantially smaller than its rival, the National Labor Federation stressed the need for a complete separation between the functions of employer and trade union, in opposition to the Histadrut, whose economic arm owns many enterprises that hire workers whose interests are represented by the Histadrut's trade union department. The National Labor Federation also advocated that basic social services, such as medical care, be provided by the state and that pensions and unemployment insurance laws be under national regulation.

ORT (Organization for Rehabilitation through Training). Founded on a small scale in Russia in 1880 as a philanthropic society, ORT has since become a global movement that promotes and develops vocational training opportunities for Jews in the skilled trades and agriculture. After the establishment of the State of Israel, ORT opened vocational courses for new immigrants, manual-training workshops in the children's village of Ben Shemen, and the first vocational schools in Jerusalem, Tel Aviv, and other sites. In various underprivileged areas worldwide, ORT has endeavored to convince Jews that learning a trade was the surest means to acquire economic independence. Gradually, ORT has begun to emphasize technical rather than vocational training, including automation and computers.

ORT's 100th anniversary.
Israel 744 (1980)

Pioneer Women (50th anniversary).
Israel 572 (1975)

Tarbut (50th anniversary of Tarbut Elementary Schools). *Israel 1206 (1994)*

Pioneer Women. Worldwide Labor Zionist women's organization. It was founded in New York City in 1925 to provide social welfare services for women, young adults, and children in Palestine and to help new immigrants become productive citizens. With

The Jewish World in Stamps

its sister organization in Israel, Pioneer Women maintains a large network of welfare and cultural projects in the Jewish State. In the United States, Pioneer Women conducts Jewish educational and cultural activities and supports youth work through Habonim.

Tarbut ("culture"). Hebrew educational and cultural organization that maintained schools in most Eastern European countries between the two world wars. Zionist oriented and promoting pioneer settlement in the Land of Israel, Tarbut provided instruction in Hebrew language and biblical and modern Hebrew literature

United Jewish Appeal (UJA). Organization founded in 1939 that has been the major means for providing American financial support for Jews in Israel and other overseas areas. It has contributed to the rescue and resettlement of more than 4 million people, about half of them immigrants brought to Israel. Since 1979, the UJA has participated in Project Renewal, a program for the physical and social rehabilitation of the lives of immigrant families to Israel living in distressed urban neighborhoods. The annual fund-raising campaigns of the United Jewish Appeal also support local programs such as Jewish day schools, day-care centers, Y's and community centers, vocational workshops, medical care, family counseling, youth guidance, home and institutional care for the elderly, aid to the indigent, and a full range of resettlement services for Jewish immigrants to the United States.

WIZO (Women's International Zionist Organization). Founded in 1920 to provide professional and vocational training for women (with special emphasis on preparation for agricultural pioneering in Palestine) and the care and education of children and youth, WIZO has expanded to defending the rights of women in Israel and the achieving of gender equality in all fields, as well as combating domestic violence and contributing to family and community welfare.

Zionist Organization of America (ZOA). Glowing reports from the First Zionist Congress in 1897 led to the establishment of the Federation of American Zionists the next year. The newly formed Young Judea (1907) and Hadassah (1912) joined the Federation, and at a convention in 1918 the various Zionist branches merged into the Zionist Organization of America. ZOA members played an active role in raising funds for the *yishuv* and in mobilizing American support for the creation of a Jewish state.

United Jewish Appeal. From left:
Israel 707 (1978), 229 (1962)

WIZO's 50th anniversary.
Israel 431 (1970)

ZOA.
Israel 636 (1977)

Zionist Organization of America (its building in Tel Aviv against Manhattan skyline). *Israel 1317 (1997)*

Sports in the Jewish World

Maccabiah Games

In a speech before the Second Zionist Congress in 1898, Max Nordau asked the Jewish people to develop an interest in sports and physical fitness. Nordau's call for "muscular Judaism" was answered by the Maccabi movement, which spread first to the countries of Europe (more than 100 clubs by World War I) and Palestine.

The Maccabiah Games, often termed the "Jewish Olympics," are international athletic events that are recognized and approved by the International Olympic Committee and open to all Jewish athletes. The first Games were held in 1932 in Tel Aviv, with more than 500 athletes from 23 countries. Many athletes and accompanying personnel remained in Palestine after the Maccabiah, so that the games became not only a tool for stimulating sports but also an important means for promoting aliyah. The second Maccabiah in 1935 was even more of an "Aliyah Maccabiah," since most of the athletes and their escorts remained in Palestine because of the anti-Semitism that was sweeping Europe following the Nazis' rise to power in Germany. The third Maccabiah Games could not be held until 1950, and the fourth took place three years later. Since that time, the Maccabiah Games have

Top: The 3rd Maccabiah; bottom left: The 4th Maccabiah; right: Maccabiah's 25th anniversary. *Israel 37 (1950), 78 (1953), 137 (1958)*

8th Maccabiah.
Israel 385 (1969)

Left to right: 9th Maccabiah. *Israel 522 (1973);* 7th Pan American Maccabiah Games. *Uruguay 1369 (1991)*

10th Maccabiah.
Israel 633-635 (1977)

The Jewish World in Stamps

11th Maccabiah.
Israel 779-781 (1981)

12th Maccabiah.
Israel 910-912 (1985)

From top: 13th, 14th and 15th
Maccabiahs. *Israel 1024 (1989), 1171
(1993), 1311 (1997)*

been held regularly every four years, with an ever-increasing participation of athletes from more than 30 countries. The program includes festive opening and closing ceremonies under the patronage of the President and Prime Minister of the State of Israel, with contingents parading under their national flags.

Hapoel Games

Hapoel is the countrywide workers' sports organization, which was founded in 1926 as an affiliate of the Histadrut. Unlike the Maccabi movement, which emphasizes competitive sports and has devoted its energies to organizing them on a national basis (as well as introducing Israel to the international sports arena), the main objective of Hapoel initially was to provide opportunities for physical education and sport for the masses of Israeli youth and to in-

9th International Hapoel Games.
Israel 443-445 (1971)

Hapoel Sports Organizations: 7th
International Congress. *Israel 203 (1961)*

volve them in the labor movement. The Hapoel Games are sports festivals that
are now held every four years.

Olympic Games

Israel participated in the Olympic Games for the first
time in Helsinki in 1952 and thereafter at all subsequent games. Tragedy struck in 1972, when Arab ter-
rorists murdered 11 Israeli coaches and athletes during an attack on the Olympic Village at Munich. This
attack, however, did not prevent Israel from appear-
ing on the international sport scene, and the country returned with a bigger and stronger delegation to the next Olympic Games in Montreal in 1976.

Para-olympics (Games for the paralyzed)

The para-olympics, athletic contests for the physically handicapped, were inspired by the work
of Ludwig Guttman, a neurologist and refugee from Nazi Germany. Guttman believed that
sport, particularly competitive athletics, was an essential part of the treatment for those who at
the time were classified as hopeless cripples. The games originated in 1948 at Stoke Mandeville
Hospital in England and were the outcome of the program of general rehabilitation of veterans who had suffered spinal injuries in World War II. Stoke Mandeville began running national
competitions against other hospitals and clubs, the first of which coincided with the opening
day of the 1948 Olympic Games in London. Israeli athletes have excelled in the para-olympics,
garnering numerous medals.

International Olympic
Committee centennial.
Israel 1238 (1994)

Los Angeles Summer
Olympics. *Israel 883 (1984)*

Para-olympics.
Israel 377 (1968)

Olympiad for the Physically Disabled.
Canada 694 (1976)

The Jewish World in Stamps

Commemorating the eleven Israeli athletes slain by the PLO at the Munich Olympics in 1972.
Guyana 3540a-i (2000)

Souvenir sheet with the Olympic torch issued in memory of the eleven Israeli
athletes, with the Israeli flag. *Guyana 3541 (2000)*

Flora and Fauna in Israel

Despite its limited area, Israel has an extraordinarily varied landscape and a rich array of flora and fauna. There are some 2,500 different species of indigenous wild plants (an extremely high number in relation to the area), as well as enclaves of tropical and European flora, the most northern and southern known. The fauna is also varied, though it is only a remnant of the wild life of biblical times, and at least 15 large mammalian species have become extinct. There are more than 400 varieties of birds (150 of which nest in Israel, the remainder being migratory or winter visitors) and about 70 species of mammals, mostly small rodents and bats. Gazelle, wild boar, ibex, hyena, wolf, jackal, hyrax, caracal, and lynx can still be found.

Roses in Israel. From left: Damascus, Phoenician, Hybrid. *Israel 791-793 (1981)*. Thistles: Scolymus maculates, Echinops viscosus; Cynara syriaca. *Israel 745-747 (1980)*

Owls (Biblical birds). From left: eagle owl, Bruce's Scops owl, barn owl, Hume's tawny owl. *Israel 956-959 (1987)*

Protected wild birds. From left: collared pratincoles, spur-winged plover, black-winged stilts. *Israel 577-579 (1975)*

Sinai rose finch; white-breasted kingfisher; mourning wheatear.
Israel C28-30 (1963)

Above from
left: Blue-cheeked bee
eater; graceful prinia;
Palestine sunbird;
houibara bustard.
Israel C31-C34 (1963)

From left: Scops owl;
purple heron;
white-tailed sea eagle.
Israel C35-C37 (1963)

Below: Ducks in the Holy
Land. From left: garganey,
mallard, teal, shelduck. *Israel
1025a-d (1989)*

Eagles and vultures (Biblical birds): lappet-faced vulture; Bonelli's eagle; sooty falcon; griffon vulture. *Israel 896-899 (1985)*

Songbirds. Wallcreeper, Tristam's grackle, white wagtail, Palestine sunbird, Sinai rosefinch, swallow, trumpeter finch, graceful warbler, black-eared wheatear, common bulbul. *Israel 1133-1135; 1137; 1141-1144; 1146 (1992-1998)*

Animals of the Bible (in nature reserves). Persian fallow deer; Asiatic wild ass; Nubian ibex; caracal lynx; Dorcas gazelle, white oryx; cheetah. *Israel 436-437 (1971), 358-360 (1967), 438-439 (1971)*

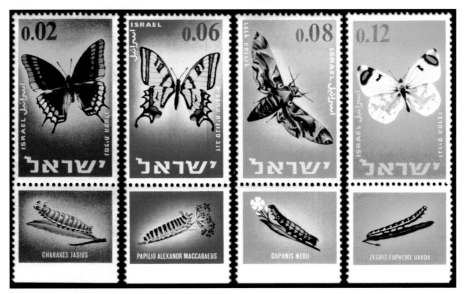

Butterflies. Charaxes jasius; Papilio alexanor maccabeus; Daphnis nerii; Zegris
eupheme uarda. *Israel 304-307 (1965)*

Eilat, the southernmost city in Israel, lies on the Gulf of Aqaba. This is the most northern tip of the Red Sea (*Yam Suf*),
a long narrow strip of water that separates the Arabian Peninsula from the northeastern corner of Africa (Egypt, Sudan,
Ethiopia) and forms the northwestern arm of the Indian Ocean. The waters off Eilat are filled with mounds of beautiful
coral and teem with clusters of exotic, rainbow-colored fish.

Red Sea coral. Balanophyllia, goniopora, dendronephthya. *Israel 932-934 (1986)*

Nature reserves. From left: Hof Dor, with sanderling; Nahal Amud,
with salamander; Huleh, with pelican. *Israel 1154-1155 (1993), 1053 (1990)*

Red Sea fish. Top: Pennant coral fish; orange butterfly fish; lionfish; zebra striped angelfish. Israel 231-234 (1962).
Bottom: Undulate triggerfish; radiate turkeyfish; bigeye; imperial angelfish. *Israel 246-249 (1963)*

The dynamic development of modern Israel has inevitably affected plant and animal ecology. Some 500 new villages and a score of new towns, as well as the rapid expansion of existing ones, have encroached on areas of previously undisturbed wild life and natural vegetation. The quadrupling of the population, the rise in the standard of living, and the vast expansion of tourism have brought large numbers of hikers and day trippers to the countryside. To protect the flora and fauna, in 1963 the government established the Nature Reserves Authority. This agency has selected some 120 areas as nature reserves in which landscape, flora, and fauna are protected in their natural condition. While most of the reserves are open to the public, some are closed to preserve their scientific value. The Nature Reserves Authority also has undertaken to reintroduce species that have become extinct.

Red Sea shells. Cypraea Isabella; Lioconcha castrensis; Gloripallium pallium; Malea pomun.
Israel 678-681 (1977)

Nature reserves. From left: Ein Zin, with wolf; Shezaf, with Negev gazelle; Ramon, with wild ass.
Israel 991-993 (1988)

Jewish Traditions and Values

The Sabbath

The Sabbath (in Hebrew, *Shabbat*, related to the verb *shavat* meaning "cease, desist, rest") is the seventh day of the week, a day on which Jews rest and abstain from work and devote themselves to spiritual matters. On Friday evening, the table is set with a white tablecloth and two loaves of *challah*, the special braided bread, covered with a decorative cloth. Ornamental candlesticks grace the table, and the family dresses in its Sabbath best. All preparations are completed before sundown, when the Sabbath is ushered into the home by the woman of the house as she lights the candles and pronounces the proper blessing. During the Middle Ages, Jews typically lit oil-filled hanging Sabbath lamps suspended by chains. These are now infrequently used in the home, though they may be seen in some traditional synagogues. The *Kiddush* (sanctification) is recited over a cup of wine, and the *Motzi* blessing is said over the *challah*. The meal is always extra special, and even the poorest householder tries to provide some delicacy for the day. It is customary to invite guests and sing special table hymns (*zemirot*) at this and the other two Sabbath meals – Saturday lunch and the *se'udah shlishit* (third meal) before the close of the day.

Sabbath plate.
Israel 631 (1977)

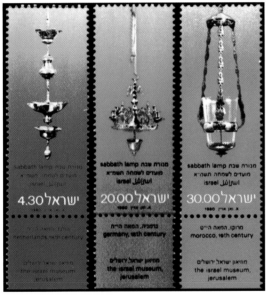

Traditional hanging Sabbath lamps. (Israel Museum, Jerusalem). *Israel 751-753 (1980)*

Blessing of Sabbath candles.
Denmark 766 (1984)

From left: Kiddush cup; hanging Sabbath lamp; candlesticks.
Israel 320, 322, 319 (1966)

Kiddush cups from Moscow and Warsaw.
Hungary 2895, 2897 (1964)

Havdalah

Ritual ceremony that marks the conclusion of the Sabbath (or a festival). A Hebrew word that literally means "separation," Havdalah is an ancient ceremony that goes back more than 2,000 years. It consists of three blessings – over wine, sweet-smelling spices, and light from a braided multi-wick candle – followed by the major benediction that deals with the separation or distinction that God has made "between the holy and the profane, between light and darkness, between Israel and the other nations, and between the seventh day and the six working days." The fragrant spices serve to refresh and revive the spirit and dispel the gloom related to the end of the Sabbath day. A more mystical reason is that the spices provide spiritual compensation for the additional soul that each observant Jew figuratively possesses on the Sabbath. The ceremony customarily concludes with everyone wishing each other a "good week," either in Hebrew (*Shavu'ah tov*) or Yiddish (*Gut voch*).

Spice box for
Havdalah.
Israel 318 (1966)

Spice boxes from Austro-Hungary (19th century), Italy (19th century), and Germany
(18th century). *Israel 1062-1064 (1990)*

Festivals

The festivals allow each Jew to celebrate the victories and successes of the people, as well as to mourn and grieve over the tragedies that have been suffered. In Hebrew, a "festival" may be termed *chag* (celebration), *mo'ed* (appointed time or season), or simply *yom tov* (good day). The festivals can be divided into those commanded by the Torah ("major") and those that were added later ("minor"). The Torah-mandated festivals include the three pilgrimage holidays (Passover, Shavuot, and Sukkot), Rosh Hashanah, and Yom Kippur. Among those festivals that were added later are Purim, Chanukah, Lag B'Omer, and Tu B'Shevat. A national day of mourning, Tisha B'Av, is also regarded as a festival since according to tradition it will become the greatest festival with the coming of the Messiah.

In addition to changes in the liturgy and special ceremonies, on most festivals (with the obvious exception of Yom Kippur) it is incumbent upon Jews to rejoice, which primarily takes the form of ceremonial meals. On the more important biblical festivals, there is both the positive commandment to rest and the negative commandment prohibiting *milechet avodah* (laborious or servile work). However, such "pleasurable work" as the preparation of food is permitted so that one can truly rejoice in the festival.

Rejoicing on the Festivals. From left: tambourine and cymbals, lyre, cymbals, shofar, trumpets, harp.
Israel 100, 121, 122, 101, 102, 103 (1955-1956)

Double oboe.
Israel 123 (1956)

Rosh Hashanah

Rosh Hashanah (literally, "head of the year"), which falls on the first and second days of the autumn month of Tishrei (September/October), is celebrated as the beginning of the Jewish New Year. It is known as *Yom ha-Din*, the Day of Judgment, when God weighs the deeds of every person over the past year and determines his or her fate for the coming year. Consequently, it is customary to greet friends with *l'shanah tovah tikatevu* (May you be inscribed [in the Book of Life] for a good year). At the festive meal, it is traditional to dip a piece of bread or apple into honey to express hope for sweetness in the year ahead. Rosh Hashanah is also known as *Yom Teru'ah*, the Day of Sounding the Shofar. The ram's horn is blown as a wake-up call for the Jew to pray and repent during the Ten Days of Repentance, before the Divine books are sealed at the conclusion of Yom Kippur. The shofar also brings to mind the binding

From left: Bowl of honey with two lit candles; man blowing the shofar.
Israel 1284 (1996), 1089 (1991)

Rosh Hashanah stamps.
Left: Flying scrolls (inscription on wine and oil jars given in tribute to the king). *Israel 10-14 (1948).* Below: Fruit and star of David. *Israel 35-36 (1950)*

Below: Israeli military insignia: air force, navy, defense army, with inscription "Happy Holidays." *Israel 28-30 (1949)*

The Jewish World in Stamps

Rosh Hashanah stamps (continued)

From left: Carrier pigeon; girl holding dove and fruit. *Israel 52-53 (1951).* Carrying a cluster of grapes. *Israel 87 (1954).* Middle, from left: Figs, lily, dove, nut cluster. *Israel 66-69 (1952).*

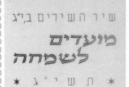

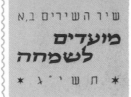

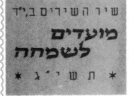

Top: Children's drawing of Bible stories (Adam and Eve). *Israel 1210 (1994)*
From left: Truth, Judgment, and Peace (Ten Commandments, scales and olive branch with dove). *Israel 606-608 (1976);*

Rosh Hashanah Stamps (cosntinued)

The seven indigenous products of the Holy Land. Top and right: wheat, barley, grapes, figs, pomegranates, olive oil, date honey. *Israel 145-148 (1958), 162-164 (1959)*

"And you may gather in your corn and your wine and your oil" (Deut. 11:14). *Israel 1173-1175 (1993)*

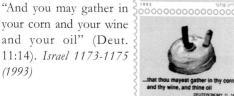

of Isaac, whose rescue from death is a prime example of God's mercy. On the afternoon of the first day, Jews traditionally go to a river or other body of water for the ceremony of Tashlich, in which each person symbolically casts off his or her sins into the water.

Old-fashioned Rosh Hashanah cards: A couple under an umbrella;
woman with Jewish flag; man giving flowers and greetings to a woman.
Israel 1417-1419 (2000)

Jewish New Year cards: Soldier; two girls dancing; child holding flowers.
Israel 1455-1457 (2001)

Yom Kippur

Yom Kippur (Day of Atonement), the fast day on the 10th of Tishrei, is devoted to individual and communal repentance (*teshuvah*, or "returning"). In the Torah, Yom Kippur is described as a *Shabbat Shabbaton* (a Sabbath of solemn rest), on which all manner of work is forbidden and Jews are commanded to "afflict their souls." According to the sages, this duty requires the prohibition of eating and drinking; bathing (for pleasure); anointing of the body with oil; wearing leather shoes; and engaging in sexual relations.

To symbolize purity of heart, it is customary to wear white. Some don a *kitel*, the white robe that is the shroud in which an observant Jew is buried. Unlike most fast days (other than Tisha B'Av) that are only dawn-to-dusk fasts, on Yom Kippur Jews fast for 25 hours. However, fasting is not sufficient in itself to secure atonement. To gain Divine forgiveness, there must be sincere repentance combining contrite confession and a solemn resolve to abandon the ways of evil. Yet, even this only secures atonement for sins committed against God and the Divine law. Therefore, on the eve of the holiday it is appropriate to ask forgiveness from those whom one may have offended during the past year.

Before the fast, it is customary among traditional Jews to perform the ceremony of *kaporot*. In the past, this entailed swinging a live rooster or hen around the head of each member of the family to recall the ancient sin-offerings and to symbolically transfer their sins to the fowl. Today, most use coins and donate the money to charity.

The Yom Kippur service is the longest in the Jewish liturgy. It begins with the mournful chanting of *Kol Nidrei*, which asks for us to be released from all vows or promises that we have made to God but have been unable to keep. A hallmark of the prayers is the confessionals, repeated ten times during the day, in which Jews collectively recite the various sins they may have committed and appeal to God to forgive them. Other major aspects of the Yom Kippur include the *Avodah* service, a recounting of the awesome Temple ritual for the day that reached its climax when the High Priest entered the Holy of Holies to beg forgiveness for his own sins and those of the entire people; the *Yizkor* memorial prayer for the dead, which originally was said only on Yom Kippur but later came to be included in all the major festivals; and the Martyrology, a remembering of those martyred Jews over the centuries who gave their lives for *Kiddush ha-Shem* (Sanctification of God's Name). The concluding service is *Ne'ilah* (closing), which symbolizes the closing of the gates of heaven at the end of the day. A single long blast of the shofar and the words "Next year in Jerusalem!" terminate the fast.

Father blessing children.
Israel 1090 (1991)

Yom Kippur by Maurycy Gottlieb.
Israel 569 (1975)

Sukkot

The Feast of Booths, also known as Tabernacles, begins on the full moon five days after Yom Kippur. Observed for seven days in Israel and eight in the Diaspora, the festival celebrates the joy of the harvest and commemorates the temporary shelters in which the Israelites dwelled as they wandered through the wilderness after the Exodus from Egypt. In Biblical times, Sukkot was the most important holiday of the Jewish calendar. As the last of the three Israelite festivals connected with the agricultural year, it was celebrated as *Chag ha-Asif,* the "feast of the ingathering" from the threshing floor and wine press.

Family seated at a harvest table. *Israel 1091 (1991)*

During this festival, Jews are commanded to construct and "dwell" in a *sukkah,* a temporary structure that must have at least three walls and be only strong enough to withstand normal gusts of wind. The sukkah must be built under the open sky, not under a tree or inside a house. Its roof is covered with *s'chach,* typically cut branches or bamboo sticks that are arranged so that there is more shade (covered space) than sunshine inside the sukkah during the day. It is customary to decorate the sukkah with colorful fruit and with signs quoting verses from the Bible or depicting beautiful scenes from Israel. Traditionally, it was forbidden to eat any major meal or to sleep outside the sukkah. However, modern rabbinical authorities, mindful of the cold and rainy climates to which Jews have wandered during their long exile, have permitted sleeping and eating inside the house during this season when dictated by bad weather.

The major ritual of Sukkot is carrying the four species – the *etrog* (citron), *lulav* (palm branch), and sprigs of the myrtle and willow. Each morning (except on the Sabbath), they are waved in a prescribed manner (toward the east, south, west, north, upward, and downward), indicating that the presence of God is everywhere and acknowledging the Divine rule over the four corners of the universe and the dominions of heaven and earth. In the synagogue, the four species are carried in a procession around the synagogue. A kabbalistic tradition is to invite seven Biblical personalities (*ushpizin,* Aramaic for "guests") to visit the sukkah during the seven days of Sukkot – Abraham, Isaac, Jacob, Joseph, Moses, Aaron, and David.

Immediately after Sukkot is Shemini Atzeret (Eighth Day of Assembly), when prayers are recited for the fall and winter rains that are essential for crops to grow after the long hot summer in Israel. On the next day (but on the same day in Israel) is the holiday of Simchat Torah (Rejoicing of the Law), when all the Torah scrolls are carried in seven processions (*hakafot*) around the synagogue amid joyous singing and dancing. The last portion of Deuteronomy is read and then immediately a new Torah cycle is begun with the reading of the first chapter of Genesis.

Biblical references to Sukkot. *Israel 454-458 (1971)*

Ushpizin (Biblical Sukkah guests):
Abraham, Isaac, Jacob, Joseph, Moses, Aaron and David.
*Israel 1312-1314 (1997),
1375-1378 (1998)*

Sukkot. *Israel 1285 (1996);* etrog box. *Hungary 2898 (1964);* Simchat Torah (inside the Synagogue). *Israel 1286 (1996)*

Chanukah

Festival of Lights that begins on the 25th of Kislev (December) and lasts for eight days. It marks the rededication of the Temple by Judah Maccabee in 165 B.C.E. after his victory over the Syrians, who had defiled the Sanctuary. According to tradition, Judah could find only a single cruse of oil that had not been contaminated by the enemy. Although the oil was only enough to keep the Menorah burning for a single day, it miraculously lasted for eight days until new pure oil could be prepared. This event is commemorated each year by lighting candles throughout the holiday – one on the eve of the first day, two on the second, and so forth until eight are kindled on the last evening – and Chanukah has become known as the "Festival of Lights."

Candles and dreidel.
Israel 1289 (1996)

From left: Chanukah lamp (Bezalel). *Israel 1187 (1998);* spinning top (Bezalel).
Israel 1186 (1997); *Chanukah* by Moritz D. Oppenheim. *Israel 567 (1993)*

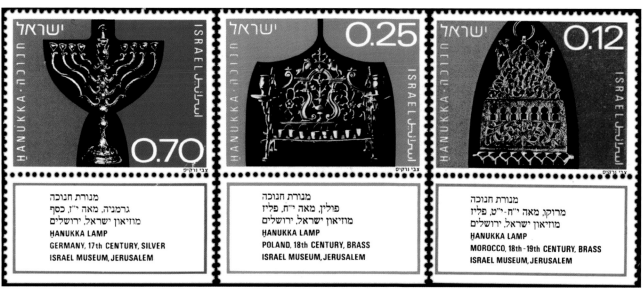

Chanukah lamps: Germany, 17th century; Poland, 18th century; Morocco, 18th-19th century. *Israel 502-504 (1972)*

Chanukah lamps: Morocco, Israel, Lodz Ghetto. *Israel 1183 (1994), 1181 (1993), 1184 (1995)*

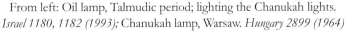

From left: Oil lamp, Talmudic period; lighting the Chanukah lights.
Israel 1180, 1182 (1993); Chanukah lamp, Warsaw. *Hungary 2899 (1964)*

Chanukah is one of the most joyous holidays. After the candles are lit, gifts are given to children and all sing the hymn *Ma'oz Tzur* (Rock of Ages) and a variety of other Chanukah songs that celebrate the courageous struggle of the Maccabees. To commemorate the miracle of the oil, it is customary to eat foods fried in oil, such as potato *latkes* (pancakes) in Ashkenazic communities or *sufganiyot* (jelly doughnuts) among Sephardim and in Israel. A highlight of the festivities is playing *dreidel*, a small top inscribed in the Diaspora with the Hebrew letters N, G, H, and S (standing for *Nes Gadol Hayah Sham*; "A great miracle happened there"). In Israel the final letter is changed to a P (*Po*; "here").

The Chanukah menorah (*chanukiah*) has spaces for the eight candles (or oil and wicks) and a ninth candle, called the *shamash* (servant), which is placed higher or to one side to differentiate it from the others. Originally, it was probably a simple, pear-shaped Greco-Roman clay lamp with apertures for the wick and for the oil reservoir. This was in universal use throughout the Mediterranean world in the centuries before and after the beginnings of the Common Era. During talmudic times, these lamps were mounted on elongated vertical bases. The richly decorated metal Chanukah menorah that developed during the Middle Ages generally had eight oil spouts and a back plate, from which it was hung against the wall. Each Jewish community developed its own style of Chanukah menorah, which generally reflected the artistic customs in the region. Today, menorahs are made of silver, bronze, brass, glass, or stone, and are designed from the most sophisticated to the whimsical.

The Jewish World in Stamps

Tu B'Shevat

Tu B'Shevat, which occurs on the 15th day (full moon) of the month of Shevat (January/February), is known as the "New Year of the Trees," the day on which God decides how bountiful the fruit of each tree will be in the coming year. Although only a minor holiday, in modern Israel Tu B'Shevat has acquired increased importance as a symbol of the revival and redemption of the land and the conquest of the desert. Tu B'Shevat has assumed the character of Arbor Day, focusing on the planting of trees. In the Diaspora, Jews either plant trees in their own communities (if the ground has thawed sufficiently) or send contributions to the Jewish National Fund to plant trees in Israel, and many celebrate by eating such Israeli fruits as figs, dates, and carob.

Tu B'Shevat: Bird singing; girl with plant.
Israel 552-553 (1975)

Purim

Purim commemorates the day on which Esther and Mordecai saved the Jews of Persia from the evil designs of the wicked Haman. Observed on the 14th of Adar (February/March), Purim is celebrated with great merriment after the fashion of the Persian Jews who made their victory over Haman an occasion "for feasting and gladness." During the reading of the *Megillah* (Book of Esther), children and adults twirl noisemakes in derision at every mention of Haman's name. *Hamentaschen* (literally, "Haman's ears") are consumed, and it has traditionally been considered meritorious to become so inebriated that one cannot tell the difference between "Blessed be Mordecai" and "Cursed be Haman." Comic plays, called *Purimshpiel*, are presented either before or after the reading of the *Megillah* or at the festive meal. Another custom on Purim is *mishlo'ach manot*, the practice of sending gifts of food to friends and gifts of food and money to the poor.

Purim players by Jankel Adler.
Israel 568 (1975)

Passover

The spring festival of Passover (*Pesach*) commemorates the redemption of the Jewish people from bondage and the Exodus from Egypt. Beginning on the 15th of Nisan (March/April), the eight-day holiday (seven in Israel) also celebrates the barley harvest in Israel. The name derives from the tenth plague, when God "passed over" (*pasach*) the homes of the Israelites and slew only the first born of Egypt. Passover also is known as *Chag ha-Matzot* (Festival of the Unleavened Bread), in memory of the unleavened bread prepared by the Israelites during their hasty flight from Egypt, when they had no time for the dough to rise. Since no leavened bread or food containing leaven may be eaten during Passover, special dishes and household utensils are used.

The central ritual of Passover is the *seder* (literally, "order"), a special home ceremony held on the first night of Passover (also the second in the Diaspora) that fulfills the Biblical injunction that parents inform their children of the deliverance from Egypt. Jews throughout the world read the *Haggadah* (narration), which recounts the events of the Exodus and expresses Israel's gratitude to God for its redemption. The major symbols of the seder are arranged on a ceremonial plate – a roasted shank bone (standing for the paschal lamb; some vegetarians substitute a broiled beet);

The Sarajevo Haggadah.
Bosnia-Herzegovina
294 (1997)

roasted egg (special festival offering in the Temple); *karpas* (parsley that is dipped in water and represents the seasonal rebirth that takes place in the spring as well as the renewal of our hope for redemption); *maror* (bitter herb indicating the lot of the people under Egyptian bondage); and *charoset* (mixture of chopped nuts, fruit, red wine and spices that represents the clay with which the Jews worked to make bricks). The three *matzot* placed on the table represent the three religious classes of Jews: Kohen (priest), Levite, and Israelite. The middle *matzah* is broken in two; one half, termed the *afikoman* (Greek for "dessert"), is hidden until after the meal. It is customary for the children to

Scenes of Passover with biblical quotes.
Israel 482-484 (1972)

"steal" the afikoman and ask a ransom for its return, since the service cannot continue until this last bit of food is eaten.

After the *Kiddush*, the seder begins with the youngest child asking the "Four Questions," to which the rest of the Haggadah is the reply. Everyone drinks four cups of wine, representing the four expressions of redemption used in the Bible. A fifth cup is reserved for Elijah, who according to tradition visits every Jewish home on seder night. At the conclusion of the seder, everyone joins in singing special songs such as the classic counting song *Echad Mi Yode'a* (Who knows one?) and the deceptively simple folk story *Chad Gad'ya* (One kid).

Paschal lamp; Passover plate.
Suriname B248-249 (1978)

Omer

From the second day of Passover until the festival of Shavuot, Jews are commanded to count seven weeks to commemorate the period between the Exodus from Egypt and the Revelation at Sinai. This process of counting, known as *Sefirat ha-Omer* (counting of the omer), recalls the ancient practice of bringing a sheaf (omer) of the newly harvested barley crop (the first grain to ripen) as an offering to the Jerusalem Temple, where it was "waved before the Lord" on the 16th of Nisan, the second day of Passover. Because of the misfortunes that have overtaken the Jewish people during this time of year, it has come to be regarded as a period of semi-mourning, when weddings and other festivities are not celebrated. The one exception is Lag B'Omer (the 33rd day of the Omer), when according to tradition a plague afflicting the disciples of Rabbi Akiva subsided. In Israel, Lag B'Omer is celebrated with pilgrimages to the Galilee town of Meron, which is the grave site of one of Akiva's greatest students – Shimon bar Yochai, the legendary author of the mystical Zohar.

Dancers of Meron (Lag B'Omer) by Reuven Rubin. *Israel 599 (1976)*

Shavuot

Also known as the Feast of Weeks (the literal meaning of its name) or Pentecost (fiftieth day), Shavuot occurs on the 6th of Sivan (late spring), seven weeks after the beginning of Passover. In biblical times, Shavuot was known as *Chag ha-Bikurim* (Day of the First Fruits), because on this day pilgrims would march to the Temple in Jerusalem to joyfully make offerings of their first ripe fruits and bread baked from the newly harvested wheat. Shavuot is also called *Zeman Matan Torateinu*, the time when the Israelites received the Torah at Mount Sinai.

Unlike Passover and Sukkot, the other two pilgrimage festivals, Shavuot has few special rituals. In the synagogue, the Torah reading appropriately includes a recitation of the Ten Commandments. Under the influence of the kabbalists, it became customary to observe an all-night vigil devoted to the study of passages from the Bible, Talmud, and Zohar, in order to be prepared spiritually for the holiday commemorating the giving of the Torah to the Jewish people. It is customary to adorn the synagogue with plants and flowers, and dairy foods are traditionally eaten.

It has long been a custom to inaugurate the education of a Jewish child on Shavuot, the season of the giving of the Torah. In the Middle Ages, a child was introduced to the Hebrew *aleph-bet* on this day (usually at the age of five) and then given cakes, honey, and sweets so that "the Torah might be sweet on his lips." A modern custom is the ceremony of Confirmation, observed by many Reform and Conservative synagogues on Shavuot, in which young adults completing their formal religious school studies confirm their loyalty to the teachings of Torah.

Illuminated manuscripts referring to Shavuot. *Israel 451-453 (1971)*

The Synagogue

The synagogue is now the most important institution in Judaism. The three He-brew designations for the synagogue indicate its major functions: *Beit Knesset* (house of gathering/assembly); *Beit Tefilah* (house of prayer); and *Beit Midrash* (house of study/learning). The Yiddish term for a synagogue is *shul* (school), reflecting that Jewish worship and learning most often take place in the same building. Early Reform Jews chose the term temple for their synagogues, indicating that in the post-Enlightenment age they no longer yearned for a return to the Land of Israel and the rebuilding of the Temple in Jerusalem, but instead considered the land of their citizenship to be their everlasting homeland.

Ancient synagogue at Capernaum.
Israel C22 (1960)

Historically, the synagogue represents the site of the first communal worship divorced from sacrifice. Unlike the Temple, which could only be in Jerusalem and was run by a specifically sanctified clergy born to the task (Kohanim assisted by Levites), the synagogue could be housed anywhere (not necessarily in a spot with some sacred connotation), did not have to adhere to a rigid architectural pattern, and had prayer leaders and teachers whose roles were not determined by birth, ancestry, or socioeconomic level. Dating back to the time of the Babylonian Exile, by the end of the Second Temple period (1st century C.E.), the synagogue as a house of prayer and study was a firmly established institution.

Wherever Jews have settled, they established synagogues as places of worship and study that assumed a central place in religious and communal life. Synagogue architecture has been extremely diverse, usually reflecting the popular styles of the dominant culture in which Jews lived. At times, these structures have been extraordinarily ornate, rivaling Christian cathedrals or grand mosques. Excavations in Dura Europos (Syria), Capernaum, and Beit Alpha in Palestine have uncovered the remains of beautiful houses of prayer with stunning mosaics, many of which featured signs of the Zodiac. During the Middle Ages, synagogues generally had unpretentious exteriors in accordance with Christian law. In some communities hostile to Jews, the synagogue took on the features of a fortress. After the cossack slaughter of Polish Jews in the mid-17th century, the Jews built synagogues with thick walls, heavy buttresses, and crenellations for sharpshooters along the roof.

Murals from the Dura Europos synagogue. *Israel 1266 (1996)*

Signs of the Zodiac. Top and bottom rows: *Israel 190-201 (1961)*.
Below, from left: the Zodiac with a biblical quote. *Israel 202 (1961)*; mosaic
floor from ancient Beit Alpha synagogue. *Israel 132 (1957)*

Traditionally, the synagogue was required to be the tallest building in town. However, Jews frequently have been unable to comply with this law, especially in Christian countries, where the Church appropriated this prerogative for itself. In the Middle Ages, attempts were made to fulfill this requirement by erecting on the roof of the synagogue a pole or rod that would rise higher than the surrounding buildings. Synagogues are oriented so that the worshipers face toward Jerusalem; those in the Holy City itself face in the direction of the Temple. In Orthodox synagogues, women sit apart from men, separated by a divider called a *mechitzah*. Reform and Conservative synagogues have abolished this separation. On entering the vestibule of a traditional synagogue, worshipers find a pitcher and washbasin for pouring water over their hands, reminiscent of the practice of the priests before officiating in the Temple.

Synagogues around the World

Synagogues around the world: Top, from left: Marble laver. *Barbados 713 (1987)*; Vienna City Synagogue. *Austria 1050 (1976)*; Great Synagogue, Brussels. *Belgium B973 (1978)*; Synagogue. *Bulgaria 3671 (1992)*. Middle, from left: Altneuschul, Prague. *Israel 970 (1987), Czechoslovakia 1478 (1967)*. New Synagogue, Berlin. *Germany 2846 (1990); Czechoslovakia 3009 (1997)*.
Bottom, from left: Great Synagogue, Paris. *France 2100 (1988)*; JCC, Berlin. *Germany 9N 226 (1965-66)*; Dohany Synagogue with F. D. Roosevelt (Four Freedoms speech). *Hungary B198b (1947)*

The Jewish World in Stamps

From left: Dohany Synagogue, Hungary; Florence Synagogue.
Israel 1416 (1999), 972 (1987); Synagogue of Luxembourg.
Luxembourg 677 (1982); Amsterdam Portuguese Synagogue.
Netherlands 523 (1975)

From left: Amsterdam Portuguese Synagogue. *Israel 428 (1970);* Winterswuk Synagogue with holy ark. *Netherlands B612 (1985);*
Tykocin Synagogue. *Poland 2662 (1984)*

From left: Cracow Synagogue, Poland; Great Moscow Synagogue, Russia. *Israel 426, 425 (1970);* Santa Maria la Blanca (medieval
synagogue). *Spain 1282 (1965);* Zabludow wooden synagogue. *Israel 997 (1988)*

Synagogues around the World (continued)

From left: Hebrew University Synagogue. *Israel 558 (1975);* restored synagogues in Jerusalem: Emtzai, Istanbuli, Raban Yohanan ben Zakkai. *Israel 541-543 (1974).*

Below: Spanish synagogues: Porta Nova, Ourense; Cordova synagogue, Jewish Quarter, Caceres, Jewish Museum, Girona. *Spain 2922-2925 (1997)*

Israeli synagogues.
Clockwise:
Ohel Moed, Tel Aviv; Ohel Aharon, Technion, Haifa; Khalaschi, Beer Sheva; Yeshurun, Jerusalem. *Israel 844-847 (1983)*

All ritual objects in the synagogue acquire sanctity by virtue of the sacred purposes that they serve. Therefore, they must be stored away rather than destroyed. In many synagogues, a special storeroom (*genizah*) was set aside for the disposition of torn prayer books, Bibles, and other holy texts that had deteriorated and become useless. From time to time, the contents of the *genizah* were removed and reverently buried in the cemetery. It was in the *genizah* in Cairo that Solomon Schechter made his discovery of a vast quantity of material that shed light on the activities of medieval Jews living in the region.

Ben Ezra Synagogue in Cairo, site of the famed *geniza*. *Israel 1306 (1997)*

Ark. The holy ark (*aron ha-kodesh*) is the repository in the synagogue in which the Torah scrolls are kept. It hearkens back to the biblical Ark of the Covenant, which housed both the shattered First Tablets and intact Second Tablets of the Ten Commandments, as well as an *omer* of *manna* and the rod of Aaron. In the Temple, the Ark was kept in the Holy of Holies, a perfect cube of twenty cubits that was entered only once a year – by the *Kohen Gadol* on Yom Kippur. With the development of synagogues, the Ark became symbolized by a cabinet housing the Torah scrolls. At first, this ark was a movable chest with several shelves on which the scrolls were kept in a lying position. The chest was situated in a side room, set off from the congregation by a curtain. Later, the chest was moved to the center of the eastern wall and made into a fixed part of the synagogue structure.

Over the centuries, the ark has been the focus of an elaborate tradition of design and decoration, heavily influenced by the artistic trends of the particular host culture. In the Middle Ages, the ark took the form of a tall niche or cabinet in which the scrolls stood upright and were appropriately adorned so that they could be seen when the ark was opened. Some arks were divided into an upper tier for the scrolls and a lower compartment to contain ceremonial objects. Some arks have a model of the twin tablets of the Ten Commandments set on top, while others have a more ornate style with columns, pilasters, pediments, and vases.

Holy Arks moved to Israel from Italian synagogues: from Ancona, Soragna, Padua, and Reggio Emilia. *Israel 497-500 (1972)*

Holy Arks in Israel: Jerusalem, Petah Tikvah, Safed.
Israel 75-77 (1953)

Ark curtain. A curtain (*parochet*), usually elaborately decorated, is hung in front of the doors of the ark (inside the doors in the Sephardic tradition). This is reminiscent of the partition between the Holy of Holies (in which the Ark was housed) and the rest of the Tabernacle and later the two Temples. On the High Holy Days, virtually all synagogues change the *parochet* (as well as the Torah mantles and lectern covers) to white, a symbol of purity and hope for redemption that is linked to the verse, "If your sins be like scarlet, they will turn white like snow." Many contemporary synagogues no longer use ark coverings; instead, the doors of the ark are elaborately ornately designed. Classic motifs for ark doors include crowns, replicas of the Ten Commandments, a pair of rampant lions representing the Lion of Judah and God's sovereignty, and the Tree of Life.

Right: Detail from a Czech ark curtain. *Czechoslovakia 1475 (1967)*
Below, from left: Holy Ark curtains (with Hebrew for festivals and the year); Peacocks
with menorah; floral pattern; menorah with two lions. *Israel 1348-1350 (1998)*

Torah scrolls. The Torah is the text of the Five Books of Moses that is inscribed on parchment by a scribe using a quill pen. The beginning and end of the scroll are attached to two carved wooden rollers, called *atzei chayim* (Trees of Life), which ensure that the Torah can be opened, closed, and rolled to any part without the hands having to touch the parchment. Sitting atop the *atzei chayim* is either a crown (*keter*) or a pair of silver finials called *rimmonim* (literally, "pomegranates"). In the East and the Sephardic tradition, the Torah is enclosed in an ornately decorated cylindrical or octagonal case (*tik*), which is divided into two pieces and hinged in the back. It opens like a book to reveal the scroll, which is not removed and is read in an upright position.

Torah scroll.
Israel 54 (1951)

In the Ashkenazic tradition, the Torah scroll is covered by a cloth mantle. This sheath of satin or velvet is usually embroidered with gold or silver threads and may be richly decorated with images of lions, crowns, and pomegranates, as well as the columns of the Temple and various implements of the service. The mantle is open at the bottom and closed at the top, except for two circular openings though which protrude the two staves on which the scroll is rolled. Overlying the mantle there is often a silver breastplate or shield (*tas*), derived from part of the ritual apparel worn by the *Kohen Gadol*.

During the reading of the Torah, it is forbidden to touch the parchment. Consequently, the reader points to the words with a *yad* (hand), literally a silver or wooden hand with pointing finger.

Torah pointer.
Israel 321 (1966)

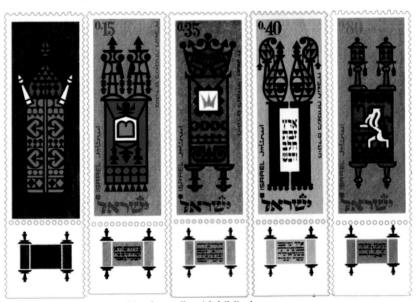

Torah scrolls with biblical quotes.
Israel 348-352 (1967)

Torah crown and Torah shield.
Hungary 2894, 2896 (1984)

Menorah. Seven-branched candelabrum, which once stood in the Jerusalem Temple and is one of the most cherished and enduring symbols of Judaism. Carved from a single ingot of gold, the Menorah's lamps were lit at dusk, and in the morning it was the duty of the Kohen to remove the burnt wicks, replace them with fresh ones, and fill the lamps with absolutely pure olive oil. Today, menorahs are often prominent features in Torah and ark decorations, stained glass windows, and architectural details. The emblem of the State of Israel combines the menorah, the symbol of light, with two olive branches, the symbol of peace. A large sculptured menorah depicting major events of Jewish history stands outside the Knesset (Parliament) building in Jerusalem, signifying the rebirth of the Jewish people after almost 2,000 years of exile.

Menorah with emblems of the Twelve Tribes.
Israel 55 (1952)

From left: Menorah in front of Israel's Knesset (mislabeled as Shrine of the Book). *St. Vincent 2306 (1996)*; Menorah with Star of David and ship (500th anniversary of the expulsion of the Jews from Spain). *Suriname 927 (1992)*

Mizrach. Calligraphic design that hangs on the eastern wall in many Jewish homes and synagogues to aid in meditation and prayer. This Hebrew word means "east" (literally, "[the place from which the sun] casts forth rays") and thus reflects the age-old custom of Jews facing Jerusalem when they pray. In addition to biblical, liturgical, or kabbalistic verses, many mizrachim are decorated with images of animals, pictures of holy places, or kabbalistic symbols, sometimes rendered in microcalligraphy. In Eastern Europe, they often were paper-cuts.

Mizrach papercuts: Menorah and lions; menorah and hands; hunting scene with deer.
Israel 1030-1032 (1989)

Machzor. The prayer book used on the major festivals of the Jewish year. A Hebrew word literally meaning "cycle," the best known *machzor* is the one for the High Holy Days (Rosh Hashanah and Yom Kippur). There is also a *machzor* for the three pilgrimage festivals (Passover, Shavuot, Sukkot), as well as separate prayer books for each.

Machzorim (High Holy Day prayerbooks).
Israel 947-949 (1986)

Ceremonial Objects

Ketubah. Literally meaning "written document", the *ketubah* is the Jewish marriage contract. Written in Aramaic, it lists in detail the financial obligations that a husband undertakes toward his wife, both during marriage and in case of death or divorce. Today, a standard form of *ketubah* is read before the bridegroom and two witnesses and signed by them. Since the 10th century, the margins of many *ketubot* have been artistically ornamented with designs and biblical verses; many of these expensive and beautifully illuminated *ketubot* have been prized for generations as family heirlooms and works of art.

Ketubot (marriage contracts) from Netherlands, Morocco, and Jerusalem.
Israel 685-687 (1978)

Marriage stone. At the conclusion of the wedding ceremony, the groom traditionally crushes a glass under his right foot. The most popular explanation is that this is a sign of mourning for the destruction of the Temple in Jerusalem, which must not be forgotten even on the most joyous occasions. Originally, the glass was broken to create a loud noise to frighten away evil spirits and demons.

Chair of Elijah. Special chair placed at the right of the godfather (*sandek*) at the circumcision ceremony, which is left unoccupied and symbolically meant for the prophet. The chair is usually richly carved and ornamented with embroideries. Since according to tradition Elijah will ultimately announce the crowning of the Messiah to redeem humankind, the prophet appears at every circumcision in order to determine whether this child will be the awaited one.

Tallit bag. Embroidered bag for the prayer shawl (*tallit*) with fringes (*tzitzit*) at the our corners that is worn during the morning service. Traditionally, the wearing of a *tallit* at worship is obligatory only for married men, but it is customarily worn by all males of Bar Mitzvah age and older. In recent years, some women have begun to wear *tallitot*.

From left: Marriage stone; Chair of Elijah; *Tallit* bag.
Israel 1244, 1242, 1243 (1995)

The Jewish World in Stamps

Derech Eretz and Gemilut Chasadim (Ethical Behavior)

Derech eretz (literally, "way of the world") is a general Hebrew term applied to proper human conduct. Based on Jewish moral standards, it encompasses the rules of etiquette and polite behavior. *Derech eretz* requires showing respect of others and the biblical precept to "Love your neighbor," as well as a renunciation of racism and violence. It also entails a harmony with other living creatures and a concern for the environment.

From left: Jewish family heritage; mutual respect; respect for the elderly.
Israel 783 (1981), 1343 (1998), 1172 (1993)

From left: "Love your neighbor" - 10th anniversary of the Universal Declaration of Human Rights; "No to Violence" (drawing of a battered child;" "No to racism." *Israel 149 (1958), 1201 (1994), 944 (1986)*

Coexistence of human beings and animals: Birds and aircraft; pets; dolphins.
Israel 1291-1293 (1996)

Gemilut chasadim (literally, "the bestowal of lovingkindness") is the most comprehensive and fundamental of all Jewish social virtues, which encompasses the whole range of the duties of sympathetic consideration toward one's fellow human beings. The earliest individual rabbinic statement in the Talmud, the maxim of Simeon the Just, mentions it as one of the three pillars of Judaism: "The (continued) existence of the world depends on three things – Torah, the Temple service (*Avodah*), and *gemilut chasadim*" (Avot 1:2). The Talmud (Peah 1:1) describes *gemilut chasadim* as among the things that a person "enjoys the fruits thereof in this world, while the stock remains for him in the world to come" (i.e., its practice affords satisfaction in this world while it is accounted a virtue for him on the Day of Judgment). Greater than charity, which can be given only with one's money and to the poor, *gemilut chasadim* also can be provided by personal service and can benefit both rich and poor and even the dead (e.g., burial societies). In Israel, *gemilut chasadim* is expressed in a host of voluntary activities and social insurance programs to ensure the basic well-being of the entire population.

Israel's National Insurance Institute: old age and survivor's insurance;
maternity insurance; large family insurance; workers' compensation.
Israel 251-254 (1964)

The Jewish World in Stamps

From left: Freedom from hunger; bread and wheat; voluntary service.
Israel 237 (1963), 891 (1984), 621 (1977)

From left: Equal opportunity; World Youth Year; Hello
first grade; youth movements in Israel.
Israel 1295 (1996), 917 (1985), 1307 (1997), 1446 (2001)

Good wishes. *Israel 1035-1037 (1989), 1059-1061 (1990), 1073-1075 (1991)*

World Jewish Communities

Middle East

Tunisia. The Jewish community of Tunisia dates back to the destruction of the Second Temple. Since that time, the settlement has been under Muslim and Christian domination in a history marked by both peaceful development and bitter persecution. Jews first received equal rights with Muslims in Tunisia when France assumed the protectorate of the country in 1881. However, in 1956 Tunisia gained its independence from France and few Jews remain.

Great Synagogue, Tunis.
Israel 425 (1970)

Aleppo Great Synagogue.
Israel 971 (1987)

Syria. The Aram of the Bible, it was the home of a considerable Jewish community during the Hellenistic period, particularly in the time of Herod the Great. With the advance of Christianity, many Jews were forcibly baptized. The invasion of the Muslims in the 7th century brought Jews greater religious tolerance, but placed them in an inferior status. In 1840, Syrian Jews suffered the effects of the infamous Damascus blood libel and were only rescued by the intervention of world Jewry. Syria is now one of Israel's most implacable enemies and almost all Jews have left the country.

Asia

India. The small number of Jews of India fall into three distinct groups. The largest is the Bene Israel (Sons of Israel), who wear Indian dress and are divided into caste-like groups of "black" and "white" Jews who have separate synagogues and do not intermarry. According to tradition, they arrived in Bombay just before the Maccabean uprising in Palestine. Indian Jews of Iraqi origin live primarily in Bombay and Calcutta and generally engage in commerce. They are descendants of the Jewish followers of David Sassoon, who came to India in 1832 and developed a commercial house renowned for its great wealth and generous contributions to Jewish charitable causes. The smallest group is the

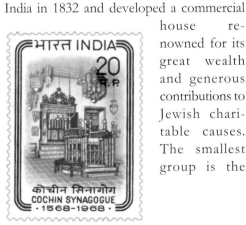

Cochin Synagogue.
India 478 (1966)

David Sassoon (by Hakop Kojoian) and biblical scenes.
Armenia 451A (1993)

Jews of Cochin, who came from Persia and Arab countries during the early Middle Ages. Although they believe themselves to stem from exiles who left the Land of Israel after the fall of the Second Temple in 70 C.E., it is more likely that the "black" ones came to India soon after the Muslim conquest of Persia in the 7th century, while the "white" ones arrived after the expulsion from Spain in 1492.

China. The "native" Jews of China believed that their ancestors arrived after the destruction of the First Temple (586 B.C.E.), though the first documented records date from 1,300 years later. By the 14th century, Marco Polo wrote of influential Jews at the court of Kublai Khan. The Western community in China was founded in the 1840's when the land was first opened to foreign trade. Its ranks were swelled by European refugees during the Nazi era, most of whom found a precarious shelter in Japanese-occupied Shanghai. Today, there are virtually no Jews in China.

Kai-Feng-Fu synagogue.
Israel 997 (1988)

New World

Dominican Republic. Occupying the major eastern section of the Caribbean island of Hispaniola, this was the site of the first Spanish settlement in the New World and possibly the first Jews in the Western Hemisphere. The Dominican Republic was one of the few countries prepared to accept large-scale Jewish immigration before and during World War II. At the Evian Conference on refugees, convened by President Franklin Roosevelt in 1938, Generalissimo Rafael Trujillo announced that the Dominican Republic would welcome up to 100,000 Jewish refugees. A farm colony was immediately established at Sosua, and plans were made for transferring refugees from Europe. However, the outbreak of the war one year later made it impossible for Jews to escape from countries under Nazi domination; only 1,200 European Jews managed to reach safety in the Dominican Republic. Today, most of the few Jews in the country live in the capital, Santo Domingo.

From top: People in the Sosua settlement; Sosua refugee settlement.
Dominican Republic 522, C113 (1960)

Star of David, menorah, Torah scroll, and
Shehecheyanu blessing. *Brazil (2000)*

Brazil. Large numbers of Portuguese Marranos who arrived in the early 16th century made this the home of the first organized Jewish community in the New World. Only when the Dutch conquered the land in 1630 were these secret Jews able to declare their faith publicly. However, when the Portuguese recaptured the territory in 1654, the Jews were expelled from the country. Small groups found refuge in Surinam and Curacao in the Dutch West Indies; 23 boarded a ship for New Amsterdam and formed the nucleus of the famous Portuguese Jewish community of New York. Jews did not return to Brazil in substantial numbers until the turn of the 20th century, when Baron Maurice de Hirsch established the Jewish Colonization Association to facilitate the mass emigration of Jews from Russia and their settlement in rural colonies in the Americas.

Baron Maurice de Hirsch.
Israel 1093 (1991)

Suriname (Dutch Guyana). This Dutch possession on the northeastern coast of South America is the home of the Jewish community with the longest continuous history in the Western Hemisphere. Established in 1630, it was augmented in the next decades by Jews from Brazil and England. In 1682, the Brazilian Jews, who had prospered in the cultivation of sugar, founded a colony at Joden Savanne (Savannah of the Jews) and the first synagogue in the Western Hemisphere (which suffered a devastating fire 150 years later). Most of these Sephardim then moved to the capital of Paramaribo, where they joined

Scenes of Suriname with biblical verses. *Suriname 359-361 (1968)*

German Jews who had settled there in the 19th century. Today, about 200 Jews remain in Suriname, which gained its independence in 1975 and maintains full diplomatic relations with Israel.

Netherlands Antilles. The Dutch West Indies consists of Curacao and Aruba, two small Caribbean islands off the coast of Venezuela. Curacao is the home of one of the oldest permanent Jewish settlements in the New World. Jews from Holland and Brazil settled here during the 1650's, prospering in farming and trade. Their Mikve Israel-Emanuel synagogue, built in 1732, is one of the oldest in the Western Hemisphere. Due to intermarriage and emigration, the community has rapidly declined and today only a few hundred Jews remain.

Interior of synagogue at Punda. *Netherlands Antilles 325 (1970)*

Community Mikve Israel-Emanuel Synagogue in Curacao. *Netherlands Antilles 475-477 (1982)*

From left: Jewish tombstone in Curacao showing Mordecai's procession; shield from a Jewish home. *Netherlands Antilles B135-136 (1975)*

Barbados. The first known Jewish settlers on this island in the British West Indies were former Marranos who had escaped from Brazil after its reconquest from the Dutch by the Portuguese. They established a synagogue in Bridgetown, but the community rapidly dwindled during the early 1880's with the island's economic decline.

Ten Commandments.
Barbados 712 (1987)

Bridgetown Synagogue restoration (exterior and interior).
Barbados 710-711 (1987)

United States. In September 1654, a group of 23 Jewish refugees from Brazil, pursued by the

Shearith Israel Synagogue, New York City.
Israel 429 (1970)

Inquisition, arrived in New Amsterdam to form the first Jewish community in what was to become the United States. After years of struggle with the Dutch governor, Peter Stuyvesant, the Jews obtained increased civil and religious rights when the English took control of the region ten years later. In 1729, Congregation Shearith Israel of New York built its first synagogue, after more than 20 years of worshiping in private or rented dwellings.

Among the colonies in New England, Rhode Island under Roger Williams provided the most congenial climate for Jewish settlers. As a result, a thriving Jewish community flourished in Newport more than 100 years before the American Revolution. The Touro Synagogue in Newport is the oldest synagogue in the United States. Dedicated in 1763, it was designated as a national monument in 1946. Other important early Jewish communities were established in Philadelphia and Savannah. Between 1880-1920, about two million Jews passed through Ellis Island as immigrants to the United States from Eastern Europe. Although only about 2% of the population, the Jewish contributions to American society have far exceeded their numbers. This is particularly true in all areas of social, business, scholarly, scientific, and artistic endeavor.

From left: Touro Synagogue, Newport, Rhode Island; Ellis Island.
U.S.A. 2017 (1982), Gambia 1313 (1992)

Canada. The Jewish community of Canada dates from the British conquest of New France in 1759. Before that Jews, like Huguenots, were forbidden admission to the colony. After the British defeated the French in 1763, Aaron Hart, a Jewish officer in the British army, settled in the small town of Trois Rivieres in the province of Quebec. In 1832, the Jews of Canada were granted full political equality, 25 years earlier than in England. Today, the largest Canadian Jewish community is in Montreal, where the Jews belong to the English-speaking minority.

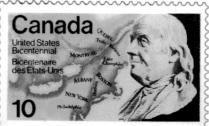

From left: Celebrating Canada's multicultural heritage; map showing first Jewish settlement in Canada (with B. Franklin). *Canada 1270 (1990), 691 (1976)*

Uruguay. Located on the Atlantic coast, between Brazil and Argentina, Uruguay is the smallest of the South American republics. However, its Jewish community, mostly living in the capital of Montevideo, is the third largest and one of the most highly organized in Latin America. Until the demise of the Inquisition in 1813, there were probably few Jews in the country. Major Jewish communal institutions were first organized in 1916, and the country's Constitution signed two years later established the principle of separation of Church and State.

From left: 80th anniversary of the Jewish community of Uruguay; 70th anniversary.
Uruguay 1619 (1996), 1234 (1987)

From top:
100th anniversary of Jewish immigration to Argentina; immigration hotel, staging area for processing immigrants.
Argentina 1660-1661 (1989)

Argentina. Some Marranos arrived in Argentina with the early Spanish settlers in the 16th century, and scattered Jews came from Western Europe in the 1840's after the country's liberation from Spain earlier in the century. However, large-scale Jewish immigration to Argentina began only in the late 1880's. At first arriving singly, Jews later came in groups, the largest of which (arriving on the S.S. Weser on Aug. 14, 1889) laid the foundation for agricultural settlements. Immigration peaked several years later after Baron Maurice de Hirsch established the Jewish Colonization Association to facilitate the mass emigration of Jews from Russia and their settlement in rural colonies in the Americas. The Jewish community of Argentina is the largest in Latin America, but a resurgence of anti-Semitism and economic decline in the past few years has led many Jews to emigrate from the country.

Panama. The first Jews in Panama were merchants from Spain and Portugal, but the unhealthy climate and poor living conditions led most to flee the isthmus. The small permanent community that remained grew only when the United States began building the Panama Canal in 1904. Panama's oldest congregation, Kol Shearit Israel, celebrated is centenary in 1976.

From top: Synagogue of the Canal Zone; Synagogue of Panama.
Panama 262 (1962-64)

INDEX

Each stamp is identified by country of issue, Scott catalogue number, and year of issue in parentheses